T0246284

LOVE LIFE

ALSO BY MATTHEW HUSSEY

Get the Guy

LOVE LIFE

How to Raise
Your Standards,
Find Your Person,
and Live Happily
(No Matter What)

MATTHEW HUSSEY

HARPER

An Imprint of HarperCollins*Publishers*

LOVE LIFE. Copyright © 2024 by 320 Media LLC. All rights reserved. Printed in the United States of America. No part of this book may be used or reproduced in any manner whatsoever without written permission except in the case of brief quotations embodied in critical articles and reviews. For information, address HarperCollins Publishers, 195 Broadway, New York, NY 10007.

HarperCollins books may be purchased for educational, business, or sales promotional use. For information, please email the Special Markets Department at SPsales@harpercollins.com.

FIRST EDITION

Page 21: Excerpt from "To the Whore Who Took My Poems" in *Burning in Water, Drowning in Flame* by Charles Bukowski. Copyright © 1963, 1964, 1965, 1966, 1967, 1968, 1974 by Charles Bukowski. Used by permission of HarperCollins Publishers.

Designed by Bonni Leon-Berman

Library of Congress Cataloging-in-Publication Data

Names: Hussey, Matthew (Relationship expert), author.
Title: Love life : how to raise your standards, find your person, and live happily (no matter what) / Matthew Hussey.
Identifiers: LCCN 2023057433 (print) | LCCN 2023057434 (ebook) | ISBN 9780063294387 (hardcover) | ISBN 9780063294400 (ebook)
Subjects: LCSH: Man-woman relationships. | Couples. | Dating (Social customs) | Interpersonal relations.
Classification: LCC HQ801 .H9553 2024 (print) | LCC HQ801 (ebook) | DDC 306.7—dc23/eng/20231213
LC record available at https://lccn.loc.gov/2023057433
LC ebook record available at https://lccn.loc.gov/2023057434

24 25 26 27 28 LBC 9 8 7 6 5

To Audrey Hussey, the woman in the elevator.

To Mum, for carrying the torch further.

And to all who not only seek love but
are brave enough to give it.

This is for you.

CONTENTS

KARMA IS A BITCH

Confession time. For most of my life, I have been a terrible person to date. I may have been an effective coach and speaker, but I was still a man in his twenties—albeit one in the surreal position of seeing comments under my videos that read: "He would be the perfect guy to date." Many people assumed that someone with my emotional intelligence had to be a wonderful person to be with.

They were wrong.

I can say with a hundred percent certainty that I have never been, by any stretch of the imagination, the perfect guy to date. And though I've always had enough self-awareness to feel uneasy reading those comments, I had no idea in my twenties—and dare I say, even in my early thirties—the extent to which the opposite of this was true.

From the moment I started my career as a professional dating coach, as a nineteen-year-old giving advice to women, I was doomed to fail as a partner. This is perhaps the fate of all coaches, therapists, and advice-givers of every variety who do not become enlightened before starting to dole out wisdom at scale—which is to say, all of us. Except maybe Eckhart Tolle . . . his enlightenment seems pretty legit. The rest of the gang fall short more times than we would like to admit. And the great joke of life is that from the moment we start ranting righteously about any one thing, life will conspire to make us trip up in that specific area.

So what exactly made me such a terrible person to date?

I dated multiple people at the same time, without exactly announcing that I was doing so. For the most part, I didn't lie about it. I just didn't actively say it because it was convenient for me not to. Sometimes I lied about it, on occasions where I told myself it was the right thing to do because I was "sparing the feelings" of the person I was with (a fluid relationship with the truth I have since worked to correct). I occasionally ghosted people. I slept with people and then let it fizzle out, without ever really acknowledging, or even always having the awareness, that feelings were being hurt. In some cases, I continued to seek the attention of people who wanted more with me, even though if I'd been honest with myself, I'd already made my mind up about not wanting more with them. I did this because the attention felt good, and life was lonely without it. In slow, quiet moments, in times when I desperately needed to sit with my feelings, work out my shit, and learn how to be alone, I picked up the phone and called somebody new.

It's one of the reasons my content has been so hard-hitting. When I tell women what to watch out for, it's often a younger, more reckless version of myself.

I'm not saying I wasn't a gentleman. Was I chivalrous? Absolutely. Was I kind? Most of the time, yes. I wanted to treat everyone well. I loathed the idea of ever hurting anybody. Did I care about people's feelings? Deeply. But in the end, I cared about mine more.

The way I dated when I dated casually just had a way of hurting people. And yet the most pain I caused was not when things didn't lead to a relationship, but the times when it did.

Why? Because even when I thought I was ready, I was not. I was not ready for real commitment or for any kind of compromise, nor was I ready to make any kind of plan for the future. I still negatively framed relationships as a sacrifice. But I was ready to enjoy being in love, and this, I would later learn, is not the same thing as being ready for a relationship.

Not that I was aware of any of this at the time. If you'd have asked me then, I would have told you with no lack of sincerity that I was a great person to be with. I felt deeply, I loved intensely, I gave a lot to the relationship, I was respectful, I was sensitive to their needs and a good talker. All of this made me possibly the most dangerous kind of guy who's bad for you: the one you don't see coming. At least with an obvious cad, you know what you're getting into. You may still go home with him for the excitement of it all and the story, but you definitely don't expect a future.

Like so many people who think they're being harmless in their twenties, I thought my job was to fall in love with someone and then strap in. But that is not a relationship. That's a fairground ride. It exists for our enjoyment. When the ride stops being enjoyable, we get off. Whatever the "You Must Be This Tall to Ride" sign reads for the roller coaster of romance, the height requirement for a serious relationship is much, much higher.

FLASHBACK: I AM TWENTY-FOUR, AND I already think, or at least desperately want the world to think, I know it all.

I find myself standing in front of the Beverly Hills sign, with a major publishing deal for my first book, *Get the Guy*, millions of views on my YouTube videos, and a brand-new prime-time NBC show called *Ready for Love*.

By this point, I'd been helping people for six years, at all stages of dating, coaching thousands of people in person, onstage, in one-on-one sessions, in small groups and large ones, at every step of attraction, through every degree of heartbreak.

But all that happened back in London, and this was Los Angeles, my new home for the next three months of shooting. I was excited, I felt confident. I wanted to be part of it. So here in Beverly Gardens Park, too new in town to know or care what a cliché I was, I proceeded to film the first YouTube video I ever shot on US soil: "3 Tips for Getting Over Heartbreak."

The whole time I was delivering my priceless tips, there was an older man standing off to the side. He wasn't interfering, but it was hard not to get self-conscious knowing I had an audience. It's a curious phenomenon, feeling comfortable with the idea of putting up a video that would be seen by hundreds of thousands of people, if not millions, and simultaneously feeling shy that a single human being is watching me record it. For his part, he seemed amused by my guerrilla film shoot on a sunny day, and when we were packing up at the end of the session, this stranger came over and said to me, "You've never had your heart broken, have you?" He wasn't being confrontational, but there was an easily detectable tone. It was the kind of tone you hear from someone who's been around long enough to have been punched in the face by life—maybe a few times, maybe a lot—speaking to someone who just doesn't get it (or more accurately, hadn't gotten *it* yet).

I felt patronized and pissed off. Who was this guy anyway? "I didn't ask you to stand there and watch me," I thought. "And now you're going to judge me?" But as much as I didn't want to admit it to myself, he had struck a nerve. It's not that the "tips" I gave didn't make sense. For what it's worth, they did. The surprising thing about the advice I was giving at twenty-two and twenty-three and twenty-four is how right some of it—not all of it, but a lot of it—really was. But on a deeper level, as my friend could see right away, the shoe didn't quite fit.

Someone who had lived longer and suffered through a real heartbreak would have known that cheerily offering "tips" was perhaps the wrong approach for speaking to somebody climbing out of the living hell of heartbreak.

I have never run into my first American critic again, but if I did, I'd tell him that since our first encounter, I have fixed that hole in my resume. My version of this formative life experience was its own cliché. I made exactly the mistakes that I tell people to avoid: I rearranged my life to fit hers; I ignored red flags; I pretended I wanted things I didn't just to be with her; I placed my sense of self-worth in the fact that we were together, putting my own career on hold and losing touch with my deeper needs; I let myself be miserable for months on end, spending my time anxiously worrying about being in love instead of *enjoying* being in love. Suffice it to say I was, perhaps for the first time in my life, not in my favorite position: the driver's seat.

I've always been a voracious note taker. Whatever most occupies my thoughts finds its way into the notes in my journals, my phone, or anywhere I can scribble down my musings on the fly. But my journals aren't filled with "Dear Diary" entries. They are filled with the things I tell myself to help me get through the day. In this sense, reading these notes paints a pretty vivid picture of whatever pain I was trying to cope with at the time. Looking back at my notes from that relationship, the scariest thing about them is not the palpable anxiety I was trying to fight off, but the "encouraging" notes I wrote to convince myself to stay.

Even a quick scroll brings up such gentle and loving self-talk as "If anyone can take it, I can." "This is warrior training. If I can handle this, then I can handle anything." "Don't wish for life to be easier. Work on becoming stronger, more resilient. This is a huge opportunity for me to grow."

You would think from reading these that this was some kind of mental pep talk in the middle of Navy SEAL training. Except I was writing about my relationship. That's how unhappy I was. I wince at the lack of compassion

I showed myself, and at just how dangerous my determination and tolerance for pain can be when directed at the wrong target—in this case, martyrdom in a relationship where most of my core needs weren't being met.

These notes weren't even hard to find. There were a lot of them, many too embarrassing to put in this book. A particularly sad line I found sandwiched in between a bunch of work-related to-dos reads:

"My expectations are what's fucking me up right now. Before, I just appreciated it for what it was, but then I went from gratitude to expectation."

Here we have the chilling justification for my then-well-practiced masochism: *My problem is not that my needs aren't getting met, my problem is that I have needs. All I need to do is get back to being grateful that I have this person, instead of having any expectations of them. Forget feeling safe, secure, loved. You're just lucky to be here!*

After the initial pain of heartbreak, it became abundantly clear that this was the wrong relationship for me. Reading these notes still makes my heart break for the Matthew in that relationship. Nonetheless, I'm thankful for them. They serve as a reminder of the frightening degree to which energy can be expended in the wrong direction.

Whenever you hear me suggesting you reevaluate a behavior that is making you miserable, don't think I'm putting myself on some kind of pedestal. I've fallen into the same trap. And never mind the people in your life who roll their eyes at the things you do. Trust me, chances are, they've done their share of crazy shit too.

When our own form of crazy leads us down the wrong path, or even when we do everything right and someone simply crushes us anyway, it helps to have a home to come back to: a place of love, truth, and restoration. For me, when I was at my worst, the first port of call was my parents, my brothers, my boxing coach, and my closest friends. I was lucky to have all of their combined experience and wisdom then. And yet, despite all these loving figures in my life offering their positivity and solutions, I still find that one of the greatest antidotes to pain is more pain. Not more of my own pain, but the pain of others—the necessity of communing with other people who are going through it.

In my darkest times, there has always been a very special place where I've been able to find this kind of communing. A place I could always go to feel less alone, to feel more like my best self, where my troubles disappeared. That place was onstage, or in sessions, listening to people, hearing them out, talking through any problems they brought up, and devising plans for dealing with both their immediate issue and, when we could breathe a little and widen our focus, helping them find the confidence they needed—confidence that, in nearly every instance, I could remind them they already had. Having this community has always been one of the most beautiful aspects of this career, and it has made me very comfortable making space for the pain of others.

Put me onstage in a conference of nuclear physicists and I'll start sweating. *(Are they, by any chance, heartbroken nuclear physicists? If so, I can help.)* But get me onstage in front of people in pain and I'm right at home.

On the last *Love Life* tour before the country shut down and there were no more in-person events for two years, I was onstage, in the question-and-answer part of the evening, and I spotted a man with his hand up near the back of the room. Now, let me be clear, in previous years there weren't a ton of men at my events. When there was one, especially when he came in the form of a gruff, stocky Texan, he stood out.

"What's your name?"

"Roy," he said.

Roy had a weathered kind of handsomeness, and he didn't seem too overwhelmed at first glance. But it takes courage to stand up and articulate your hurt or worry or confusion, so I asked . . .

"Hey, Roy, how are you?"

"Good, Matthew. Thanks. I've had an ex talk about you a lot, so I thought I'd come check you out." That got a big laugh from the entire room, followed by a spontaneous round of applause, and Roy noticeably relaxed.

"Well, thank you for being here."

"Yeah, yeah. I enjoy everything you have to say, but I'm a man." Roy deepened his voice a bit when he said the word, in a plainspoken way. "So I'm just trying to figure out what I can take from a male perspective." He spoke slowly, not out of nervousness, it seemed, but emotion. "I'm very . . . I guess, 'reserved.' And I dwell on my hurt, because . . . we're people. But I have a problem." He plunged in. "My ex moved on fast. And it hurts, man. We were together for like five or six years, and when they move on fast, it makes you feel like you're not good enough. And I just want to know, how do I change my perspective on letting stuff go? Because that's what I need to do. I need to let stuff go or I'm going to be unhappy for the rest of my life."

When he reached the end of his question, the room broke out in applause, in recognition of Roy's honesty. Then there was a long silence as I considered how much I related to what Roy had said, not just about the pain of heartbreak, but the dizzying bewilderment of watching someone you're not ready to let go of move on at breakneck speed. The silence was broken by a voice from another part of the audience: "There are twenty women who are going to give you their number!" The entire room—including Roy—laughed.

"Roy, you're going through an incredible amount of hurt. When did this happen? When did she move on?"

He explained how recent it had been—a matter of months.

"So," I said, "it's incredibly painful. Part of the pain is you continuing to convince yourself that this must, on some level, have been the right person. And that your 'right person' is now with someone else. Now, I don't believe that. I believe that the right person can only be the right person when it's two people choosing each other. As much as you may have loved someone, and as incredible as they may have been, if they don't choose you, they cannot be your true dream relationship.

"You're mourning because you think you've lost the person you're supposed to be with. But I can promise you, you haven't. Because unless someone chooses you, they're not the person you're supposed to be with. You can be disappointed that she wasn't the right person, but you can't grieve like she was, because she's not. Disappointment takes a minute to get over, but it's much easier to recover from disappointment than the idea that you've lost the love of your life. You didn't lose that. That is still to come. Something better is coming for you, I promise you, brother."

Allow me to restate to you what I said to Roy, in case you yourself are struggling to move on from someone who didn't choose you:

It's OK to be disappointed that someone didn't turn out to be the one. But don't grieve as if they were the one. If they didn't choose you, they're not.

And while we're on the subject, by the end of this book, I want your confidence to be in a place where someone "not choosing you" is the biggest turn-off in the world. The problem is, and this may be where you find yourself right now, that if your confidence isn't currently in its best shape, when someone doesn't choose you, you default to fundamentally questioning your worth.

So I continued to Roy:

"Then there's the ego element: She chose someone else, why not me? What did that person have? Why wasn't I good enough? One of the greatest pieces of advice I ever received was: Kill your ego. A piece of you has to die. Right now, you're going through hell. It's been awful. Somebody ripped your heart out. That is hell. But I *want* that version of you that goes through hell and comes back out alive and has something to tell us at the end of it. Do I want the version of Roy that hasn't been through that? That's boring. I don't want that Roy. I want weathered Roy, scarred Roy. We become far stronger by what goes wrong in our lives than what goes right. So all this you're going through is like a great stew, adding flavor. It's going to make you more complex, more compassionate. It's going to make you kinder, more empathetic to other people. It's going to allow you to bring more to your next relationship. And it's going to make you such a strong person. And after you get through this? What is there left for you to be afraid of? I've died already! You can't scare me!"

You will, of course, have noted that I did not, having been through it myself, address Roy's heartbreak by proceeding to tell him I had three tips to get him over it. Luckily for Roy, a more weathered, humbled Matthew had laced up his shoes that night. Just as I believe of Roy, my value to everyone in that room and everything in my life had expanded through my pain. I had become a better partner to my audience, just as Roy now had the ability to become for the person waiting for *him* on the road ahead.

A real relationship requires bravery from both sides. It requires us to be vulnerable enough to allow ourselves to be seen. It requires curiosity and vision to fully take in who the other person is. To really see them. To accept their on-camera selves, and their hidden behind-the-scenes mess. To view their worst parts with acceptance and generosity, not contempt. And to have enough faith and strength to trust the other person to offer the same latitude to our darker sides. On top of all this, it requires two people who actually have a vision for where they want the relationship to go, and the daily execution to move toward that vision. Exceptional relationships are not found. They're built.

In the pages that follow, I will share with you the lessons and stories that have changed my life, and the lives of the millions of people who follow my work, whose trust in me I look to earn in the way I show up, both in public and in private, every day.

Who are these millions anyway? Fifteen years ago I may have started making videos for heterosexual women, and while they still make up the majority of my audience, today it's more diverse. There are many more Roys. And people from the LGBTQ+ community have found help with this work as well. Love is universal and flows in all directions. The advice I offer is rooted in human nature. I am grateful to all for seeing past the limited range of pronouns I've used in the introductions to my videos, pronouns that could make many feel that the message wasn't for them. In this book I've tried to remove those barriers and to use more inclusive language. Whatever the gender or sexual preference of the people featured in this book, we are all capable of stumbling in the same ways; which is why, whoever you are, I trust you will find yourself somewhere in these pages, and in doing so, I hope you feel seen, regardless of who and how you love, or how you identify.

I'm still learning to be better at the concepts I cover in this book myself, but I'm a whole lot better than I used to be. We will, all of us, find ourselves in need of advice in our love lives at some point. I have always found the subject of dating and relationships to be a wonderful *way in*. It's a way into our demons, our insecurities, our trauma, our hopes and dreams, and the ways we might also be stumbling in other areas of life.

It is my experience that one cannot talk about love without talking about life. And one cannot truly have a great relationship with love if one does not have a great relationship with life itself. To have an exceptional love life, we must also cultivate a love *for* life. Whatever stage you find yourself in, I invite you to discover, in the pages that follow, the tools we will need for both.

LOVE LIFE

1

BEING SINGLE IS HARD

I started giving dating advice more than fifteen years ago, mostly to small groups of guys. A handful of women saw that the advice helped and asked for sessions of their own. As women began to outnumber men, I sometimes had attacks of conscience: Who am I to peddle advice about what a woman should do or feel? What do I know about being a woman? But these attacks almost always came in the luxury of hindsight, after a session, when I had the chance to run things over in my mind, or once I started recording the events, when I could listen to the audio or watch the video all over again. It never happened in the actual moment, onstage, when a woman was telling me about a crisis in her life, expecting relief, insight, or some kind of plan. In that situation, I can only trust in experience, as I try to pass along everything I've learned from answering questions like hers before.

By now I have spent literally thousands of hours in situations like this. It doesn't matter who someone is, or what their background is, or how they identify . . . the right response is the one that helps them out of their imme-diate trouble, and hopefully nudges them toward a long-term strategy. This book is full of the answers I return to again and again. I prefer practical advice over pallid positive thinking. I want people to go out into the world knowing there are real steps they can take—things they can do and things they should stop doing.

One small thing that's given me a shred of understanding for the kind of constant pressure women can feel from their families and married friends—and sometimes it must seem like it's coming from all sides—is the pressure I got as a guy talking about dating and relationships. When a journalist or someone in my audience asked me if I was single, I always felt a combination of boredom at being asked that question for the thousandth time, and frustration at the farce of it. If I told them I was in a relationship, they'd say, "Oh, that's great," and move on. If I said I was single, they'd respond, "How come? You're the relationship guy, after all."

Can I admit that this got to me? Not every time, but more than every twentieth time I answered that question, it made me doubt myself, so that it felt impossible to let that part of my life work itself out organically. I found myself backing into the situation I warn against: putting so much pressure on myself to meet someone significant that I had to constantly resist making bad decisions, all because I wanted the check mark of being in a relationship—something I had to remind myself wasn't important in the first place.

Let me answer the question once and for all. First of all, I'm not the "relationship guy." What matters to me is not that someone is in a relationship, but that they are happy with whatever their status is right now. I've never preached that people *should* be in a relationship; I've just helped them find one if they want to be. And second, I don't think my being in a relationship is my strongest qualification. I happened to get engaged while writing this chapter, which is a happy circumstance for me, but the label alone shouldn't be a badge of honor. Simply being in a relationship doesn't make me or anyone else a success—many people I've coached could proudly count themselves more successful the day they left their relationship. And we all know at least one couple whose relationship has all the social media hallmarks of a blissful union, but behind the scenes is on the brink of annihilation.

Let me paint the more honest picture:

- If you find love as a result of my work, I'll be happy.
- If you break up with someone you shouldn't be with and become single again because of my work, I'll be just as happy.
- And if you decide you're not in such a rush to find a relationship after reading this book because you're loving life and being you, and you're not trying to fill a hole by finding someone who will make you feel good enough, then that's the jackpot.

None of this makes being single easy. Even if we shake off the outside pressure to meet someone, we still have to deal with our own feelings about the need to connect. In fifteen years of coaching, I've worked with countless women who feel their dating life isn't going anywhere. Disenchantment and hopelessness follow rejection and heartbreak until a person starts to feel that the old ideal that there's someone out there for everyone applies to everyone except them. You stop seeing the point in dating, since you either never feel a spark, or everyone you feel a spark with ends up screwing you over or wanting different things than you. You say to yourself, "Maybe I should make peace with the reality that I'll never find anyone." Then everyone you used to spend time with begins to pair off and disappear from your life, and this disappointment hardens into a conviction: Since I'm the one who's still alone, there must be something wrong with me.

These thoughts grow louder with every failed connection. And even though we try to stay positive, we carry the persistent fear deep down that, well, maybe the world has simply changed too much. Maybe real relationships don't even exist anymore. Or, even more damningly, maybe they don't exist for me.

It can be depressing when a relationship we've invested months or years in goes wrong and we find ourselves back at square one. There doesn't seem to be an account where we build wealth in our love lives. Whenever someone leaves, we have to start all over again with a new person; the relationship clock resets to zero. But there's no reset button on the clock of our life or our body. Those keep winding down. If our love life were a board game, it wouldn't be Monopoly, with its steady accumulation of houses and hotels. It would be Chutes and Ladders. Each new relationship is a ladder to climb, and every breakup is the chute that seems to instantly drop us right back in the same old loneliness we were in before. But this isn't necessarily a bad thing. We get to start over!

When we get this feeling of being left behind as our friends pair off, it's worth remembering that anyone can find themselves back in the single state at any time. Longtime couples split. Is it worse for them after twenty years of marriage or partnership than it is for someone on their sixth (or sixteenth) heartbreak? There is no one answer. Some people emerge from a breakup with a sense of accomplishment and a serenity about their newfound independence. Some people feel absolutely abandoned without any of the comforts or friends or the certainty they had in the life that just ended.

But whatever state you find yourself in—dating, dumped, divorced, defiant—everybody has to face the emotions that come with being single. Compared to the trauma of heartbreak or the apocalypse of divorce, the day-to-day challenges and stress of being single can feel frustratingly elusive. How do you tackle a problem when the problem is an absence at the heart of life? Still, it can hurt not to have someone, and once you start adding up all the little aches, you wind up with a chronic condition. Some days, when you have a lot on your plate and feel confident, or at least happily preoccupied with life, the stress is manageable. Other days, it can feel like a constant battle against an opponent only you can see. Sometimes the pain of being single hits you on the best days of all, when you're carried away with a peak experience, and it's exactly the exceptional quality of this happiness that reminds you that you have no one to share it with, no one to listen to you when you're doing something that excites you, no one beside you if you just want to take it all in in silence.

Some people feel this absence as an actual loss, as if every year that you're alone is another year lost with the person you haven't met yet. This idea of a particular predestined partner is dangerously close to something we'll debunk in the next chapter. But the feeling of loss is also a fact of life. The writer Christopher Hitchens said, "A melancholy lesson of advancing years is the realization that you cannot make old friends." This is just as true in relationships: You can't go back and marry the high school sweetheart you never had. And some people, especially people in a position to compare themselves to their married friends, feel this acutely. If an old friend has been with her partner for ten years, it's easy to compare yourself in your current single state and say, Even if I met someone today, I'd still never have that ten years of history.

I think there's reason to hope. As we get older and more attuned to what we like to do and the kind of people we gravitate toward, we catch up more quickly with our counterparts. I don't mean that you zip through a checklist of red flags based on all your previous dating disasters, although certainly don't ignore that. But there are people you can meet later in life where there is an instant soul connection. I'm usually allergic to language like this, but it's not really that mysterious. You've both been on your own road and you know the ways that life has humbled you, and after all that experience, you're better able to recognize and appreciate the tender spots in another person.

Whether we live miles from our first home or around the block from the place we grew up, we go out into the world hoping to be something different than what we were when we left. And at some point, you run into someone who reminds you of that fact. Even though they came from a completely different place, they had the same urges. People are so often defined by the things they want, the drives they have, and everything they're determined to accomplish, but we are also shaped by the things we reject—everything we have to say "no" to just to get to where we hope to be. It takes a lot of living to know the things you can't put up with. And each time you put one more of them behind you, it takes you further from the person you used to be and the choices you once would have made. Then someone appears in front of you who has arrived at that same place, and you recognize in each other the distance you've traveled from home. That isn't magic. Or if it is, it's not a magic that was ever available to you when you were nineteen.

BEING SINGLE IS HARD; IT can feel like an ache that never goes away. One core purpose of this book is to give people a set of tools that will help them bring exponentially more opportunity into their love lives. But another cornerstone is to help people live with a sense of presence, enjoying the beauty of the life they have while remaining open to opportunity. But that can get tricky. Sometimes "remaining open to opportunity" can morph into "waiting in hope" or "waiting around, feeling like the rest of your life isn't worth living until the one thing that is definitely not happening today (or maybe ever) finally happens."

In Greek myth, Pandora couldn't resist opening a box she was told not to open. Once she did open it—and how could she not?—she saw that the box contained all sorts of unspecified diseases and evils that were now flying out to plague humankind forever. Quickly realizing her mistake—and we'll ignore for now that this myth, like the story of Eve, just seems like an excuse to blame anything that's wrong in the world on a woman with a healthy sense of curiosity—she quickly closed the lid, just before hope escaped. It's a curious detail. You might think, "What's wrong with hope? How could hope be as devastating and pernicious as disease?"

For years, I had to struggle with chronic pain. The diagnosis I was given was tinnitus, a buzzing in the ear, but on many days—really, most days—the buzzing came with every variety of crippling headache you could imagine: pain, dizziness, a throbbing in my head and ear. Fixing this became the obsession of my life for several years running. If you think I didn't live in hope, you'd be dead wrong. I chased practically every cure I ever heard of, and living in California, I heard of a lot. I went to an osteopath who cracked my neck and spine until it felt like he was separating my head from my body. I signed up for something called "sound bath therapy," where I sat in a room while somebody played a "concert for one" on bowls and another guy played a didgeridoo "into my heart," as he put it. I went to a migraine doctor who put me on a triad of meds that required me giving myself an injection every month. I went to one ENT after another. One of them told me to cut out "coffee, alcohol, sugar, salt, and spicy foods," and another told me the next step was antidepressants. I felt like I'd really need the antidepressants if I ever did cut out everything they wanted me to.

I did yoga. I drank celery juice every morning. I went to a dentist for a six-hundred-dollar mouth guard. I went to an acupuncturist who gave me an inner-ear and jaw massage that involved sticking his fingers simultaneously into my mouth and my ear and manipulating the entire area from the inside. I went to a Chinese acupuncturist who prescribed a complicated concoction of herbal tea sachets that was unbelievably foul-smelling and tasted like mud mixed with hot water. I kept that up for a month, which was practically the definition of the triumph of hope over experience.

I flew to Munich, in the middle of the pandemic, for a treatment that involved withdrawing buckets of my blood (well, that's what it felt like), which was then spun in a centrifuge to separate out the anti-inflammatory proteins, and then that serum was reinjected into my jaw, the back of my neck, and my shoulders, twenty times a day for four straight days. This was right before Christmas, when all I wanted was to be with my family. Instead I was one of a handful of guests in a giant hotel, each one of us some variety of invalid or another, wandering through this empty mausoleum of a German hotel like ghosts. I spent an obscene amount of money to feel lonely and miserable, and all I got out of it was a lifelong tolerance for needles.

You could say I was plagued by hope for years. Every time I heard of some new remedy, I lived in anticipation. I'd be flooded with a sense of relief that the fix was coming—that this new treatment would finally make a difference. My nervous system would calm down because I was no longer in a catastrophic mode of thinking. I could imagine—I could almost feel—the end of the condition; it now even had a specific date: namely, the day I would start the treatment. I'd talk with my friends about this new miracle cure with a sense of excitement that bordered on joy. Even though I could still feel the pain, the mere possibility of relief seemed to do something to my brain. All of this is to say I understand the emotional state when somebody who isn't in a long-term relationship starts excitedly telling friends about the date they went on that was actually pretty interesting. I get it, completely. They're starting to entertain the possibility that this depressing trajectory they've been on for what feels like forever might be coming to an end.

I'm drawn to this connection to chronic pain because scientists have found that chronic pain reconfigures the brain—with persistent pain, the pain receptors become disinhibited, so they're now on a hair-trigger response, activating faster than they would in pain-free people. That means that now you can't just treat the pain, you have to rewire the brain. But even when I was in this state, there always seemed to be a small escape hatch: Every day, there was a moment, just after I'd woken up, before I'd fully come out of the dream I was having and remembered exactly who I was, where I got a quick glimpse of what it felt like to be pain-free.

Anybody who travels knows this moment: You wake up and ask yourself, Where am I again? Austin? Singapore? Is this an airport Hyatt or my friend's house? It's a familiar feeling for anybody who's had their heart broken: You are granted ten or fifteen unmiserable seconds when you just wake up, before you piece it all together and remember how you feel, a short reprieve before you see the day's headline, the same one as yesterday's headline, telling you you're heartbroken. Once you spot that, you say, OK, I'm ready for the day. Now I remember how shattered I feel.

You can get replays of that feeling of reprieve during the day. I'd be happily caught up in something I was doing, and someone close to me would ask, "How's your head feeling today?" And I'd have to admit, "Oh, you're right, it's not so great. But in the ten minutes before you asked, it was actually OK." All the people who kept telling me "Trust me, it'll go away" weren't helping, because that gnawing hope took me out of my life. Waiting for the day when everything would be better made it impossible for me to enjoy my life as it was. It set me up for disappointment every time it didn't get better.

I finally learned to change my relationship to the pain, which I noticed changed from day to day. I began to get curious about that. I started tracking what was going on during a day when the pain was a 7 or 8 that was different from the days when it was a 4 or 5. Because when you're dealing with pain on a day-to-day basis, those two degrees of difference are a big deal. These calculations help with the difficulties of being single too: There's a way to cultivate a curiosity about experiences that are a few degrees different from the ones we usually have. It's like that moment waking up: The longer I could stay curious, the longer it took for the pain to settle back in.

This kind of curiosity, which we will talk about throughout this book, can allow you to take the perspective of a social experimenter in your own life. Say you normally go into a panic when someone you started dating doesn't text you back as fast as they have been, and now you're thinking you're going to get hurt because you like them more than they like you. Maybe that's enough to make you go cold the next time you meet, or take an aggressive tone. But if you try a different reaction—admitting that you were a little sad because you like hearing from them—maybe the vulnerability, this honesty that's not part of your normal practice, gets a good result.

It's also possible that it doesn't, and that's OK, because the result is not the point. Now you're starting to study the range of reactions that are available with a slight shift of gears. We can get so settled in our own groove that we don't understand how vast the spectrum of possible experience really is. But when we allow ourselves to test a different way of thinking, it's like breaking out of jail. In this way, curiosity helps you step out of fear, and by doing so you rob the thing you're afraid of of the power it has over you. This attitude—remaking your own life into a social experiment—can produce results you never could have anticipated. Even when the results are just barely different—the difference between a 7 and a 5 on the pain scale—that still represents the wedge you can use to reshape your life. From the outside, this tiny shift in behavior may not seem remarkable at all. But from the inside, it can feel mind-blowing. It's not that you got a slightly different reaction. It's that a different reaction is possible, thanks to your engagement and curiosity. And that can feel like a huge relief. It's a sign that you're rewiring your brain.

2

HOW TO TELL
LOVE STORIES

A friend of mine recently ended a relationship. From the beginning, she dropped hints about wanting to get married. After a while, she graduated to just saying so. Still no proposal until they entered their seventh year together and went on a romantic vacation to Cabo. In such a perfect setting to pop the question, what did her boyfriend do? He spent the whole two weeks happily snorkeling around and soaking up the sun. That did it. She broke up with him. After seven years.

A month later, she surprised her friends by landing in another relationship. That one ended quickly. In the months that followed, she replayed this sequence several times over: She'd meet a new man within weeks, start complaining about him to her friends almost immediately, then break up. The behavior was baffling, not just because she seamlessly hopped from one relationship to the next, but also because the men she dated had nothing in common. There was no type, no pattern in her attractions. They were just men it didn't last with. But what they did all have in common was that each one provided her with a new love story to tell. She was a highly functioning woman with a pivotal job in the New York banking industry, but being a friend of hers was like having a front-row seat at a Kate Hudson or Drew Barrymore movie.

Every man provided her an exciting starring role in a brand-new love story, one that she could tell to her friends, and to herself. Even if they turned out to be more of a tragicomedy, these stories allowed her to feel involved, and not on the sidelines. These kinds of stories, even when they aren't going to plan, can make us feel we aren't alone in the world. When we are at our lowest, any story can feel better than having no story.

But her recounting of these spicy new tales belied a more painful truth—that while on the surface her behavior could be dismissed by friends as a compulsion to be the actor-producer of her own serial love stories, there was a fearful sense of desperation that was motivating it all. After spending years being seen as the one most likely to land in a happy marriage, she'd suddenly been pushed to the back of the line as one friend or another raced ahead of her into successful relationships of their own, while her search for a replacement at whatever cost highlighted one of the greatest paradoxes when it comes to love stories: Sometimes the most important step to finding your own love story is learning how to be happy outside of one, and that was the step that was terrifying her.

THERE'S A DANGER IN LOVE stories that are more fun to tell because of just how heightened, dramatic, or unlikely they are. There's a Barry Manilow tune, "Somewhere Down the Road," where, as the song begins, it feels like Barry's doing the mature thing you do at the end of a relationship, reframing the breakup to make everybody feel less awful. He talks about their bad timing and her dreams calling her away; he almost sounds like a healthy adult. But then comes the chorus, where the music swells and he envisions them crossing paths again, belting out with total certainty that one day she'll figure out that she belongs with him.

Despite how creepy it would be to get a text like that from an ex, whenever this song comes on, usually when I'm in some waiting room, ol' Barry still manages to evoke the romantic in me—all because of the way he tells the story. Who doesn't suspend their rationality radar for a well-told love story? How many times have I watched *Titanic* and cried, despite the fact that Rose, at circa one hundred years old, doesn't seem to be over a guy she knew for four days when she was seventeen?

I never want to lose touch with the part of me that can be overwhelmed by the drama of stories that make my heart ache. But if I promote that part of me to be chief executive of my life decisions, I'm fucked. We have to separate the sentimental feelings we have for a love song or a gut-wrenching movie from the sober reality of our real life. It's an essential adjustment not just for our happiness, but for our survival.

Sometimes, if we want to start living again, we need to let go of the story we tell (or the way we are telling it) to ourselves and to the rest of the world. It isn't easy. Many of us know that familiar twinge of regret, years after a breakup, over a relationship we know ended for a very good reason. God forbid any of these momentary daydreams come true, and my high school girlfriend and I find ourselves back together on some ski lift in Switzerland or on a whale-watching cruise in Patagonia. It's important to counter these feelings with a strong dose of reality. Letting go of an old love story starts with resetting what it is we actually value in life. And to do that, we need to decide what a love story worth having actually looks like. Only then can we start telling ourselves different and healthier stories.

Can the one who got away—or, in the case of Jack and Rose, the one who froze to death and sank into the North Atlantic—ever actually be "the one"? Could the person we once happened to have an amazing connection with actually be the right person for us for life? If that actually were the case, MDMA would be the most valuable substance around because of the overwhelming feeling of love it can produce for a few short hours. But that's an experience and not a relationship, which is, by definition, ongoing. You don't find the pattern for a relationship worth having in a brief connection that produces a burst of peak sensation and then disappears. It would be absurd to wake up the next day and tell your friends that your MDMA buddy is your destiny. But too often that's the love story we want to tell.

All this begs the question: Where do we look for someone who really is worth our time and emotional energy?

The Limitations of Dropping the Handkerchief

In my first book, I tried to solve a problem I saw over and over: women dating men they weren't excited about, guys who treated them badly, guys who checked too many boxes on the bad-boyfriend checklist, women with no activity in their love life at all. I wanted them to have more choices. Better choices. Since so many women were struggling to meet great guys only to wind up dating terrible ones, I thought the problem could be fixed if I just helped them get more opportunities with great guys.

The problem of not meeting many great guys seemed to start because people were being passive about that first exchange. Too many women had been taught that it was a man's job to make the first move. This has shifted somewhat, and dating apps do make it easier for anyone to make the first move, but our conditioning still gets in the way, so in an awkward situation, people go to their default behavior and just wait around for somebody to approach them.

What kind of person approaches you when you're alone in a roomful of people? Often, it's someone who does that all the time, which isn't in itself a red flag, but certainly can be. At the very least, playing the waiting game usually leads to missing out on anyone who doesn't have that habit, or doesn't feel like it that day. How many women in the past did I want to talk to but never found the courage, in some non-awkward-enough way, to cross the room and say something to? And I'm not the only one who feels this way. Our hesitation alone doesn't make us bad partners, just awkward instigators.

Enter the Handkerchief Technique: Any woman who thought she was old-fashioned because she wouldn't approach a man herself has lost sight of what the "old-fashioned" actually did. A hundred years ago, in the days of calling cards and formal introductions, a woman would still walk past men, and when she spotted one she fancied, inadvertently drop her handkerchief (directly in front of him) and keep walking. That man, sensing an opportunity to be useful, would pick up said hanky and venture in a chivalrous tone:

HIM: Madam, ahem, I believe you dropped this?
HER (more to herself than to him): Oh, dear, did I?

And out of nowhere, the potential for conversation arose, a conversation he believed he started—though we know he didn't, since she chose precisely the man she wanted when she dropped the handkerchief in the first place.

That was the lesson: Too many people (and not just women) have gone through life waiting to be chosen, and now it was time to do the choosing. While this specific tactic landed with women, everyone can take something from it. I was always looking for someone to give me permission to speak to them before I dared try my luck. But the handkerchief flipped that sequence of events around and offers a subtle way to give someone permission to approach us, someone of our choosing. In doing so, it becomes a low-risk first move with the added benefit that the other person would have no notion that the encounter was not entirely their idea.

In that book, I talk about some practical ways one could "drop the handkerchief" today. I wasn't wrong about the power in the gesture. So many women have told me they're now married as a result of putting this advice to use to meet someone they might never have met otherwise. But I made one big miscalculation: I underestimated people's ability to make poor choices in their love life even when they had an abundance of choice.

When the guy she initially wanted to pick up the handkerchief turned out to be a genuine asshole, why did she still give him so much attention? Why not just take it back and drop it in front of someone else? Women were spending months, even years, with the wrong guy, even when they had plenty of other choices. The handkerchief hadn't solved it. It almost didn't seem to matter who was doing the choosing: something in the wiring was leading to bad choices, making people overvalue the wrong qualities in one person, and undervalue the right ones in someone else. Without fixing these instincts, people will keep defaulting to the kind of decisions that bring them pain and misery.

In fact, people were even becoming obsessed with someone who barely picked up the handkerchief in the first place (if at all!). Back in 2018 on my *Love Life* tour, I found myself in front of an audience in Dublin, inviting the audience to ask me questions about the issues troubling them the most right now. I've done this my entire career, and it has always been seen as a risky move by those on my team who value predictability. But there will always be a question that sells me on the value of the unexpected. Dublin was no exception. A woman in black, with black hair, and a smile playing over her features, stood up and asked, "How do you get over someone you never dated?"

The immediate laugh from the audience told me she'd struck a nerve. It felt like the perfect example of needing to change the story we tell ourselves. I said to her: "It comes down to what it is you want to romanticize—whether you want to romanticize someone from afar, or whether you want to fall in love with the reality of life. The days of me getting excited about someone who's not excited about me are over. I can't find the energy to get excited about someone who doesn't want me. If someone doesn't want me, it kills it for me, because I know this person will make me so unhappy."

After that, another woman at the back of the room stood up. She spoke confidently into the mic with a slight Eastern European accent, and her voice rang across the room as she started to tell her story: "When we meet a guy, and we are in the beginning, and the guy wants to show all the beautiful sides of his personality, values, and life, and he's perfect, and he's amazing, nothing bad about it, so you fall in love. Stupid. Me." She slapped her own forehead in an "Oops, I did it again" motion, while the audience, now completely on her side, laughed along.

"And then, three months, four months after, the guy goes to the dark side, and then everything falls, and then he's completely different, and treating you bad, and it just gets worse and worse and worse. But you are already there, and you are already in love. Two questions. First, how to recognize the traps. What is his true personality? And second, how to get rid of him when you're already in love?" At the second question, the audience practically gave her a standing ovation.

I jumped in: "I'm probably going to say at the end of this little rant of mine, 'You should probably leave the guy.'"

She was way ahead of me. "No, I did. We broke up this morning," she said in a tone that was both proud and nonchalant. The audience erupted in laughter and applause at the unexpected twist—she had already apparently done the very thing she was asking me to tell her how to do.

"Oh, OK. Very good. How long were you together?"

"One year and three months."

"How quickly—be honest—how quickly did you know it was wrong?"

"Honestly . . . Really?" The hand went back up to the forehead, a motion that had now become a tell for feelings of embarrassment or shame at ignoring things she shouldn't have.

"Seriously."

"Seriously, since the beginning."

"So you stayed in for a year and three months. Why?"

"Because I didn't want to be alone."

"Thank you for the wonderful honesty. 'I didn't want to be alone.' By the way, what a great morning to break up with someone!"

"That's what I thought!"

I loved this woman's confidence, the way she timed her breakup on the off-chance that she could stand up at our event and tell a version of her own love story that was hot off the presses. It served as a reminder not just of how powerful our stories can be, but also how much the impact can change depending on where we tell them. Certainly there's a difference between telling your love story to a stranger you will never see again and to a roomful of people who will find it hard to forget you—and will probably remind you of your tale if they ever run into you later. I don't think I'm exaggerating when I say that her story felt like her own personal Declaration of Independence.

Her two-part question captures so much of why I decided to write this book. "How do I recognize the traps?" was the first question she asked, and in the first half of this book we'll be focusing on the things that are worth paying attention to, in both dating and relationships. Once you know that, you can't un-know it. So when someone starts doing something that makes them a bad investment, you'll be fully aware of it.

Her second question sums up one of the big themes of the second half of this book: "How do you get rid of him when you're already in love?" This boils down to an age-old question: How can I get myself to do what I know I should do? It's almost like asking, How do I get myself to go to the gym? I know I should, it would be good for me, make me live longer, feel better, have a better quality of life. I know my current lifestyle makes me feel insecure and unhappy, the things I eat mess up my moods, I don't feel proud of myself, and it might lead to major problems with my health at some point if I don't stop.

Too often, we give the word *love* a special significance. "But I love them" sounds romantic. On the other hand: "But I love pizza, I just can't let go of pizza, I'm not ready." Actually, when I say that about pizza, it feels entirely justifiable. But still, you get the point. You can hide a lot of things inside that word *love*: fear of being alone, addiction to a person because of the cycle they put us through (the so-called "trauma bond"), a mistaken belief that we need them for our survival, the glorification of another person that we use to justify shortchanging ourselves. We'll focus on each of these in the pages ahead. For now we can say that this woman was asking two questions that are fundamental: How can I know what to do, and how can I find the internal resources to do it once I know?

The Castle

Let's start with the knowing. In order to know what to do in any given situation, we need to begin by asking ourselves a basic question in our dating lives: What is worth valuing?

It's important we ask this question out loud, consciously, even skeptically, because if we leave it up to our unconscious mind to decide what to value, it will often default to some incredibly dangerous miscalculations, such as *This person is important because I feel so strongly about them.* So not true. One does not equal the other, at least not automatically. To determine the value of a person in our lives as a serious candidate for a long-term relationship, we can use a model I call "The 4 Levels of Importance":

Importance Level 1: Admiration

This level is pretty self-explanatory, and we've all been there. We find ourselves drawn to someone. It may be that they have qualities we respect and admire, or want to have ourselves. Or they have a charisma that draws us in. A smile that makes us weak. Maybe they're just hot. Whatever it is, there's something about them we can't look away from, unless they look our way, in which case we may find ourselves hurriedly looking back down at our book, or our friend, or whatever it was we were doing before they hijacked our attention. If the person we can't stop thinking about is someone we get to see more than once, we begin to think of our situation as infatuation. A persistent, deeply annoying feeling of not being able to get this person out of our mind. A feeling that makes us act like an idiot. I remember listening to comedian Bill Burr talking about what happens to a genuinely funny person when they're suddenly faced with a live audience:

> The amount of times I've heard comedians say something so funny in the green room and I'm like, "Dude, that's so funny, you have to do

that on the stage," and they're like, "Nah, man, that's not me, that's not me," and I'm like, "It is you, you just fucking said it." . . . I have this theory that you walk onstage, and the weirdness of looking at people and talking, you become "This is me onstage, oh, I'm holding a microphone," and it just becomes weird. And you spend eight, ten, twelve, fifteen years trying to get back to who you were when you walked in, who was this guy who was making people laugh in the bars. Because you just walked into the bar and something happened and you were riffing on it, but you were comfortable. Then you go onstage and it's just like, "Oh shit, everybody is looking at me and I have to handle all this, uh, what am I doing with my hand, and how do I get this out of the stand?" and it just becomes this whole, you know, just looking at yourself, and who you are just goes right out the fucking window.

That pretty much sums up how most of us are when we become attracted to someone. Just like a comedian who gets nervous because now she's in front of a live audience and wants the audience to like her and the stakes feel really high, we forget our playful, relaxed, authentic selves when we are face-to-face with someone we like. The mere fact that we like them makes it feel as if the stakes are really high. As we will find out, there's nothing high at all about the stakes at this stage. In fact, level 1—admiration—isn't really important at all. It is nothing more than a mind trick.

Importance Level 2: Mutual Attraction

Now we are into more interesting territory: The person you like seems to like you back. At the very least, they're focusing their attention on you. Maybe they're complimenting you, asking to see you, remembering some offhand thing you happened to say the last time you spoke. Maybe it's just a mutual physical attraction, what we call chemistry. Maybe it's a synergy in the way you think, something we think of as a real connection. Perhaps it's both. But in this stage, your heart and mind vibrate with excitement for having stumbled on that most elusive of delights: wanting someone who wants you back!

I remember the feeling I had in high school when I found out a girl I'd fancied for a long time fancied me too. *Fancied* was the word we used in Essex where I grew up, which sounds like something fleeting and frivolous, not the angsty, nauseating longing I felt constantly in the pit of my stomach. I might fancy a chocolate biscuit (cookie, for Americans) or a cup of tea. It seemed impossible that my unimaginably complex feelings (namely that my life would only be complete if this one girl would just make me her boyfriend forever) could somehow be reduced to "I fancy you." But looking back on it now, it seems like the perfect word for trying to play it cool on the outside while our insides are pretzeling into all kinds of knots.

Back then, this fancy of ours felt like the most important thing in the world. And the fancying business doesn't get any easier after high school. As we get older, and our lives contract as our obligations grow, many people discover that finding someone they like in the first place can become an increasingly rare experience. The older we get, the easier it becomes to feel less visible to the world, as if our moment onstage has passed. To add to that, our standards tend to be higher, or at the very least more particular; many of us find ourselves attracted to fewer people as we become clearer on what we are looking for. So when we meet someone we like, and that person returns the attraction, it feels both rare and valuable.

This alchemical moment is responsible for most of the pain in people's love lives. Level 2—mutual attraction—seems so important, because whether it lasts years or it only seemed to occur for a night, it contains the hope of attaining something we have always deeply wanted: our own happily ever after. There's another song I feel deeply about: In *Hello Dolly!*, Michael Crawford sings about his overwhelming feelings for a woman he's just met. Clearly an innocent, he seems certain that it "only takes a moment to be loved a whole life long." Watching the movie, I get swept away by his mixture of innocence and idealism, even though I know, from a professional perspective, that he is attaching far too much meaning to an initial stirring of love.

I really do love the song. It captures the promise of love that we feel in that spark of mutual attraction. But it doesn't come with a warning: It also only takes a moment for us to create an entire epic in our mind of what this love story should be. Our heart may seem to know in an instant, but that's no guarantee that the other person's heart has jumped to the same conclusion.

Importance Level 3: Commitment

In the way that finance ads will say that past performance is not indicative of future results, mutual attraction is no guarantee of matching intentions in the field of love. One person may be planning to build a lasting relationship; the other may be angling for a passionate month-long affair. In both cases there is passionate attraction, but the outcome of each scenario couldn't be more different. This is why the third level of importance is such a vitally significant step on the road to someone taking on real importance in our lives.

Commitment is simply two people agreeing on a path forward together: I choose to be with you, and you choose to be with me. For most people (though not all) this will come with an agreement on the generally accepted conditions of monogamy.

Most people I coach know that, sooner or later, commitment is an important condition of a relationship. What they sometimes miss is how important commitment is as a gauge of how much to value the relationship. In other words, having "such an amazing connection with someone" isn't nearly as important or valuable as you think.

I've lost count of the number of women who have come to me for advice that begins like this:

I have this amazing man in my life, we have amazing conversations, we can talk for hours, we have such a great time when we are together, we have such great chemistry, and a really deep connection.

And I ask: So what's the problem?

Nine times out of ten they will offer some version of:

- I don't know where it's going; he isn't progressing things.
- Sometimes we go days without speaking and I don't feel like I exist to him, but I'm afraid of bringing it up.
- I want to be exclusive but he's not ready.

Without a mutual agreement to build something, there is no relationship. Having mutual attraction (Importance Level 2, above) is equivalent to two people discovering a plot of land together that seems to have potential. Maybe it's on a hillside, or by a lake, or in a prime spot in the city. It's a great, picturesque plot of land. But nothing is built there yet. What it needs to realize its potential is two builders, two people who both say, "Yes, let's build a beautiful castle of our own here." Too often I find a woman still admiring the plot of land long after the other person has disappeared into the brush. Every now and again, he may come back and breathe life into the fantasy, but he's never really setting down stakes, and he certainly isn't building. Ask yourself, Do I have a builder, or is it just a connection? Connections don't build castles; builders do.

That's why I try to temper the reactions of people who are crying too hard over lost connections. They're not really crying over what they had, rather what they thought could have been. If someone you had mutual attraction with disappears or moves on (or if you're the one moving on), don't grieve too much. The right person is someone who says yes. It will never be someone who says no, no matter how much potential you give them credit for. If they don't say yes, then by definition, they have lost any value once attributed to them, and they cease to be an option in our love lives.

Think about it for a moment. If there's someone in your life you have mutual attraction with (level 2), who also commits to you (level 3), and they suddenly get hit by a bus, that's tragic. No one would blame you for grieving in a situation like that. But now imagine (you might not have to) that you are going through the same emotions over the loss of someone who told you they didn't want to commit to you. That person didn't die; they're still walking around, or sitting at home ordering ridiculous things on Amazon. They're just choosing not to be with you. How important to your love life can they possibly be?

There's a verse in a Charles Bukowski poem that goes:

but as God said,
crossing his legs,
I see where I have made plenty of poets
but not so very much
poetry.

In the course of your love life you may run into a lot of poets, but I assure you, you'll find a lot less poetry. A poet may talk a good game, but poetry takes effort and has to actually be written for it to exist. Poetry grows out of a relationship, being surprised by the beauty in the things you build together, piece by piece. The poet may gaze handsomely over the plot of land, but there's no poetry in a relationship until the two of you start working together on something that will stand the test of time. Don't overvalue the poet when there's no actual poetry.

Importance Level 4: Compatibility

It is said that love conquers all. In life, maybe. But in love, ironically, love doesn't conquer all. Compatibility does. Two people may say yes to each other—that is, there may be commitment—but being able to work together gracefully is a different story. How well do you work in a team together? Do you have the same idea of what a great relationship looks like? Do you have the same goals? What about goals you each have that are different: Are they synergistic or do they represent two completely incompatible futures?

Compatibility is different from mutual attraction. I've encountered many people in my life that I felt an attraction with, in business, friendships, and love, but that didn't make us compatible. I may have an acquaintance I feel connected to, but if that person is unreliable, has a very creative relationship with the truth, and is late all the time, we're going to discover that we're incompatible as friends. This isn't just true for negative qualities. It's true for mere differences in behavior and the way we want to live our lives. In a relationship where there is one extreme introvert and one extreme extrovert, neither is inherently good or bad, but the difference may be enough to cause severe practical problems in the relationship, even if the two of them started with a strong connection.

Relationships aren't sustained on connection alone. The true test is how naturally compatible your beliefs and behaviors are, and how competently you're able to negotiate with each other when differences arise. One of the simplest questions to ask at this stage is: "Are they good at handling me?" Isn't that one of the most romantic things anyone can do? We spend so much dating time trying to decide who's right and who's wrong for us—and there's certainly a level of wrong that's just a nonstarter—but in a relationship we are all going to be right and wrong a lot. Who's great at managing our inevitable freakouts? And whose inevitable freakouts are we great at managing? Does the person you're with enjoy the process? Are they patient or amused helping you manage something that they have a completely different view of? Can you turn around and do the same? Can even your differences be a source of pleasure? And on the days that they're not, will you still be spooning at the end of the day? Compatibility has nothing to do with agreeing on everything. It has a lot to do with enjoying the drama and dynamics of the day-to-day decisions you make together. Only through this fourth and final level of importance—compatibility—does a love story get to become a life story.

3

RETRAIN YOUR INSTINCTS

One of the love life myths is that somehow love is a special realm where we can be guided by instinct. But this assumes that in childhood we all developed great instincts for every situation. In reality, through no fault of our own, there are areas where we have developed instincts that are completely counterproductive for our happiness and well-being, and can even be dangerous. In fact, in some situations, our instincts can get us killed. This was what my boxing teacher, Martin Snow, told me when he caught me blinking in the ring. "Your instincts can get you killed, kid!" he said. He wanted me to think of a riptide where our instinct, when we feel it pulling us out to sea, is to swim back to shore. But the current is more powerful than we are. So we have to fight this natural instinct and go the long way by swimming parallel to the shore, even if the riptide carries us farther out, until we're safely out of the current and can head back to the beach through calmer water.

In the boxing ring, it's the same thing. With a punch heading at my face, my instinct was to blink. I had to train myself to overcome that natural instinct—one that essentially blinded me at the most crucial moment—and learn instead to block or parry or slip the punch that's heading straight for me.

That's what it's like in the early stages of attraction just when we decide we like someone. There's a temptation to just surrender to the feeling, clear our schedule, and see if they're game to fly to Paris together or begin inquiring as to whether our company has offices in a town near them that wasn't even on our radar a month ago. In our excitement over a person we've only been on one or two dates with, we get ahead of ourselves. We give in to our romantic instincts and rocket into a realm of fantasy romance.

As much as you may want to, it turns out that just about the worst thing you can do at this stage is tell four of your best friends, who, of course, share your romantic instincts. This amplifies the danger. You show them the latest messages from the new and incredibly attractive figure in your life and suddenly you're all scrolling through his Instagram while they're pointing out the ways you're perfect for each other. "Look, he's a musician, that's hot!" "Aww, check out all the pictures he shares of himself and his nephews. He seems like such a great guy!" "Look at his style, he's so your type!" Next thing you know, your friends have appointed themselves managers of your love life, checking in to see whether and when you're going out on a date with this dream man. How can reality stand up against that? How can any connection develop organically after you're so amped up just because he has a man bun and a guitar?

All this excitement puts you into hyperdrive, moving at the speed of light toward some fantasy scenario. Then something shifts in the universe and that planet you were aiming for suddenly begins to recede. The object of all that imaginative effort begins to pull away.

The energy between the two of you changes. Communication becomes inconsistent. Texts grow short. None of them contain the future tense. All the little things that were stoking the fantasies, the sexy ineffable things that got you excited, don't seem to be happening anymore. How could something so right vanish even faster than it appeared?

Why Do People Go Cold?

What changes? There are too many reasons to list. They got a text from an ex. They like the drama of attraction but feel crowded by an actual person. Work is a bigger priority than dating. They're dating multiple people and just started getting serious with one of them who's not you. They fed off your excitement until they realized they couldn't match it. Their brother went into the hospital. They bought a horse.

The first thing to realize is that there's no way to know. And the instinct to play detective until you nail down a reason can quickly become dangerous. Here's a hard truth: We often don't get to know, and frustrating ourselves in pursuit of the unknowable is a recipe for unhappiness. Remember the last time someone in your friend circle wanted to hang out and you didn't feel like fitting it into the hundred things you had to do that week? Did you helpfully tell them, "Hey, you're not one of my closest friends, and while it's possible that it could be fun spending time together, I'm just not motivated, OK"? Or did you say: "Hey, super-busy week over here, but when things free up, I'd love to"? We often can't be truly honest because it would be dreadful or time-consuming or inconvenient or rude, so why should we expect full disclosure from someone we barely know (even if we slept with them and like them)?

Nevertheless, when someone pulls away, it's natural to wonder if there was something we did to cause their disappointing exit. An explanation that falls on our side relates to another dangerous instinct we have early on once we've decided we like someone: the instinct to make someone too important, too quickly.

People tend to pull away when they sense they've become too important too quickly. No one wants to be someone else's top priority before they've earned it. Imagine going to a job interview and being told, "How would you like to be our CEO? Starting tomorrow?" That may have happened at some company somewhere once or twice, but usually if you're getting the top job—and what is dating if not a search for a suitable candidate for a top job?—you'd expect to come back for multiple interviews. On this score, dating really is like a business: The top spot can't really be given away, it can only be earned. So when things do start moving so quickly, it's natural for someone to think, "Why me? How'd I get so valuable when they don't know me and I haven't really done all that much? Is there something wrong with them? Do they not have options?" It's a deadly combination in a new romance, this double whammy that makes your value plummet as your intensity goes up. When that happens, no one should be surprised if the person who seemed so perfect just a few days ago starts vanishing from your DMs. We have to be incredibly wary of the instinct to transfer the importance we feel for the position we are looking to fill to a new person who only *might* one day fill it.

Unfortunately, this is the stage where another questionable instinct can kick in: We feel a new relationship slipping away, and we decide to fight for it. Suddenly this romance is important enough to mobilize all our resources to keep it. Why? This pit-bull instinct may be useful when we've messed up at work and have to show our boss we're willing to do whatever it takes to correct it, but it's not likely to help in early dating, for many reasons. First, it's illogical, based on a false notion that something increases in value when you think there might be less of it soon. But is a potential connection really such a scarce commodity, as if they were the romantic equivalent of a nationwide search for a suitable liver transplant? Probably not, if you first ran into them at the coffee shop around the corner. Second, it's a sign of impatience; if we want results and we want them *now*, we'll place a greater value on something just because it's here in front of us. This is what happens at closing time at bars all over the world, and the results are generally not as persuasive in the light of day.

Third, and most troubling, are the self-esteem issues that contribute to our overvaluing this person we barely know and undervaluing our own self. Where did we get the idea that somebody who's pulling away and growing uncertain (ABOUT US!) is just what we need, when exactly the opposite is true? This lukewarm reaction on their part is all the proof you need that they're not right for you. The appropriate response in that situation is to say, "Hey, things have felt a little different between us recently, and although it's been really fun getting to know you so far, I think maybe we should hit pause as I sense you're busy in your life right now and that (correct me if I'm wrong) we might not be looking for the same things." It goes against all our instincts to be the one to "hit pause" at the very same time as we desperately wish it would continue. But inspect this message more closely and you'll see you're not closing the door; you're extending an invitation for them to make the effort you've been wanting all along.

If we find ourselves drawn to someone who's pulling away, we have to suspect ourselves. What is it that's so great about this person anyway? They're hot? Tall? Self-assured? Charismatic? Charming? None of those are the traits that make a great partner. I had a terrific talk recently with Dr. Ramani Durvasula, who specializes in helping people recover from relationships with narcissists, and she warned that vague responses like that ("There's just something about them!") set off alarm bells and are a likely indicator of a trauma bond: You're attracted to them because they have something you can't name (and will only discover when it's too late), but the feelings in you they are able to generate are what compel you to keep trying.

So if that's your first instinct (to keep trying because of some mysterious quality or feeling) it's good to keep in mind the easily recognizable qualities that do make a good partner: They're kind and compassionate. They show up for you, consistently, reliably. They communicate well. They're honest and trustworthy. They make a great teammate. They care about your day and the challenges you face, and they want to support you as you face them. (And if those sound like qualities that make you head for the hills, you're not looking for a relationship!)

But those are rarely the qualities people describe when they're trying to list what they like about a new person. When people talk about someone they can't get off their mind, they usually list things like charisma, confidence, boldness, sex appeal, connection, the fact that they can talk about all sorts of subjects, that they "have such strong feelings for them"—and these can all be wonderful things to have. But they're not the traits that make you say, "This person will be an incredible teammate."

If *you* have those teammate traits—if you're the one who's trustworthy, kind, committed, communicative, consistent, generous—then you've got the rare stuff that's worth fighting for. It's also the rare stuff you should protect. And if someone doesn't recognize those qualities in you, they'll never value what's valuable in you. You should keep them at arm's length until they do. In the meantime, they're definitely not a person worth fighting for.

You will meet people who are wonderful to hang out with, but do they have what it takes to build an amazing relationship? If they're already pulling away after a few dates, probably not. One of the greatest things you can find in a partner is a sense of certainty about you. There are definitely times you should be willing to fight for someone—in the right circumstances. Romeo and Juliet, despite the war between their families, had a relationship they both wanted. They weren't fighting uncertainty, they were fighting outside circumstances, and (setting aside for a moment the fact that they were both children who never even reached the point of a real relationship) their feelings for each other were definitely not lukewarm. Romeo wasn't saying, "Should I be worried that I climbed to her balcony and found her writing saucy letters to Paris? Never mind. I'll still fight for Juliet and our love!"

Ask yourself if you're playing Romeo and Juliet with someone and the big obstacle is their uncertainty. Because if that's in the script, why take the part? The only person worth having in our love story is the one who values what we have to give. Part two of that rule is that they won't value what we have to give if we don't put a high price on it ourselves. If they get the idea that we'll fight for them even when they're pulling away, first they're going to think we're way too intense, then they're going to wonder what this one-sided intensity says about us, our confidence in ourselves, and who we are.

Our reaction to their pulling away should be to let them know that this indifference, this sudden change of heart, has consequences. Sure, we were trying—they got a taste of what we're capable of—but the moment they started projecting their ambivalence, they became less worthy of the effort we can lavish on someone we have feelings for. They took themselves out of the running for all those wonderful things. And they need to know it. You can still be kind, but let them see that your intensity is like a solar flare—it can stop as quickly as it starts. Tell them, "Yes, I'm attracted to you. We have fun. You make me laugh. And sure, you can be exciting. But none of that is more important than what's right for me."

Lowering the Intensity

If I'm coaching someone, the last thing I want to say is "Be less intense!" because, well, it's too intense. But it's good to remember that, as intoxicating as the very beginning of the relationship can be, it's also when you're most likely to experience uncertainty (both theirs and your own). Connection and intimacy grow at an unpredictable pace, with retreats and advances. It's natural to feel that you've overextended yourself, and think you have to compensate for some (imaginary?) mistake by pulling back. You can't overcome this unpredictability—which is natural and even appropriate on both sides—by overwhelming it with a certainty of your own. Recognize these swings, as erratic as they may feel, as part of the natural flow. There is no such thing as a permanent feeling. Feelings pass. As the poet Rainer Maria Rilke wrote, "Let everything happen to you: beauty and terror. Just keep going. No feeling is final."

I sometimes get offers to speak somewhere or be part of some opportunity that sounds like it could be amazing—*if* it ever actually happened! Since there's no way to know whether the complicated arrangements will even work out, I put it out of my mind. I have a saying in those situations: "We'll see." It's not a very exciting saying—it may actually be boring—and it sometimes frustrates people on my team who want to fantasize with me about all the good things that could come from these incredible opportunities. But just saying "We'll see" does lower the temperature and reminds me (and anybody I'm bumming out) that nothing is real until it is. It also keeps me focused on the things I can actually control, like making sure I continue to progress in other important ways in my life instead of waiting and hoping for this opportunity to be realized.

Dating is the same way. Date One shouldn't come with expectations. If we get too excited about it (or too judgy!), we can muddy our view of what's really happening. Of course, there are basic things we can expect, like common courtesy. If they're an hour late, they've fallen below baseline expectations of respect. But outside of that, Date One is just about having fun, and, on our side, being great company. On a first date, we want to see if they're great company, but we want to *be* great company too. After Date One, we want to maintain a nice balance to make sure we're being present. It's a kind of mindful dating: If it's Date Three, be on Date Three. Don't skip ahead to Date Fifty-Six. Let yourself enjoy every stage. Slow down. See the other person for who they are, and you will both relax. Be careful not to project onto them amazing or mythic qualities they don't have.

It's hard to tell someone all of this. Asking someone to question their instincts can feel tantamount to saying, "You shouldn't trust yourself," which is the opposite of the message of this book. It's more about recognizing these instincts as extremely normal and deeply human features that can hurt us: surrendering to something that superficially resembles what we've been looking for our whole lives; clearing our schedule for someone; getting ahead of ourselves; becoming swept up in our friends heightening the stakes with their excitement about it; moving at breakneck speed; wanting closure when someone disappears; making them too important, too quickly (while undervaluing ourselves); basing our feelings on hard-to-describe qualities and not ones that actually make a great partner; fighting harder when they pull away; overcorrecting when we think it was our mistake that made them pull away.

We must defy these instincts in ways that can at first feel extremely counterintuitive, but will lead us to much more peace and happiness in our love lives: slowing down; lowering the temperature; "hitting pause" when someone isn't respecting or reciprocating the energy we are giving; valuing someone who is present over someone who is scarce; substituting easygoing curiosity—one that allows our counterpart some room to be themselves—for overwhelming emotions; balancing optimism with a "we'll see" mindset; and keeping our eye on real qualities that make a great partner. Like in the case of the riptide, it may initially feel counterintuitive to take the longer route back to shore, but the results will be far more real and lasting.

These things all help you find the right perspective in the earliest days, and as a bonus make you more attractive to the person in question. As Martin the boxing coach says: "When life happens, we don't rely on our instincts, we rely on our training." With time, your new training can even become your new instincts—instincts you become increasingly grateful for as you experience a more straightforward, and ultimately more rewarding, love life.

The worst instinct of all is the instinct to undervalue all you have to offer. Don't ever sell yourself short by giving everything to someone who isn't worth it, or hasn't proven themselves to be worth it yet. This is the ultimate reason you have to protect your heart from getting swept up in a fantasy before you've actually gotten the chance to know someone. In the beginning, all you're seeing is their early (and often best) behavior. How someone makes you feel early on is not a reflection of their character; it is a reflection of their impact. True character is consistent; it can only be measured over time.

4

BEWARE AVOIDERS

But First, a Note on Liars

It's nearly impossible to spot a genius liar. But they're out there, the brilliant con artists and certifiable psychopaths who can beat a polygraph or fool an FBI agent. And, to tell the truth, spending time with gifted and talented liars (before you realize who they really are) can be a lot of fun. What amazing backgrounds they seem to have! What incredible lives! It's almost unbelievable! They make it feel as if anything is possible and they may even promise as much. They're one reason there are cults—and epically horrible relationships. Liars on that level, the kind for whom living and lying are indistinguishable, are hard to recover from—and, depending on how long and how intimately they were able to operate, the damage can be devastating, and often creates serious trauma. I've worked with plenty of individuals who've experienced that level of deception.

But, luckily, people with that level of mendacious skill are rare. It's much more common—it's nearly universal—for us to overlook the more garden-variety dissemblers. Admittedly, we can't notice everything about a person we've just met, but nearly everyone looks past a few things when we think we're becoming attracted. Practiced liars rely on this selective blindness. What's amazing is how little they have to say to pull this deception off—all because we want to believe.

In the beginning, a liar doesn't depend on your complicity in order to lie to you. But to keep up the act, liars need a willing audience—because if you're spending a lot of time with a liar, you do start to notice certain inconsistencies, the big or small disconnects between what they're saying and how they behave in everyday life. When you first catch them at it, you might even feel an impulse to look away. You don't want to appear neurotically suspicious or ruin something that feels like it has potential.

But with a liar, the dissonance between their words and actions never goes away. At some point, if you don't agree to ignore these incongruencies, their whole performance—because that's what lies really are, a charade, a fantasy they want to make you the costar in—falls flat. Just the way a magician needs an audience willing to suspend disbelief (does anybody really think that card tricks demonstrate psychic powers?), a liar needs someone who'll buy their act and then sit back to enjoy the show.

But underneath it all, there's a real person whose words are out of sync with their behavior. If we recognize this and decide that we would like to do something about it, branding them a liar is probably not the best place to start. But pointing out the disconnection, letting them know you've noticed a difference between what they say and what they wind up doing, brings the conversation into more neutral territory. It also puts them on notice. There's a whole spectrum of reasons why people lie—from insecurity and lack of a sense of control to addiction and psychopathy. But the only way to address any of it—to find out whether you're going to soothe the insecurities, help treat the addiction, or dump the psychopath—is to see what happens when you bring the topic out in the open.

We'll talk later about why we maintain relationships with people we know are causing us harm, and how you can break that cycle for yourself. But now I want to talk about a type that's far more common than the blatant liar—someone who can deceive you without ever telling a lie: the avoider.

Beware Avoiders

I think we use the word *liars* too broadly. There really are compulsive liars in the world. But most people don't run on the same mix of manipulation and insecurity that drives this compulsion—which is not to say most people tell the truth, but rather they don't have the pathology to tell bald-faced lies or whip up a nearly coherent alternate reality on the spot.

Instead, they give easygoing evasive responses that feel almost as normal as the full truth. If you ask someone where they see your relationship going and they say, "Look, I'm having a great time with you, but I just got over someone and I'm still not sure what I want right now"—well, there's your truth. Maybe they didn't spell it out explicitly—avoiders never will—but there's no reason to waste your energy trying to decode their words. Anything that isn't a clear "What are you talking about? It's you and me, baby!" means it's time to reassess how much time and energy to invest in this situation.

Liars go out of their way to lie to you—lying is their drug, and they're truly happy to offer you a line. But avoiders are aiming for nearly the opposite effect. On certain topics—usually the ones that lead to a true sense of intimacy—they go out of their way not to share a single word. While most of us are clumsy or obvious liars, we can still be very skillful at avoiding subjects we don't want to discuss. Liars and avoiders do share certain traits: To start, both enjoy an uncomfortable relationship with the truth. But while the liar is passing out falsehoods like chocolates on Valentine's Day, the avoider is deftly changing the topic or deliberately missing the point.

There's a telling moment in the 2006 movie *The Holiday* that perfectly captures both the classic avoider and the response his behavior deserves. Jasper (Rufus Sewell), the ultimate dashing manipulator, has flown from England to Los Angeles, where Iris (Kate Winslet) has finally been enjoying some happiness without him. Jasper has one goal: to bring her back under his spell.

Iris, excited despite herself by Jasper's sudden invitation to accompany him on a trip to Venice, asks if he's really free to do that. When he responds with a classic avoider line ("I just traveled halfway across the world to see you, haven't I?"), she realizes that wasn't exactly an answer to her question and she asks him directly if he's broken up with his fiancée. When Jasper again tries to avoid answering ("I wish you could just accept knowing how confused I am about all this"), she does what she realizes has been called for for years, and tells him, "I'm miraculously done being in love with you!"

As the classic avoider, Jasper never lied, but he also never gave her a truthful answer. Nevertheless, by answering a direct question with a carefully worded evasion, he did reveal his true nature. Once she saw him waffling under direct questioning, Iris finally found the courage to shut down the toxic dynamic he kept trapping her in with his artful evasions.

It's not productive to worry about liars. We may, from time to time, fall victim to a lie. Usually there's nothing we can do about it. Our only job is to decide what to do once we discover that we've been lied to. But an avoider can be more dangerous than a liar in the long run, because avoiders make us their dance partners. They depend on our unwillingness to turn the conversation to any topic where we might have to face some painful truths.

We've probably done some avoiding ourselves, when it's suited us. Have you ever realized someone liked you more than you liked them? Did you tell them immediately? Unless you're a saint and always have been, the answer is likely no. We've all changed the subject when there's a price we're not yet willing to pay. Avoiding difficult conversations is human, on both sides.

Unfortunately, by avoiding difficult conversations, we run the risk of conspiring in our own unhappiness. *Because there can never be only one avoider in a relationship.* If we never ask uncomfortable questions when they come up, we're just playing along. This isn't something that only happens in the "limbo" stage of a relationship when you still don't know where you stand; this plays out in marriages all over the world that follow one script on the surface and ignore the drama building up everywhere else.

It's not enough to simply beware an avoider. We have to actively ensure we aren't enabling them by being an avoider ourselves. But if you want to make sure you're not enabling an avoider, you have to ask scary questions. The questions themselves may not be inherently scary; it's the consequences of finally knowing the truth that make us hesitate to put them into words. But you lose nothing by communicating. The right relationship is one where things get better when you communicate. If your relationship gets worse when one of you speaks the truth, you're in the wrong relationship.

Ask Scary Questions

There's a question I often ask at the beginning of live events: "Who here is single?" The majority of hands go up.

I then ask, "Who's in a relationship?" That usually encompasses about 20 percent of the room.

My next question catches people a little more off guard: "Who here isn't sure if they're in a relationship?" Sheepishly, hands start rising across the room.

Something about their situation has left them confused about what, exactly, their situation is. These are the same people who'll send me messages on social media asking where they stand with the person they just started dating. Midway through writing this chapter, I received a well-timed message from a woman named Maria asking me exactly that:

> I have been talking to/dating this man for close to five months now and everything is going well. We talk every day and we try to see each other as much as we can (at times there is a huge gap when we don't physically see each other due to our busy schedules). He's like no other man I have met, a gentleman, kind, and intelligent, and I feel very comfortable with him. However, I'm terrified of having the conversation with him on where we are in the relationship. Are we exclusive? etc. I see that he's interested in me, and I'm interested in him. My question is: How should I ask where we stand without going too deep into it?

There are many conversations we prefer to avoid, and some, like the one Maria hasn't had, that terrify us. But to be afraid of having a conversation is to be afraid of what we'll learn from it. Month by month, our rejection of a conversation turns into a rejection of the truth—the *actual* state of the relationship, of all the feelings and intentions we can't say out loud. Little by little, the longer we avoid this one honest conversation, our real-life relationship may increasingly depart from the imaginary one we have constructed in our mind: a delicate ideal we don't dare expose to the light of reality.

We especially avoid asking direct questions if we think they'd precipitate a new dynamic and hasten the end of an old one we're clinging to. Difficult questions force relationships to change form—either in reality, or in the form they've taken in our minds. Too often we choose to stay in relationships because of the relationship we're having with someone in our mind, and not because the one we're actually experiencing in real life is providing us with what we really want.

I thought of calling this chapter "If You Don't Know Where You Stand, Ask!" But that ignores the difficulty that surrounds this process. Asking one question may require a few calories of effort, but bracing ourselves for the consequences, the potential heartbreak, and even the agonizing uncertainty that the conversation may well turn into the final one of the relationship (even if that relationship is just OK), that takes real, genuine energy. It takes bravery. It means preparing ourselves for a lost future—a new reality we have not readied ourselves for, a different life that we didn't plan to begin today.

If we're not ready for the answer—or ready to do what's in our best interest upon getting such an answer—we then find ourselves in a situation where the reality of our circumstances no longer matches the idea we have built up in our mind—an idea that, in light of new information, has risked veering into the world of fantasy.

Let's say that Maria, hoping that the man she's been dating has intentions for them to be together for the long term, learns that he doesn't want a relationship, sees their time together merely as a bit of fun, or still wants to see other people. She now finds herself in an incompatible situation. Having come face-to-face with the limited potential of this relationship, she is now in danger of knowingly and willingly wasting her time.

If she never asks, she can pretend she doesn't know she's wasting her time. She can be a victim when he finally reveals he's never been serious about her the whole time they've been together. But if she asks the scary question and he confirms that he's not serious, she may find herself more than just hurt by his answer. In a way, learning the truth and moving on would be a best-case scenario. The worst would be if, despite her hurt, she doesn't have the strength to walk away. Perhaps she already doesn't trust herself to be able to, which is why she's avoiding the conversation in the first place. Finding herself in such a situation would not only mean dealing with disappointment; it would also be a major blow to her identity as a strong and self-respecting woman.

If she doesn't walk away, she will have to embrace this new world—a world where if she wants to continue to invest in this unserious situation, she will have to find a way to make 2 + 1 = 4. This world is the birthplace of cognitive dissonance—and not just for her. After this conversation, he too will have to create his own form of cognitive dissonance to keep the courtship going.

Having been forced to answer questions he has no welcome answers to, and not at a time of his choosing, the situation will now feel very "real." If she continues to see him, her negative feelings about the lack of progression—which were previously just a subtext he could ignore—will now be an unwelcome guest on every date, a conscious and lurking downer replacing the carefree tone of their previous interactions.

Until this point, he'd been enjoying the freedoms that *not* having this conversation had presented. He hadn't actively lied because they'd never talked about it. But now that they *have* talked about it, his intentions (or lack thereof) are on the table, at which point it all becomes a little less romantic. His dissonance will consist of ignoring the ways his romantic—but ultimately hollow—gestures feed her hope of progression while she lives with the ongoing anguish of the progression she'd once happily imagined never being realized.

So she thinks, "No, it's better to have the conversation at another time and keep enjoying this romance." After all, she likes this guy. A lot. And what does she have to look forward to by blowing up this situation? Being on her own again with no one she feels real chemistry with? Going back on the apps for a string of disappointing dates? Surely better to let it play out with this person she *knows* she likes where there's at least a chance some good may come of it. Besides, the more time she spends with him, the more attached he's going to get, right?

A client recently said to me on one of my webinars: "It all works until you start making waves." Her word choice highlights the sleight of hand we use when our lack of confidence is telling us to suppress any direct statement of our needs. "Making waves" here should be replaced with "communicating your needs."

Why would we want to be in a relationship that only works if we go silent about what we want? Clearly, there's a time when asking "What are we?" would be a crazy thing to say. (Imagine the Kathy Bates in *Misery* vibes of someone turning to you at the end of the first date to say, "I had an amazing time. So, what are we now?") But avoiding conversations that reveal intentions is an incredible waste of time and demonstrates a lack of respect for oneself.

If you've been seeing someone consistently for months and you still have no idea what the two of you are, or if it's even exclusive, it's time to have the conversation:

> "Hey, I'm having the best time seeing you, I like you, and I can feel myself liking you more and more each time we see each other, but I find myself not really knowing where we stand . . . I didn't want to just assume we were exclusive, but I want you to know I'm not seeing anyone else right now because I've been giving this a real chance. I wanted to know if you were in the same place or if you're still wanting to remain open to seeing other people. If so, then that's OK, but it's something I should probably know before I keep investing more time and energy into us."

Say all of this kindly, but be ruthless in your response. After all, your time and energy are at stake here.

We're all afraid of unwelcome answers in life. I'm aware of how powerful that fear can be in stopping us from having a conversation we really need to have. But I also know that by nurturing your confidence and cultivating a wider perspective, that will change. You'll see that even the answer you once thought was your worst nightmare is merely a signal pointing you in the direction of something that's more worthy of your time and energy. When you do land in that situation, asking the question will be natural, because when you are truly valuing yourself, it will be your time and energy you work hardest to protect, rather than the fantasy of what you currently have—and perhaps even more dangerously—the fantasy of what *could* be. We'll never rid the world of avoiders, but we don't need to. By asking scary questions and acting on the answers, you'll never need to worry about having your time wasted by one again.

Still, it's possible that, despite the advance warning, you fall for an avoider and all their tricks and emotional loopholes and blind spots and brick walls. It happens more often than anyone likes to admit—which makes sense, because not admitting that it's happening is how it happens in the first place! But when we avoid confronting the exact thing we're afraid may actually be happening to us, a strange dynamic starts to take over. We begin to sell ourselves on the avoider's twisted logic, sometimes so successfully that we're surprised when other people seem skeptical of the line of thinking we've come to accept. If you suspect this might apply to you, then please consider the warning in the next chapter.

5

DO NOT JOIN
A CULT OF TWO

Whenever someone stands up at a live event or appears online with an urgent question, I've learned to take a beat before starting in with a response. Partly that's to help someone relax—it's not so easy to talk to a crowd, virtual or in person, about your most intimate concerns—and teasing out the circumstances a little always helps. But I've also learned that the question someone asks is not necessarily the same thing as the problem they really want to solve. So talking around their question a little lets us get closer to the real issue.

I've faced thousands of questions. Some of them are profoundly individual and take a lot of time to untangle. But some of them are not. If there's anything close to a one-size-fits-all piece of advice that would spare people the most heartache at the beginning of a relationship, it's this: Assume exclusivity at your peril!

Some will argue that after so many dates, it's simply implied that two people are exclusive based on the fact that they've been seeing each other a lot, talking every day, texting nonstop, etc. It doesn't seem unreasonable, especially when the two of you have been together so much that you'd need a Time-Turner clock from the Ministry of Magic in order to see other people.

I never want to be the romance-killer, injecting skepticism into something that should be a beautiful and organic process of two people falling madly in love or lust. But having watched so many get hurt this way, I can say, simply from a statistical standpoint, that the conversation about exclusivity is one you should have, proactively and preemptively, because the downside of *not* doing it is so much worse than any immediate discomfort you might feel in bringing up the subject.

In any case, the only truly awkward conversations are the ones where you find out that the two of you are operating in completely different worlds—for instance, when they tell you they want to see other people and you tell them you don't. But that's exactly the conversation that will spare you more pain down the road.

In fact, conversations like these won't necessarily interrupt the romance. When done right, they can even *add* to it. If you're on the same page about wanting to jump each other and *only* each other, the conversation can actually be quite fun. "I'm the only one you want? Why, I'm so glad you said that because you're the only one *I* want. Now let's go celebrate in a stairwell somewhere . . ."

Here are some ways of bringing it up, as well as some variations for different situations. Let's say you're in the early stages of dating. You can say:

> "I'm having the best time with you, but right now when someone asks me out, I don't know what to say to them. I don't want to put any undue pressure on this because I'm enjoying the process of getting to know each other, but I like you, and while we're deciding whether this could really be something, I'd like to give it a proper chance to see where it goes and not date other people."

Or:

> "I'm not seeing anyone else and I wanted to know where your head is at with things."

You can also adapt it to really own your vulnerability and show who you are:

> "I'm sensitive and I know I'd get hurt if I found out later that you were seeing other people, because I'm really starting to like you. We don't have to decide what this is right now or put labels on it, but I know I'd be treating this differently if we were still open to dating

other people right now versus giving it a shot with just each other. What do you think?"

Intimacy can also be the precursor to exclusivity. If you're getting physical, but clarity as to where you stand is important for you before you do, you can say:

> "I like you and I'm really attracted to you. But I don't want us to get more physical if you're in a casual place in your life right now, even though I'm sure it would be a lot of fun. By the way, it's absolutely fine if that's where you're at, but I just wanted to put it out there, because I'm not looking to be intimate with someone who is looking to do the same thing with other people. That's just not me."

I want to stress that it's not about using this to put pressure on someone. Putting pressure on someone rarely works. It's more about staying true to yourself and what you want, while demonstrating that you're not judging them for the phase they're in, even if it means the two of you need to go your separate ways:

> "That doesn't mean we have to rush anything . . . it just means if that's not where you're at, I'd rather take it slowly for now until you feel the same—and if we don't arrive there that's OK too, since not everything is meant to be."

This is true power: being kind, composed, and willing to walk away without anger if they aren't on the same page as you.

If you recognize that you've gotten stuck in some kind of situationship, statements like this can help. There's a warmth and a charm to all of them, but there's no lack of candor. By all means, make them your own, and express your unique voice through them; but no matter what, you must own them. Owning them means understanding why they work, so that you have conviction in using them and sticking to them. Remember, standards aren't tactics. Tactics are transactional. Standards stay consistent, even when they don't get us the result we'd hoped for.

But sometimes I'll get a question from someone in a nearly identical predicament: They're with a partner who seems lukewarm or elusive or invisible whenever the conversation comes around to the subject of commitment. But instead of challenging that situation, whatever discomfort it might cause, they've come to accept the terms they've been offered. They even seem ready to champion them in front of their friends, as if they were now part of some exciting new love alliance where the best thing about it is not knowing when or if you'll ever see them again.

In one of our webinars, a woman named Cora appeared online to ask—well, it was hard to know what she was asking. She presented her relationship of nearly a year as one between two "entrepreneurial people" with busy schedules who find it hard to see each other or speak on a regular basis. It was starting to bother her that her friends (who could probably tell she liked him more than she was letting on) kept wanting to know what the nature of the relationship really was.

As she described how the two of them related to each other, there was a strange absence at the heart of her question, as if she were selling me on something that she wasn't entirely convinced by, so I finally asked, "Is the reason you don't want more because you're happy for things to be casual, and finding love is a lesser priority to you than your work right now? Or is the truth that this is how *he* feels, and you're using the same excuse, when deep down you do want more from him, but you're just worried that if you ask for more, he'll freak out?"

She laughed, and said, "Yeah, I guess if I'm being honest with myself, it's probably that." She had appropriated his excuse in order to stay in rapport with him, and in doing so, had silenced her own voice. When she was speaking to her friends, it wasn't Cora speaking, but the guy, who was ventriloquizing her to maintain a status quo that he was happy with. Even though Cora's case might sound unusual, her predicament is not uncommon. But complexity is so much harder to confront. Situationships like hers are the opposite of love at first sight. They're strange compromises that get created incrementally. You get nudged over and over, until you can almost become untethered from reality, as if you'd joined a cult of two.

The dodgy relationship logic that leads to cognitive dissonance takes months to create and it's hard to untangle. On a webinar, a client who called herself Songbird (did she feel that she'd been stuck in a cage?) tried to explain her situation, but the more she explained, the harder it was to understand. She lived in Michigan and had been seeing a Canadian citizen "for months," but recently he'd stopped texting as often as he had been— nothing for almost a week. Communication was hard, she admitted, and gave a number of reasons why: Phone service was spotty where he lived; he was a doctor who was busy and had three jobs; she hadn't been able to download the app on her iPad that he could text her on most easily; mostly they'd been seeing each other on Sundays, both in the US and Canada, but lately he'd been waiting for a visa and couldn't travel to see her. She seemed happy that they'd been getting more physical lately—he was playing with her hair, putting his arm around her, and she had spent the night at his place recently—but he seemed like a guy who waits for his moment. Then she said, "So he still hasn't kissed me."

There were so many warning signs in her story and so many questions to put to her, but the fact that she was regularly traveling to another country and, after months of dating, still hadn't asked why he hadn't kissed her? It indicated how complicit she had become in the construction of their odd situation, that despite all the excuses she gave (she'd been getting over something in her past, their shared natural shyness, his busy schedule) she'd been living in a fantasy. She was afraid to ask the simplest of questions that might threaten that fragile setup. The more I tried to get an answer from her, the more dissociated and emotional her responses became.

By this point we were nearly twenty minutes into our conversation, and despite all the red flags she was planting, she hadn't even gotten around to a real question. But the call in to the webinar was itself a sort of question. She might not have been willing to ask her doctor friend anything direct that threatened their relationship, but his lack of courtesy, evident in this last whole week gone by without a text, had now gone on so long that it presented a real challenge to her cognitive dissonance. So she finally spoke to someone who she knew wouldn't bullshit her.

Being real about what we are seeing is one of the most basic kindnesses we can provide each other, especially when you spot a friend in the early stages of a relationship getting so overwhelmed by all the new emotions that they seem to have lost the basic capacity to distinguish fantasy from reality. It's a corollary rule to "Do not join a cult of two": "A friend is not an echo chamber." Be the reality check you want to see in the world.

But Songbird's situation, like Cora's, is not uncommon. It's not that men, en masse, are gaslighting women, or even that it's always the man who is the primary engineer in every deviously tortured relationship. But there are a lot of guys who like the place they're in, and they don't want to venture beyond their comfort zone, and consciously or unconsciously, they start to sell the woman they're seeing on their way of looking at things. They'll say, "Every time you bring this up, you're just messing with a good thing" or "You're overthinking our attraction." That's not a sale a man can make all at once. But by degrees, he shifts her further and further from anything she originally wanted, until, by the time it gets so bad that she's going online to talk to me, I, along with everyone listening in, want to say, "How on earth did this go so far?"

There's a simple way out if you've reached a point in a relationship where you're stuck in something that doesn't quite feel right. Don't worry about ruining the party; be clear about what you want. Your certainty will do one of two things: chase away someone who can't handle what you're asking for, whether it's exclusivity or just a kiss after a dozen dates, or excite the person who is ready for the same thing.

There will always be someone who tries to sell you on their logic of why they can't give you what you want or show up in the ways you need. You don't need to assess whether the excuses they are giving you are legitimate, you just need to be honest with yourself about whether the reality of what's being offered is enough for you to be happy. That avoids all the effort of trying to decode what someone is saying. Tell yourself: They have their reasons (real or not), but I have my reality, and it is my reality, not their reasons, that determines whether I choose to keep going.

6

RED FLAGS

I just looked up "red flags" on YouTube just to see what kind of advice is out there. (As it turns out, a lot of it is mine!) As a field guide, however, all these sightings can become both confusing and overwhelming. Here's a sampling from the many channels: He doesn't compliment you? Red flag—withholder. He compliments you too much? Red flag—love bomber. He never asks questions about you? Red flag—narcissist. He asks you too many questions about yourself? Red flag—too controlling. He's disrespectful to his mother? Red flag—not fully grown. He's too close to his mother? Red flag—ditto.

Once you start scrolling through this catalog, you can forget that people are just people, flawed, prone to making mistakes. Not everyone has entirely recovered from their traumas before going out on a date. What if the scanner's turned on us? Do we see any red there too? Is it even helpful to know all this? If the extremes of every trait turn out to be major red flags, who's left in the middle, in the tiny pool of "relationship material" that remains?

The obsession with red flags focuses our attention in two directions, toward the past and the future. We can't grasp how valuable a red-flag warning could be (or how damaging it is to ignore one) without first performing a kind of forensic investigation into our own relationships (with a bit of perverse pride in the worst of them), asking ourselves what went wrong—trying to match every ex to one red flag or another—and how quickly we realized it. There's something cathartic in knowing we knew—even if we ignored it for too long, at some real cost to our well-being and self-esteem. On one level, it's an inventory of our scars, proof that we have lived and loved. On another, it's a way of telling ourselves: "No, in hindsight, I was not blind or crazy. I knew all along it was Professor Plum in the library with the candlestick."

Looking ahead, we can convert this catalog into a time-saving (and pain-sparing) manual. If I can spot a disqualifying behavior on Date Three, then I won't have to waste a year only to bring it up on Date Fifty-Three. This kind of preemptive strike is good for everybody. Time is limited. Why suffer needlessly or dive into situations we know will cause us pain?

But which red flags are worth focusing on? In a crowded field where seemingly any trait can be construed as grounds for termination, which ones truly will hurt you the most, either now or down the line? Below is my attempt at distilling the list down to a small handful that are disproportionately responsible for wreaking the most damage; the ones likely to cause us the most pain, should we choose to ignore them.

Talking Badly About Multiple Exes

I wanted to call this "Talking Shit About Your Ex," before I remembered that some people truly do have a disastrous ex. And no one should feel stifled when it comes to talking about the suffering they endured in a previous relationship. Learning about someone else's pain (and sharing your own in return) is a valuable stage on the way to intimacy.

OK. But then you run into someone who says that "all my exes are assholes" or "crazy." With such a person, one of two things is true. Either they're someone who can't take responsibility for all the ways they can be hard to deal with, and so instead of looking at the traits they need to change, they'd rather turn the conversation to the ways someone else was awful to them. (People do the same thing when they're fired from a job.) Or the second possibility: They're someone whose exes truly were extremely toxic people—because that is precisely the kind of people they're drawn to! The first person will turn on you at the first sign of conflict, and you'll wind up as the latest example in their litany of "crazy exes." The second person will test you to see if you can become—or if they can turn you into—the kind of crazy that turns them on, feels comfortable to them, or the kind of crazy they need to reject, just to feel good about themselves. If you don't want to be part of their drama—and that is the healthy reaction—they'll call you boring, or find you threatening, and likely hurt you before moving on to someone who will play that role for them.

Treating People Badly When They Don't Think You're Looking

This red flag occurs when someone who's trying to impress you, seduce you, sleep with you, or make you fall in love presents a selective version of who they are. Bad actors do this, sure, but so does anyone on their best behavior. Let's be honest, we're all different when we're acting moody with a sibling than when we're out on a date. But sometimes you really will be dating Dr. Jekyll, only to see them turn into Mr. Hyde when they interact with others.

We all know to carefully observe how people treat someone they believe isn't useful to them, especially when that person is just doing their job: the waiter or barista, the valet parker, the senior citizen in customer service. But good reviews here can't always be trusted: Maybe your date was aware of you watching. As long as there's an audience, it's still a performance. The real test is how they treat people when they don't think, or have forgotten, that you're even there. I'm not recommending tapping phones or hiding cameras in their workplace. But pay attention. Are there dead zones in their performance? Be wary of being so blinded by the adoration they direct at you that you fail to see how capricious their attention really is.

One final warning: It can be tempting to enjoy the fact that someone treats others badly at the same time they're treating us so well. Sometimes when people who are rude to others are kind to us, we feel the validation of having in some way tamed the beast. We feel special; it's wonderful to feel like we're someone's soft spot. It gives us a unique status. Who didn't watch *Game of Thrones* wanting to be Daenerys Targaryen, Mother of Dragons, having the unique affection of fire-breathing beasts who didn't let anyone else come close? In real life, we must be wary of getting on that pedestal: It's a trap. The light someone shines on you should never go hand in hand with treating others with an absence of dignity and respect. As a corollary to this, don't ignore what your experience would be if they ever decided to exchange their light for their fire.

Love Bombing

A woman at one of my events described a guy she'd met as "very intense" in the early stages, citing the poem he'd written for her about what a goddess she was. When I told her that I thought he'd turn out to be a disaster, a good portion of the audience let out an audible groan at my cynicism. But—spoiler alert—as the woman kept talking, it turned out he already had been a disaster, and had disappeared as quickly as he'd shown up.

Love bombers—like this mirage of a man—get the name from the way they carpet-bomb you early on with a level of adulation that's completely disproportionate to how well they actually know you. They dive headfirst into love, they want you to keep up, and they're often quick to take offense if you don't seem to be as excited as they are about the ride.

There's something fascinating about love bombing. Running into someone who falls in love that fast can feel like walking onto a movie set. That's what they're counting on—all those romantic fantasies that make us such suckers for a love story. It's worth noting that there are different kinds of love bombers, ranging from those who have immature ideas of what love is combined with poor impulse control, to the truly malignant actors, who know that when we're eager to find love, moving fast may feel like just what we've been pining for. It's the instinct the malignant love bomber preys upon.

So we have to pay attention, and not let our desire for our very own Technicolor love story blind us to the uncanny feeling that something seems off about the oddly rushed pace this person has chosen. Why is someone who barely knows me telling me I'm the love of their life? To mean this much to them that quickly defies logic. Sure, it'd be nice to find someone who sees how special I am. But really? After one coffee?

So how can we distinguish the love bomber from the well-intentioned person who just happens to be really excited about us in the early stages, and can't quite contain it? A good starting point is to ask yourself if the intensity has been a mutual phenomenon, or is being directed solely by them. Ask yourself: Have I matched their energy? Have I ever said, "I miss you dreadfully too"? Or "Yes, I do want to drop everything to be with you"?

Remember, if a person is deeply into you, they're just beginning to realize what's at stake between the two of you, and the last thing they want to do is screw it up by coming on too strong or letting out all their irrational feelings. You're both feeling your way cautiously. If anything, people who are sensing they're falling for each other can wind up being quite formal and awkward together, almost old-fashioned in their give-and-take.

If you do notice a speed and intensity coming from their side that feels unearned at this early stage, it's not necessary to have perfect judgment on whether it is in fact a red flag. Instead, simply try suggesting a slower pace. The reaction will be revealing. Do they, perhaps with a little embarrassment, apologize and back off a bit, hoping that would be a good way for the two of you to fall back in sync? (Perhaps not a red flag after all.) Or do they carry on as though you'd never said anything?

Patience, restraint, and the ability to delay one's urges can be solid signs of someone who values the relationship they are looking for over the immediate experiences that their heart (or any other part of their anatomy) wants to have. If someone has no interest in your carefully expressed desire to move at an organic pace or shows no shame in showering you with proclamations of love in ways that seem disconnected from your reactions, beware.

At best, it usually means their view of love is immature and unrestrained, or that their image of you is a projection of perfection that you can't possibly live up to, both of which mean that the peaks of their "love" will likely be followed by an equally severe drop-off in feelings when your flaws and humanity appear. That is, watch out for the love bomber who's using their waves of outrageous affection as a cover for their fault-finding. One viewer summed it up perfectly in her comment on a video I put up on my YouTube channel called "How to Tell If a Guy Is Love Bombing You":

> Lol . . . I remember briefly dating a guy who confessed after we broke up that he starts every relationship thinking she's his future wife. Then slowly he discovers she's not it, so he pulls away over time until he breaks up with them. It was ridiculous! I did the inner work to make sure I repel those kinds of men.

At worst, it means your love bomber is deeply manipulative, maybe even malevolently so, and this is a conscious strategy to extract from you a level of investment and a depth of feeling that you would never naturally give at this stage. Experts will tell you these are the hallmarks of narcissism. First, it's selfish to create incredibly intense feelings only to drop someone at the first sign of human imperfections—in other words, just when the connection starts to shift from fantasy romance to real commitment. Second, it's objectifying. The narcissist (or at least the person behaving narcissistically), only wants you to fall in love so they can feel validated as a supreme love being. They don't care what the consequences will be to you. "You're in love with me? Great! Now I can finally move on." That's why I tell people to beware of extraordinary first dates. These kinds of people give great first dates, because they desperately need to blow your mind. You can be forgiven for thinking it was about you, but it was about them all along. Remember, an emotionally healthy person who's serious about finding a relationship isn't looking for an audience, they're looking for a connection. And a real connection never flows in only one direction.

Not Saying Sorry

You've probably dealt with someone who can't apologize. Someone who can't even mumble an "I'm sorry" presents an unsettling combination: a shortage of humility and a surplus of insecurity. Saying two simple words should be easy, and choosing to remain silent when an apology is called for is infuriating. But even worse, it's a barrier to growth in the future. When someone admits the wrongs they've done, or the hurt they've caused, it's a fundamental act of recognition that can also serve as a bridge to change and growth. A partner who can't apologize either cannot grow, or can only grow in secret, removed from the loving support that flourishes in openness and mutual recognition. Instead, they come back later, after coming up with their own version of change on their own timetable, ready to take credit for the new and improved version of themselves, but never apologizing for the person they used to be or acknowledging any hurt they might have caused. Shutting down any exchange of apologies means denying the benefits that come from a successful argument: the communication of needs, the exploration of sensitivities, the reassurance of knowing that individual pride is less important than being part of an evolving relationship. Instead, their failure to apologize forces you to be with someone who insists on a solitary journey, which means yours will be too, and you will likely find yourself alone in your pain.

Beyond missing out on the benefits and connections that grow out of an exchange of apologies and forgiveness, the failure to say "I'm sorry" threatens to rob us of our sanity. Why is that? Because one trait that accompanies the inability to apologize is the tendency to manipulate others into thinking that they are always wrong, or that they have completely misunderstood reality. Sometimes that manipulation crosses over into intimidation or worse. In a predictable series of steps, someone else's failure to apologize leads to the decline of our own self-esteem. This is why not saying sorry is such a big red flag. By avoiding romantic partners who can't say they're sorry, we keep ourselves open to the possibility of true connection.

Consistently Not Keeping Promises, Big and Small

None of us does everything we say we will. That doesn't make us liars for having said it in the first place. It just makes us normal, well-intentioned people who can't get around to everything on our list. But there are people who reliably break the promises they make, who consistently say they'll do something, then don't. When this becomes a pattern, it should concern you.

The inverse is also true. If someone says they'll do something and they consistently follow through—if they actually send you the link they promised or put you in touch with the person they know in your new neighborhood—that's worth taking as a green light. While these may feel like simple acts, the signs early in a relationship of an ability to follow through are an important way someone can show they are the kind of person who will be there for you.

People give all sorts of reasons for breaking promises:

- They really wanted to get to it but they have so much on their plate.
- They're not great with time management.

- They take on too much and try to please everyone.
- They have ADHD.
- They didn't think it was that big a deal if they didn't since it wasn't a super important thing.

I've been guilty of most of these. We probably all have. So how do we tell the difference between someone just doing their best who deserves a chance, and someone who is a terrible person to rely on and will fail you in fundamental ways over the course of a relationship?

At a certain point in life, all we have is our word, and how much the people who care about us believe it or feel they can count on it. Which is why we should all fight to build it, maintain it, or repair it. When you meet someone who either doesn't care that their word has come to mean nothing, or condemns anyone who distrusts their word when all evidence makes it reasonable to do so, run.

It's worth noting here that having two specific red flags—the inability to keep one's word and an unwillingness to apologize—is the most dangerous combination of all. This is what I call a "dark pairing," two qualities that when found in the same person make them particularly, even exponentially, destructive. I don't mean to send you on a search for an unattainable paragon of virtue. But ask yourself these four questions when someone you're attracted to repeatedly fails to follow through on their promises:

- Has it happened multiple times with different kinds of promises?
- Do they ever acknowledge missing the mark? (That is, did they bring up their failure on their own?)
- Did they apologize?
- Did they repair the value of their word by making sure to follow through the next time they promised something?

Or did they . . .

- Carry on and hope you wouldn't notice?
- Try to convince you you're making a big deal out of nothing?
- Lie about having ever promised it in the first place and make you feel crazy?

- Tell you they don't need to apologize for being busy/stressed/not having the time to do it/not being able to honor what they committed to?
- Deflect by attacking you for the things you've done wrong that they never mentioned because they're "not this nitpicky with you"?
- Continue to break promises—knowing that now you're scared to bring it up because of how badly it went last time?

Clearly, this is a sketch of the pathway to emotional abuse. Don't jump to conclusions—go easy if someone brings you a Dr Pepper when they said they'd get you a root beer, or innocently forgets to do something they said they would. But when someone makes a pattern out of failing to do what they promised, cut your losses and start looking for the kind of teammate you can rely on.

Inconsistency in Communication

It's easy to get excited when someone starts a campaign of texting us relentlessly. But this runs the risk of measuring someone's potential by the peaks of their intensity, and not by the consistency of their communication. Still, who hasn't dealt with someone who will rapid-fire fifty texts over the space of an hour, only to give you the silent treatment for the next week?

It may not be as thrilling when a person texts you at the end of their working day or gives you a call consistently every couple of days, but that level of consistency counts for something. Whether or not that amount of communication is enough for you is a matter of compatibility, but it's not a red flag.

What is a red flag, however, is when communication is inconsistent. At best, it means they don't want anything serious with you. They're not looking for a relationship, they're looking for experiences. If they wake up on a Saturday and suddenly want affection, closeness, and company for the day, there you are. But then they disappear again, back to everything else in their life that apparently doesn't include you. They don't care that this predictable lack of consistency kills momentum—in fact, the setup does them a favor. The moments they reach out to you maintain your attention, while the black spots in their communication make progress impossible, thereby freezing the relationship exactly where it is.

At worst, it means they're living a double life that you don't know about. When the communication has stopped with you, it means it's started up again with the other person in their life. If you begin to pull away from someone like this, don't be surprised if they suddenly try a lot harder. That's often just a way to keep you in the fold for the next time they need a hit of your attention.

The Cost of Ignoring Red Flags

In one of my master classes, I asked my Love Life Club members to look back on their relationships and say what it had cost them to ignore a red flag. The chatbox started to fill immediately, almost before I could finish the question. The answers tended to fall into three categories:

Being left abruptly:

"Getting my ass dumped out of the blue and having major anxiety"

"Eventually me getting ghosted"

"Marriage: they dumped me after four months of being married to them"

There are often early warning signs that someone isn't who they say they are, doesn't feel the same way as you, and isn't committed to the same level that you are. You may feel that things ended suddenly, or that the disappearance feels inexplicable given the feelings they expressed to you or the actions they took toward you, but a more honest look reveals that there were red flags predicting their abrupt departure all along.

Winding up in an abusive relationship:

"My body, I was sexually assaulted, and years in therapy to not blame myself for his abusive behavior"

"Everything I worked hard for, the future I wanted, my savings, my job, my sanity, everything"

We ignored the red flags early on when we weren't feeling safe, our needs weren't being met, and there was little to no consistency in the attention we received. We may have even convinced ourselves that with more investment, these feelings would go away. But they never did. In fact, we had to deal with the opposite situation, where the more we invested in the situation, the worse it seemed to get.

Wasting our lives in a situation where their long-term intentions are not aligned with ours:

"He didn't want a relationship and I accepted friends with benefits, eventually he fell in love with someone else and let me go"

"Twelve years and the opportunity to have children and the family I always wanted"

You want a deep, committed relationship and they don't. You want monogamy and they don't believe in it. You want a family and they categorically aren't interested in having kids. When we ignore misalignment in intentions early on, we can continue investing time and energy without realizing we're not on the same path at all as our traveling partner. Only years later do we realize, or finally accept, that we've been headed in a completely different direction the whole time.

AFTER THE COLLAPSE OF THE relationship, we can look back and try to spot the early warning signs that should have clued us in that the whole thing was doomed from the start. It's easy to punish ourselves for ignoring what in hindsight seem like obvious red flags. It's like watching a horror movie where the person who knows there's a murderer on the loose hears a noise downstairs and instead of grabbing their keys and peeling out of the rented house, slowly opens the basement door armed only with a malfunctioning flashlight. Except that the person everyone's yelling at ("Why on earth are you doing that? Get out!") is us. We're the oblivious victim.

The truth is this can happen to any of us. It's tempting to feel humiliated by our inability, or unwillingness, to act on the red flags. But we can also take it as a reminder never to let ourselves be hijacked again, to go too fast to spot the warning signs, to get swept away by our own desire to be swept away. Instead, we have to stop for the speed bumps, and have clear conversations about our needs and reservations well before giving in to the impulse to just fall into something that is then disproportionally hard to emotionally, or logistically, disentangle ourselves from.

One of the trickiest aspects of dealing with red flags is knowing whether something someone has done or said meets the qualifications. If it does, do you cut and run? Do you stay and see if it happens again? Should you say something before it's too late?

Author Robert Greene gave this advice: "One of the things you look for are patterns, in judging their character, because people reveal themselves in the past. They reveal who they are through their actions. They try to disguise it, but they reveal it . . . nobody ever does anything once."

If Greene is right about people, it may be well worth looking into someone's past relationships, how they ended (if you are lucky enough to hear the truth), how they treated others before you, and how they are treating people, and you, now. "Nobody ever does anything once" is a pretty good rule of thumb. I'd certainly include it in any kind of "how to stay alive" manual I wanted to give to someone I love—which is why it's here right now.

If we're truly living by this advice, then it's worth asking: "How bad was that thing that just happened? And if it happened over and over again for the rest of my life, what kind of life would that be for me?" If the answer is somewhere on the spectrum between "completely untenable" and "at odds with my idea of a happy and peaceful life," it might be considered wise to get out.

But again, to turn this camera back on ourselves: We've surely done things we resolved never to do again. Maybe hurting someone recklessly and knowing the harm it caused changed us forever. That ability to change is the mark of character. But if we can consider some major screwup of our own as an anomaly and not a predictor of future behaviors, shouldn't we give this same chance to someone else?

The whole point of this catalog of red flags is to help you recognize behaviors that I believe will reliably cause you future pain, no matter how generously you try to interpret them. Still, even in those cases, we know life isn't always simple. There are degrees of bad.

Are they truly love bombing me or just getting a little carried away? Are they someone who has a disqualifying issue with saying sorry, or has their ego just gotten the better of them in this one instance? Are they struggling to commit because they're genuinely unable to, or are they ever so close to breaking through the trauma that's had them shutting down all along? Are they inconsistent with communication because they have another life, or simply because we are very early in the process and I haven't become that important to them yet, which is understandable? Even the act of cheating, however reprehensible to most, leaves many people on the receiving end asking me whether they should presume it's a sign of who someone is, or accept it as a genuine regret that they will never repeat.

It's tricky.

The truth is, despite offering up some important red flags in this chapter, the whole idea of red flags makes me uneasy. They are inherently reductive. Life is rarely so simple and the choices are not always stark. I wasn't ready for a serious commitment when I met my wife. Then I changed. People do sometimes. To rely on such a change or to stake your future on it would be a bad idea—this is just a means of deferring the problem to become the pain and responsibility of our future selves to have to deal with. But getting more clarity in the present can help you get the closure you need on whether something truly is a cue to stop, or an invitation to greater understanding and even intimacy.

If you think the trait in question is worth a conversation to see if things could improve, I call it an "amber light." Let's say you experience something that you don't like, but you want to explore a little before deciding it's time to throw in the towel. That trait or tendency temporarily becomes an amber light. Amber lights either turn green (keep going!) if the situation improves, or flash red (get out!) if it doesn't.

How does that happen? How do you find out which way the amber light will turn? By starting a conversation. This is a core principle in my work, that tough conversations improve our lives. Mr. Rogers used to say: "If it's mentionable, it's manageable." Well, in romantic relationships, everything has to be mentionable or we'll never really know whether it can improve.

When people come to me with their problems, so many of their questions follow this pattern: "Matthew, he did this, and I didn't like it. Do you think it can get better?" But when I ask the obvious follow-up—"Have you talked to him about it?"—their answer is almost always no. I should be the second person they've talked to about the problem. A big part of the problem is that I'm usually the first.

I've watched as people who see the signs that someone isn't looking for something serious simply ignore them, hoping that simply getting closer to this person will change their mind. One year later, they find that the person remains precisely where they began: not in the market for a relationship at all.

Often we don't speak to the person directly involved because we're afraid of scaring them off. But if we let our fear and discomfort guide us, we are simply ignoring the red flags that will one day haunt us. Putting our fear of scaring someone off over our need to know whether that person can actually live up to our standards is a recipe for unhappiness. We need to reverse that equation: *My greatest fear should be wasting my life on someone who won't make me happy, not scaring someone away.* Even the person we think is right for us is wrong for us *if they're not invested in our happiness.* Happiness, not the person, is always the prize. To find happiness with a person, we must be brave in our willingness to communicate around the things that give us pause. This bravery is easier to demonstrate once we realize that the relationships worth having are actually formed in the crucible of hard conversations.

7

HAVE HARD CONVERSATIONS

About eight years ago, Trojan condoms hired me to be one of their spokespersons for a public-service campaign about safe sex. As a "world-renowned relationship expert," according to their press releases, I was sent out to talk about the many ways people stumble into risky behavior. First they flew me into New York City to chat with a number of media outlets and magazines, each with their separate audiences with risks unique to their demographic. At one magazine, for instance, the editors told me there still existed a machismo culture where too many men didn't want to wear a condom, and too many women were afraid to have the conversation, let alone make some man put one on.

In many ways, safe sex is ground zero for hard conversations, for straight couples and queer couples, for everyone. How many lives have been forever changed because in a crucial moment someone felt too awkward or embarrassed—or worse, intimidated—to have an uncomfortable conversation? Our culture doesn't help. I remember being ushered into a sound room in my role as spokesperson to be patched into one radio station after another. I did so many drive-time interviews in a row that I couldn't tell you who was on the line or what part of the country I was talking to, but this particular radio host must have been broadcasting in a conservative area, because he welcomed me to so-and-so FM by saying, "Now we have a gentleman here, Matthew Hussey, who's going to talk to us about—and I will say this word just once—'condoms.' So, Matthew, what do you think is going on here? Why are so many people having unsafe sex?"

I didn't think twice before saying, "Well, it has to be partly due to people like you, who apparently think it's an offense to say the word *condom* more than once in a radio interview!" Honestly, if I had thought twice, it would only have been worse. At least it was over quickly.

Another hard conversation that will come up: kids, although "kids" is what you call the conversation when it's an easy one, when it goes, "Of course, who doesn't want kids?" In the more fraught version, the subject is the biological clock (something we will discuss at length in chapter 11). I have watched people time and again avoid hard and (to be fair) potentially relationship-ending conversations with their partners over misaligned views on having children, leading to far greater devastation down the road and a profound sense of regret. My up-close experience with this kind of regret has convinced me of one thing: any painful conversation today that saves us from the anguish of future regret should be moved to the top of our list of priorities.

Our willingness to have hard conversations is an outward reflection of a newly decided upon internal standard—a standard that has arisen out of full acknowledgment of the kind of life we want to live. Knowing your standards and having hard conversations go hand in hand. Once you've made up your mind about what you want and can communicate it—"Sexy as you are, I can't go further without a condom" or "You're fun, I have the best time with you, but I can't continue if you're not interested in committing yourself to a relationship" or "I do love being with you, and I'm sad we disagree on this, but my plan is to have a child, with or without you, before I hit forty"—you can find the clarity and strength you need to walk away from situations that can't provide it.

The rules of negotiation don't change because you're in a relationship and emotions and sex are mixed up in it; you always have to be willing to walk away. If you're job hunting, you wouldn't consider leaving your current job without getting a bigger title or a salary increase or one that was more in line with what you wanted to do. If you're selling a house, you know the price you have to get to make moving worth the effort. In either case, if your basic conditions aren't met, you politely end the negotiations.

Hard conversations both arise from having a standard on the inside, and are the route to establishing that standard on the outside. One woman who follows me on YouTube sent a guy she was dating a sample text message I had created for times when a relationship wasn't going anywhere. He texted back, This doesn't sound like you. Pushback like that is completely normal and to be expected. In family therapy, it's called "homeostatic pull"—the desire in any system to keep things the way they are. When I hear that response, my reaction is: "Great! Now you're on your way to a different result from the one you've been getting." Clearly this guy senses things heading in a new direction, and he's testing to see how firmly she believes in it. He wants to know if this is some halfhearted resolve that will disappear at the first sign of trouble—in other words, merely a tactic—or whether she is setting out a very real new standard, and letting him know that now they will both have to play by a new set of rules.

The right response to his text is: The truth is, this is me. But because I like you, I've been going along until I could see where this was heading. Now I see it's not going in a direction that excites me, so I have to be honest with myself, and with you, about what I need. Instead of doing that, she panicked and said: You're right. It doesn't sound like me. There's this relationship guy on YouTube, and I sent you one of his messages because I feel sad that nothing is happening between us. Just like that, she had given up on the boundaries she had only just drawn. The truth is, he was right: It didn't sound like her, but that was the whole point. It was a new standard designed to signify that she was now taking herself and her needs seriously. Unfortunately, it wasn't supported by a deeper confidence and therefore fell apart at the first sign of resistance. By backtracking like that, all the progress she'd made toward changing the dynamic between them disappeared, and the guy learned that any standard she tries to establish can be ignored because she'll drop her resistance at the first sign of confrontation.

This is why hard conversations (that are underpinned by a standard) are so important: We can't improve what we don't confront. (The negative corollary of that rule is that anything we ignore, any behavior we turn a blind eye to, we tacitly approve.) Still, it's natural to shy away from getting into this situation. First, we're afraid of saying it all wrong, and we get bent out of shape because we're worried about being tongue-tied or embarrassed. Second, we're afraid of scaring someone away, and of the loneliness and regret that might follow if we did. And third, we're afraid of facing the reality of the situation we're actually in, that confronting whatever the issue is—asking about inconsistent communication early in a relationship or bringing up marriage or children later on—will end things between you and force you back into the jungle of dating.

Let's acknowledge how tough any of this can be. If you haven't gone on a date or been with anyone in a serious way for months or even years, it can be terrifying to start a conversation about standards (or about anything, really) that risks losing the first good thing to come around in ages. It's like laying out all your terms and conditions while you're still trying to make the sale. In those circumstances, you're more likely to remove a few terms just to close the deal. If you haven't experienced any intimate attention in a while, it's almost inconceivable to treat it as if it could be replaced—the essence of what we call the scarcity mindset.

By focusing only on how you might scare someone off (setting aside for a minute that anyone scared off by a hard conversation is probably not someone you want to be around), you lose sight of all the positive outcomes that can come from trusting someone with your real concerns. Being vulnerable enough to let someone know that you have something at stake is brave, endearing, and creates an intimacy in itself. You're telling someone about you.

You're also telling someone how to see you. Life isn't simple and people do need cues. Letting someone know that this isn't a casual hookup to you, or, later on, that you're ready to build something real and lasting, lets them know what category to put you in. You're insisting on a value that sets you apart from less serious relationships. There's a percentage of women who are passive out of fear, or who were taught that being passive is proper feminine behavior. Too often they'll lose out not because the guy doesn't like them enough, but because they continued to carry on as if they were quite content to remain in the "casual category." This is the true hidden danger of hoping that love, and a relationship, will happen *to* us. Sure, love is a two-way street, but you still have to direct traffic sometimes!

The truth is, it almost doesn't matter what standard ends up being the subject of your hard conversation; the conversation itself adds gravity and intention to the relationship. A friend who'd hung out a couple of times with a woman he liked went away to a work conference in Houston, then decided to tack on a long weekend in Austin to his trip. When he got back and called her, she said, "I got concerned while you were away and I didn't hear from you. It made me wonder if maybe you were sharing your bed with someone." For the record, I'm pretty sure he was, but that wasn't the point. Her saying that instantly made him consider her in a new light. Not only did he realize she was not someone he was going to be able to treat casually, but he even found it a bit of a turn-on. The two of them ended up in a serious relationship because that combination—the realization that she was serious about him and the sexiness of her saying so—snapped him out of a period where he'd just been floating along between hookups. Maybe it all would have happened anyway, but it sure seemed like the conversation changed the conditions.

The Hardest Conversation Is With Yourself

It's not a secret that I'm a fan of hard conversations. As we saw in chapter 5 with Songbird, some people join my programs because they're in a tricky situation and are having a tough time being honest with themselves about it. They know that if they present their predicament to me, I will happily play the role of the friend who will never avoid the difficult conversation with them. This is not a scientific observation, but my sense is that somewhere around half of the hard conversations that people really need to have are with themselves. When that's the case, the best thing I can do is model the kind of conversation they're having trouble framing, on their own, with themselves.

A conservatively dressed Australian woman who attended one of my tour events in Sydney stood up to ask a question. She waved around the mic in one hand and her iPhone in the other as if she'd been standing in front of a crowd like this for years. But her fragility began to show as soon as she started laying out the contradictions of her situation: She'd been single for eight years before she met this man nearly a year ago, and she really loved him, but "we don't have a title." They "try to make an effort to see each other every fortnight," but when they're apart, she said, and here she choked up, "I feel like he's forgotten about me." She was certain about the intensity of her feelings—she was ready to marry him if he ever asked; she even said she would "take a bullet for him"—but the two of them kept arguing when they were apart.

"It feels so good when you're together," I said, and from the way she answered, with a less-than-enthusiastic "yeah," it confirmed the feeling that she wasn't braving the crowd because she wanted affirmation. After she admitted that they were only together two days every two weeks, because he works nights and lives a few hours away, I asked her to do the math over a lifetime. At almost forty, given current life expectancies, she might optimistically count on being on the planet for another fifty to sixty years, with the prospect of happiness available only two days every two weeks. "But you're probably arguing a bunch when you're together," I guessed, "so you're not even happy all of that time."

"I have to admit, the arguments start with me."

"Of course they do, because you're not happy!" I think she could tell that I was outraged on her behalf—this idea that she was the one with the problem because she happened to have needs was a deeply corrosive one. "How many more lifetimes do you think you'll get? I think it's just one. I'm certainly not going to take a chance that there's lots more." As she was regaining her composure, I introduced her to the dangers of adopting a "future-vacation" approach to life—referring to the type of person who lives fifty-one weeks of the year waiting for the one week they go on vacation to feel happy—and how she was in danger of running down the clock on her life doing the same thing.

"There isn't time for you *not* to be happy today," I said. "You don't have the time that you're pretending you have by wasting twelve days every time you leave him, anxiously waiting for the next time you'll see him."

Like someone moving through the stages of grief, she turned from denial ("But we want to be with each other!") to bargaining ("But I've hurt him so badly in our arguments . . . It's my fault.")

"OK," I said. "Let's pretend it is your fault. You might be doing a really good job of being sweet and vulnerable here, when behind the scenes you're just a terrible nightmare!" The laughter in the room suggested that everybody thought this idea was absurd.

She laughed too, and played along. "When I'm angry!"

I asked her the number one reason the two of them argued, and again her voice broke as she said, "Because he ignores my texts or he doesn't respond. He doesn't initiate. He doesn't ask about me."

"So even though you may not argue in the most productive way, at the root of it you're not getting what you need from your relationship. So you could start arguing more productively, but if the root of your relationship doesn't change, you're still going to be unhappy. And you could spend your life this unhappy. Do you want to be this unhappy in five years?"

She shook her head.

After she admitted that she didn't want to feel this way for the next five or ten years, I spoke very plainly about the truth of her situation: "This thing you're convincing yourself of, this happy thing you're holding on to—it's not a happy thing."

"But why is he still hanging around?"

"Because *you're* still hanging around! There are people who will be weak if you allow them to be weak—who will take advantage of you if you allow it." This was classic avoider behavior—on his part, certainly, and to a lesser extent, on hers too. I'm not proud to say I'd behaved this way in the past too, which is one of the reasons I felt so passionately about helping her realize that he would continue to treat her casually if she let him. Even those who go on to regret the ways they may have hurt people or wasted their time don't have the power to return to that person their time or unhurt them. Which is why it's so important for us to have our own backs in the moment, and not assume someone is having our back on our behalf. "Right now, you can't see it because you're blinded by your love for him. But him not giving you what you want and still remaining with you is selfish. He's being selfish and you're not protecting yourself."

None of this was easy for her to hear, and it required incredible bravery for her to put herself in a position where she must have known she would be likely to hear it. But protecting her feelings was beside the point. Given how much was at stake, how many decades she still had ahead of her, no short-term pain compared to the importance of planting one seed: Every week she wastes with a man who's telling her that he doesn't love her as much as she loves him is a week she's not spending with the person who's right for her, or in her own peaceful company. There is someone out there who is right for her, who deserves her and whom she deserves, even if she doesn't know him yet.

The room broke into applause, signaling their agreement and support for her. "I'm going to lay out your choices now. You decide what to do. Leave. Live your life. Meet someone who can meet your needs. Be happy. . . . Do you have kids?"

"Two boys, sixteen and eighteen."

"So you can either show them an example of what a strong woman looks like, or you can show them someone who allows people to treat her however they want." I wanted to orient her focus toward the real ways she was being mistreated that she had been ignoring: "It's mistreatment when you are care-less with someone's heart. You don't do that to someone you love and care about. You don't keep them on a leash just so they're around when you need them . . . seeing them every two weeks because it suits you."

She then did something very common, turning the conversation away from the deeper truth that he didn't want what she wanted, and onto a less painful barrier to their being together: "What do you do in that situation?" she asked. "When he lives far away . . ."

"You remind yourself that if two people want to be in a relationship, they make it work." This woman's predicament clearly resonated with the people at the event, who again broke out into applause. It also resonated with her. Especially when she connected with how much her ultimate decision would impact her sons. They could see her meet someone who is ready to meet her needs, which means they could see her happier, peaceful. Or they could watch her continuing in this unfulfilling relationship, one that regularly sets her in a state of high anxiety. When we boiled it down to those stark choices, it barely seemed like a tough decision at all. I had one last piece of advice: "By the way, if you do leave, and he has a miraculous turnaround and realizes what he was missing, then you have a real decision to make. But right now, there's no decision because he's not even offering you an option you want."

I urged the audience to give her a huge round of applause, and while they did, I went over to hug and reassure her and quietly reaffirm what I'd just said publicly, that her person was out there. In truth, the hardest conversation wasn't the one she needed to have with him, but the one she needed to have with herself, where she came to terms with the fact that he wasn't that person.

Have Them Sooner

Part of what made this woman's hard conversation so hard one year in is how long it had been left. Hard conversations tend to get harder as time goes on. The longer our needs go unmet, the more they harden into deep resentment and anger. Our identity becomes fixed too as the one we've been playing so far, and it feels more difficult to suddenly convince someone of the new *us* we want them to respect—in other words, we are used to being seen the way they see us now, and it feels scary to ask, or demand, to be seen as something else. Then, of course, there's the fact that over time we tell ourselves the stakes are higher because now we have so much to lose: what we've built with some-one, the time we've invested, the ways we've oriented our lives around this relationship—what's known as the sunk-cost fallacy. So we make what I call the "One-Day Wager": the terrible bet that one day they will miraculously change to become everything we need them to be.

If we can learn to have hard conversations sooner, we will find ourselves being able to have them more casually, with the ease of someone who is merely educating someone about who we are and what we need, before all of the scar tissue of them having gotten it wrong for so long has developed. And we'll never find ourselves having to stake everything on the One-Day Wager. We don't have to make big bets when we are running small experiments with hard conversations that lead to real data about someone's potential.

But even in the early stages, when we're facing a hard conversation, we can't discount the fear of saying things all wrong, of wading in, and screwing things up in a royal fashion out of nervousness, and winding up in a whole second discussion that boils down to "No, that wasn't what I meant at all."

Hard conversations are a language to learn like anything else, and like any language, there are more eloquent ways to speak it that get better results. When learning languages, it's usually more useful to be shown an example of it at work than to be taught it in the abstract. If you're worried about coming across as too intense, or saying the wrong thing in a hard conversation, I've laid out an example below we can work through together. The following example is not intended to be a catch-all for hard conversations, but it's a good example nonetheless. See if you can spot where your own way of saying something might have differed from the example here. That doesn't mean your way is wrong, but it will highlight how different our results can be based on the language structure we choose . . .

Seek Neutral Ground

In the scripts that follow, I want to offer a few phrases that can help steer things away from more emotional territory into a kind of diplomatic middle ground. When I first imagined the following conversation, I used a hypothetical situation where you felt you'd been lied to. Being caught in a lie is not the worst of sins—we all misrepresent things once in a while—and bringing it up is a small-scale introduction to the world of challenging conversations. But the language I've outlined could work in other circumstances where someone has done something that has hurt you or given you pause—so in the places where I had originally used the words "lied to me" or "lying to me" you'll see I've left a blank, like Mad Libs. Let's imagine you've already had a messy/over-emotional/reactive argument and this is the follow-up where you clear the air.

> "Knowing that you _____ (insert activity) made me feel weird/
> hurt/scared. I've been going over it in my mind and I realized I
> should just be talking to you about it. In truth, I can't have some-
> one as close to me as you are _____ (again, name the offending
> activity). It's unacceptable to me and I want to talk about why that
> happened, because I want to understand what led you there so we
> can make sure it never happens again."

Let's break down the language here and why it's useful:

Weird, hurt, and *scared* are good words to use because they don't cast judgment on someone else, focusing instead on a feeling we're getting, one with some ambiguity that allows you space to maneuver. It's almost like you haven't decided how you feel yet.

"I've been going over it in my mind and I realized I should just be talking to you about it" is great for gray areas where you don't know if you're in the right about the issue at hand. It's saying, "I don't know if my fears are war-ranted, or if I'm slipping into irrational rumination, so this is me being vulnerable enough to actually have the conversation with you out loud." This has the effect of bringing you closer despite the circumstance, reaffirming that you trust that what you have together is robust enough to handle a per-ilous discussion.

"I can't have someone as close to me as you are (blanking)" almost feels like a compliment. It's saying that he/she is close to you, and therefore holds an important position, but because it's such an important position, there is a standard you expect from them. Somehow it gives importance to the person, while depersonalizing the standard you have. It's not about them, it's about the position they hold in your life. Compare this line with something we are often tempted to say in a situation like this: "You can never do that again." Nothing wrong with this; it's bold and assertive. But it's more likely to bring ego into the equation. We want them to hear you, not blindly fight against what they perceive as aggression, judgment, or being told what to do.

Now that you've removed ego from the equation, you're free to speak the rest of your part in the conversation with a little more force:

> "It's unacceptable to me and I want to talk about why that happened, because I want to understand what led you there so we can make sure it never happens again."

"It's unacceptable to me" is where you clearly state your boundary.

"I want to talk about why that happened, because I want to understand what led you there" is a moment of compassion. It shows a desire to get behind why they did what they did, which is also an opportunity for you to find out whether this person is able to be introspective, self-aware, and appropriately self-critical.

"So we can make sure it never happens again" actually demonstrates a spirit of teamwork in solving the problem. If *we* are doing this (that is, having a relationship), then *we* need to ensure this never happens again, because it's beneath the culture of the relationship we both seem ready to commit to.

Having hard conversations is one of the key ways we assert our boundaries and standards, and these two things are at the core of a better love life. If you're anything like me, or the thousands of people I've worked with, there is a people pleaser in you that likes to run the show; one that is so afraid of making waves that they'll look for any excuse not to speak up. But by becoming more competent in this area using the skills in this chapter, and seeing how practical they can be, we can finally start working on this muscle that may have atrophied until now. Eventually, speaking up for ourselves will become a part of our identity, one we will never live without again.

Like anything else in life, hard conversations require practice, and get easier as we become more competent at having them. But it can be an exhilarating realization to discover the extent to which the right language in a hard conversation can open a door and make walking through it more appealing, while the wrong language can have someone turning around altogether. This doesn't just apply to having a hard conversation where someone has done something we don't like. It can also apply to saying things that feel hard to say when all we want is for someone to like and accept us.

I remember a weekend event I held in London many years ago, back when it was still part of my program to have people go out and practice what they learned during the day with me in the city at night. This was possible when there were thirty women going out to a specific location (sending two thousand women to a specific area now would feel a little much). On the second day, I asked for feedback on how it went. One woman said to me: "Matthew, I had fun, but it never stopped being in the back of my mind that I have kids and I don't know when to bring it up." Another woman, seeming not to have a question but simply excited to tell her story then shot her hand up and said: "I exchanged numbers with a really attractive guy!" "Nice! How did you get talking to him?" I asked. Here's what she said, without even realizing it related to the first woman's struggle: "Well, I noticed that he had a chin dimple, so I said: 'I like your chin dimple. It's not quite as cute as my daughter's cheek dimples, but I like it!'" The audience laughed and instinctively picked up on the kind of fun, attractive energy that the guy must have felt the night before when she said that to him.

Here was a perfect example of how a hard conversation never came to be for one person, but remained a hard conversation for another. The first woman talked as though she had Darth Vader waiting at home for any guy who got close to her. The second woman managed to talk about her daughter in the same breath as she used to flirt with someone.

This highlights a vital point about hard conversations—people take their cues from us. If we are scared to have a conversation, people can feel the fear. If we are worried our baggage is going to scare someone away, they are more likely to see it as baggage. But we can learn to carry things more lightly, even things we once thought would make us invisible or unlovable to the world. It's hard to think of a better example of this than my client Angela, who one day in spring 2019 stood onstage at my Retreat and told nearly an entire room, myself included, overcome by emotion, the story of her own hard conversation.

Angela

Angela is a Scottish woman who'd originally attended one of my earliest retreats back in 2010, when they were small affairs and we could still fit everyone in one big rambling house outside Orlando. She had been to other events, like a series of talks I'd given in London on confidence, but before we first spoke at that early retreat, she'd remained mostly a studious presence, dressed a little out of place for Florida, in floor-length skirts with long sleeves.

Then, at one point in the week, she pulled me aside and asked if she could talk with me one-on-one, something that was much more common in the earliest in-person retreats when the attendees numbered in the tens and not the hundreds. The place had a little home movie theater that was quiet, shadowy, almost church-like, and Angela and I went in and took our seats together facing the empty screen. She didn't say a word once we sat down, which wasn't as odd as it sounds. I finally broke the silence and said, "You know I'm going to sit here until you tell me what it is." As she crossed her arms in defiance, I told her I could sit here all day and assured her there was nothing I hadn't heard before.

Then all at once, her story tumbled out: When she was twenty-three, she'd been walking home from work when she was struck by a drunk driver going 70 miles per hour, who left her lying on the ground and drove away. She lost a leg, and, after surgery, her arm was crisscrossed with scars; the doctors told her she might never walk again, or feed herself, or have a family of her own. But she had enough of what she called her "Scottish stubbornness" that she walked out of the hospital on crutches, and now got around completely on her own, "wearing," as she put it, a prosthetic limb.

After she'd blurted out all this devastating news she'd been withholding in one emotional rush, I said, "And what?"

Well, she said, she was worried now that when she goes on a date, the guy is never going to want her because she's missing a limb.

In times like this, as a coach, I've learned how powerful it can be to break someone's pattern by giving them a response that's radically different from the one they have been preconditioned to expect. So I said, with a kind of incredulous faux-outrage, "How arrogant is that? Do you need everyone to want you? Like everyone you go on a date with has to fall in love with you and choose you?" Angela looked at me quizzically for a full fifteen seconds, then cracked up. Then she cracked up some more, before the two of us burst into laughter together, which must have gone on for a full thirty seconds. She instantly and instinctively got it: In love, we don't need everyone to want us. We only need one person. And rejection just helps us get to that person faster.

It was a full eight years later, in late 2018, that Angela reached out by telephone, eager to tell me her good news, how my only partly flippant response gave her the confidence to do something she never dreamed she would be able to do. I was excited for her. Despite her silence in the movie room, Angela was a great storyteller—"A bit of a gab," as she put it—and I asked her to come talk about the big changes in her life at an upcoming event before Christmas. She demurred. An upcoming procedure at the hospital would pose a conflict, she said, so we agreed that she would instead come to the next retreat that spring as my guest.

When I called her up to the stage some five months later, I had no idea, really, how moving what she was about to share with us would be. She chatted confidently about the accident, and my reaction to her problems in the little movie theater, and she won my heart by recalling an incident one morning in the kitchen, when she'd slipped and fallen and spilled coffee on her long dress, and felt embarrassed, partly because the fall had exposed her prosthetic leg. Apparently, my mum, who was there, came over to her, put a hand on her, helped her up, and offered to wash her outfit for her if she went upstairs to change. Angela waved to my mum, Pauline, who was at the back of the room that day too, and thanked her again for her instinctive kindness that morning when she'd felt so exposed.

"By the way, guys," she said to all the women in the room. "This is pretty much the first time I'm wearing a skirt with my legs out," she said, referring to her blue and white cotton skirt that showed off her legs and pale suede half-boots. The women applauded. She was getting warmed up now and explained how, after she left that retreat, she'd started taking the techniques she'd learned through my programs and putting them into action, and she met a guy, and after a good first date, she resolved on the second to "just put it on the table."

Angela said, "And I was so worried that I was going to tell this guy what my accident was, and what scars I have, and what I wear." She pointed down to her prosthetic leg . . .

"And he said the same thing Matthew said:

"'And what?'

"I knew then and there that this was the man for me," she said, laughing, which the crowd returned. "But the truth is, because of what Matthew had taught me, even before meeting with this man, I said, 'If he doesn't like me for who I am, then stuff it. I'll just keep going. My worth doesn't depend on his interest.' So"—she was directly addressing the women now—"If I'm standing here and you can see what I wear, my scars, my insecurities. Any insecurities you've had, I've seen it, done it, got the picture. If I can get that, you can certainly get that," she said, relaxing into her full Scottish dialect.

She then told the story of how, a few months later, her new boyfriend took her to St. Andrews and booked the honeymoon suite, telling her sheepishly that it was the only room they had. When they went out to eat that night, he was really nervous, his hands shaking so badly as he passed her a plate to try that food flew across the room and hit another table. She remembered thinking, "Seriously, he's this nervous? I've still got it!" He took her out under the stars and told her to close her eyes, and she said to him, "What are you doing down there?" And, there on his knees, he proposed. Six months later, they were married.

At this point, everyone cheered. When the room calmed down again, she said she had two more things to share. "My story—this thing I couldn't speak about, the thing that caused me the most torment, the thing that's most holding you back—Matthew got it out of me. Now I've started this charity to help families and children who've been harmed by drunks and drunk drivers."

Then Angela tricked us all a little, saying that she'd gone in for a procedure around Christmas and it wasn't good—it was life-changing, in fact, and she talked about the saddest thing in the aftermath of the accident, being told that, because of the severity of her injuries, she couldn't have a child. How do you console yourself after something like that? She rummaged around and pulled out her phone, and called my mum up to the stage and showed us all a picture of her in the hospital, with her husband at her bedside—and a baby in her arms! Her own baby daughter, Hannah. I'd thought she was going to say a few words about the charity she'd started, but instead she'd waited five months, taken two flights to get to Miami, kept her secret all week long, then timed her reveal perfectly. I was flabbergasted and delighted.

"That's why I told all of you: This works," she said. "There's no sugar-coating it, no putting a pretty bow on it . . . I wanted my life to go in one direction and it went in a different direction. But I now have fulfillment in all areas. I know there are going to be dips, but I have tools now for my self-esteem and confidence. And I know what I've learned from you, Matthew, I'm going to teach Hannah, and what an amazing little person she's going to turn into."

8

ATTENTION IS NOT INTENTION

When we feel starved of romantic attention, any amount from someone we consider desirable can feel like sunlight. If it felt so hard to get that kind of attention in the first place, we don't want to let it go lightly. But when we want a relationship, our standards have to be higher than that.

If you've been following my work for some time, you'll have heard me say: *Don't invest in someone based on how much you like them, invest in someone based on how much they invest in you.*

It's a great rule for protecting ourselves. It redirects our attention away from how good it feels when someone's energy is on us, and instead on how much they are consistently investing *in* us. It stops us from justifying giving our time and energy based on how great we think someone is, or how special we believe our connection with them to be.

While this rule works for avoiding being taken advantage of, if followed to the extreme, it can make us so passive that nothing ever happens. If we all waited for each other to invest before we ourselves did, no relationship would ever get off the ground. Someone has to make the first move on the day two strangers see each other, someone has to send the first text after a date, say the first "I love you" . . . propose. We can't all move in unison all the time. Indeed, someone's decision to step forward can be the very thing that makes us step up our own game. Therefore we all have to find the balance between our pride and proactivity. Too much pride and we never take a risk to do anything. This is the case in many people I coach who don't create nearly enough romantic opportunities to stack the odds in their favor to find love.

Too much proactivity and we become an overeager chaser liable to be taken advantage of.

One way I've helped people find this balance is by adding a precursor to my original rule that my brother Stephen Hussey coined: Invest—then test.

If you take a half-step forward, do they step forward too? See each proactive step you take as a mini-experiment, and watch to see how they turn out. For example, you could be sending the person you are seeing a morning text that says: Hi, you/handsome/lovely. Hope you have a great day. It may not seem like much, but a lot of good can come from a message like this. You're not making some huge effort to get their attention. You're not even asking a question to try to elicit a response. But it's open, kind, and vulnerable. Once you've done this, I want you to pay close attention to what happens. Do they send *you* an early-morning text the next day? In other words, does your proactivity lead to proactivity on their part? People will tell me, "I know they like me because they always text me back," but that's just reactivity. My question is, "Sure, but do they ever text you *first*?"

This is the inherent danger of the beginning of any relationship—once you start to have feelings for someone, any attention you get back can feel like a drug, reordering your rational thought. It may be even more dangerous than other drugs, because however good a person might feel when they're on cocaine, they don't wake up the next day and fantasize about growing old with it. They don't imagine taking cocaine home to their parents. But the attention you get from an attractive stranger, a text from the ex you never quite got over, the prospect of a romantic weekend with someone you have plans for—these things feel like hope, and are so easily mistaken for deeper intention.

Notice I said, "someone you have plans *for*." That's the problem; at this stage, you don't necessarily have any plans *with* them yet. "With" suggests shared intentions, plans that have been communicated on both sides. But we can all recognize the overexcited part of ourselves on the emotional high of love's promise, scheming and hatching plans *for* someone because of how perfect we've decided they are for us.

We begin imagining ourselves with them in some future scenario. Before we know it, we're deeply involved in the love story we've worked up in our mind—one detached from the reality of how much they're actually investing but based instead on the excitement created by the attention we've received.

I've seen so many people get badly hurt because they mistook someone's *attention* at this dangerous stage for *intention*. Remember, attention is simply energy someone is giving you in the moment. Intention signifies a genuine desire to see where things might go, which can be harder to identify. Don't let the attention you're getting showered with now distract you from their intentions—or their lack thereof.

Hot and Cold

One of the most crazy-making examples of this confusion comes when someone showers you with attention when you're with them. It seems like they can't get enough of you. Then as soon as you're apart, you feel like you don't exist. It's like straddling two parallel universes, one with a person who's extremely into you, and the other with a person who barely thinks about you at all. This can be dangerous for your time and energy, as we saw with the woman from Australia in the previous chapter. The same person who shows you plenty of attention in the moments when they want a *romantic experience* soon proves—by their nearly total disappearance—that they have no intention of backing up those feelings by taking any real steps toward progressing things.

And what of the excuses they give when they finally do get back in touch? They're busy with work or friends, they got caught up in some family matter, they spent days away for some hobby they're really into? Any of these could be true; they could be legitimately busy with these other priorities. But is this a good enough reason for someone to have ignored you for the last week? Should it make you tolerate inconstancy and behavior that makes you feel terrible about yourself? What should you do here?

The easy mistake to make at this point is to mirror their behavior. By returning their attention when they're pointing the spotlight on you, then shutting down when they turn off their high beams, you may even think you're following my advice to invest in who invests in you. The problem with that is you're almost certainly giving this romantic Houdini exactly what they want, making yourself available when they're ready to play, then not bothering them whenever they're not. Not only does this reward the behavior you want to discourage, but it may also play into an even more dangerous cycle, where you end up attracting someone who gets excited by your withdrawals, then loses interest whenever you return their affection. That's a game nobody wins.

So how do you break the hot-cold cycle? You have to be willing to withdraw your attention *through direct communication*. This means you withdraw, but first you educate them on your reasons for doing so. Note that the right time to do this is not when they're in the middle of one of their cold periods—if they aren't reaching out to you, then there's no leverage. This is only effective in a situation where they pop up wanting something from you, when you do have leverage. This might come directly in the form of "I really want to see you this weekend" or indirectly through a simple "I miss you." Whatever form it takes, both situations are a play for your attention.

At this point, you text back:

> If I'm being honest, I'm a little surprised you want us to see each other. [Or: A little surprised to hear you miss me.] I haven't felt like we've been that close recently since I haven't heard from you very much, so I guess I just assumed we weren't in the same place.

You're not expressing any strong emotions here. You're matter-of-fact—you've practically put any issue you might once have had in the past tense, based on their lack of investment. Maybe they quickly text back their excuse (see above: work, friends, family, hobby). This is your opportunity to educate them about what your standards are:

> I totally get it. I have a lot going on, too, so I know what it's like. Something I really value is consistency, though. You know, you and I are really great when we're together. But I don't feel like we're very connected when we're apart.

You're being compassionate and understanding, but letting them know that their lack of consistency hasn't gone unnoticed, and isn't something that will work for you. You're bringing awareness to how you feel when you're apart, and inviting them to step up and be better, without pointing fingers.

We've already mentioned the dangers of "playing it cool" by mirroring their level of investment, shutting down when they do, but there's an even greater risk you take by not sending a text like this. Not only does silence constitute a tacit approval of the wrong behavior; it denies you the opportunity to awaken the right behavior in the right person. There are those for whom this message will make them come alive and think to themselves, "This is exactly the kind of vulnerability and strength of character I've been looking for." If you fail to announce what you really want here, you run the risk of becoming invisible to the kind of person who wants exactly the same thing.

Six Steps for Sorting Attention From Intention

Attention feels good, but how can you tell what someone's intentions might be early enough that you're not wasting your time, without getting too intense too soon and scaring someone away? Here are some simple things you can do—and some simple things to watch in their behavior.

1. Get Curious

Ask questions about their nature, their plans, what they're looking for—not a formal interrogation, just some relaxed and sincere curiosity about the person in front of you. Try this early on when you're out for coffee or a drink, when there's not a lot at stake. It's the ideal time: You haven't risked anything significant, you haven't been sleeping together for months. There's nothing emotionally overwrought about a coffee. Keep it loose; there are no wrong answers. Just objectively look at the person across the table and allow yourself to wonder—out loud!—what made them what they are. They're like a human scratch-off at this point, and each new area reveals a new part of them.

There are two important reasons to take this approach:

- It will allow you to set aside any expectations or projections and focus on genuinely getting to know the person in front of you.

- Genuine curiosity is more likely to lead to truth. People respond to amused interest and a neutral tone more than immediate judgment. The more you can understand who someone is now, the less likely you are to waste your time later on.

Exceptions to this strategy: Beware of the person who, in response to your first curious and nonjudgmental questions, answers the question and then barely lets you speak again! Curiosity is one of the few things that gains in value the more times it's exchanged.

2. You Notice *Them* Being Curious

Sometimes the person across the table wants to get to know us. Other people are just chasing a hit of pleasure. How can we tell the difference?

One way to tell is whether they're genuinely curious about *you*. Someone who wants a relationship will ask questions that will help them figure out:

- Your Values
  For example: Is this person kind? (It's a simple thing that's important to me.)

- Your Background
  For example: Do they have a good relationship with their family?
  (And if they don't, has it made them want to invest in creating great friendships/a sense of family elsewhere?)

- Your Lifestyle
  For example: Do they enjoy partying regularly? (I'm really more of a 10 p.m. "chamomile tea in bed" type now.)

Ultimately, they want to figure out who you are as a person, just like you're doing with them. A person who's evaluating you for a bigger role in their life works on a different timeline than someone who's eager to jump in the sack with you right away. That's why it's dangerous to rank a date based on how totally fascinating a person was, or how good a time you had. Sure, a horrible time tells you everything you need to know, but having the greatest date ever can prove to be a surprisingly unreliable index.

Immensely charismatic people who know how to charm and excite you are *giving* you a great date. Players love giving the *best* dates, not because they're into you, but because their ego thrives on you being so into *them*. They enjoy seducing, and what they want to hear is: "That was the best date I've ever had!" You might actually say that only to have them think, "Fantastic! More women must experience these phenomenal dates."

Exception: The interplay of genuine interest on both sides can be phenomenal too. But it may also be easy, conversational, even quiet. This is the opposite of the showy player: the person who makes room for you.

3. They Follow Up

They don't leave you wondering if they want to see you again. This isn't the same as immediately booking a date for tomorrow night. In a busy life, a turnaround like that might not be possible. But they won't wait until next Friday, then send you a message saying: I must see you tomorrow. No, tonight! Where are you? Can you meet an hour from now? My God, I'm so excited to see you!

That's just selective focus masquerading as excitement. They're deciding to focus on *you* tonight—perhaps because they're horny, or their other plans canceled, or they've finished an intense workweek and their mind is finally free to think of something fun. Who knows?

By all means see them. But if you want more with them, don't do anything that would make you feel used and resentful if it never progressed beyond the current stage, because all you have now is sporadic attention rather than real signs of *intention*.

4. They Are Scheduling

I wanted this section to be called "They Are Planning," until I remembered that when you're both excited to do something together, planning isn't a commitment; scheduling is. We may plan to go on safari one day, but it's not real until you're both booking flights and arranging time off work.

Plans can be dangerous. They give us all the satisfaction of talking about an idea, and even some of the enjoyment of it, but without any of the effort it takes to make it happen. There are those in dating (and in business) who love to get excited about future plans. It's a demographic with a disproportionate percentage of time-wasters.

Exception: There are also people who have no intention of being serious with you who will still happily schedule you into their lives, spiriting you away for New Year's Eve, including you on a family vacation with their parents. It's tempting to interpret this as a sign of real intention, because for the most part, these are only things people would do with someone they have real intentions for. Unfortunately, these people (often the love bombers we mentioned earlier) love the feelings that these experiences produce. It has nothing to do with being ready for a commitment. There are plenty of people who desire the experience of having a partner but have no real intention of being a partner themselves.

Somebody who schedules something is much more likely to be serious than a dreamer who never cracks open their calendar. But one-off whirlwind sentimental lovefests are far less valuable than consistent effort. That doesn't mean that somebody who throws out a fun idea of something you could do together deserves a dressing-down. ("Don't parade these flimsy fantasy getaways to me, Brian, unless you've got some firm dates in mind!") In the early stages, it's fun to float ideas of future activities you could do together, and there's nothing wrong with playing along. It's fun and flirtatious to improvise things you might do on some extravagant getaway together. There's no need to make everything about seeking investment at this stage, as long as you can tell the difference between role-play and real progress.

5. They Involve You

Dating someone you're serious about doesn't mean they now have to involve you in every decision they make. But once you're past the tricky first stages of attraction and you both recognize your connection, it's important to notice how they handle things that could significantly affect:

- The amount of time you are able to spend together.
- How far apart you might be for an extended period.
- Your trust in them.
- The possibility of the relationship progressing.

Them *involving* you, depending on the stage of the relationship you're in, won't necessarily mean you get a vote or a veto. If someone has to go away for a month for work, they may not ask your permission. But you might expect to get a forewarning and plenty of communication around it. One thing is for sure—they'll want to make sure that them leaving doesn't make you doubt their interest in you, or their intentions for continuing the relationship.

The key questions here are:

- Are they actually taking your feelings into account?
- Do they care?
- Are they concerned about bringing you on board in the process, or are they indifferent to your experience?
- Do you feel like the last one to know about the things happening in their life, and generally outside of the circle of information?
- Are you collateral damage whose reactions go unnoticed until your hurt or frustration becomes impossible to ignore?

One way you can tell you're not being taken into account: Your reaction (when you get to have one) is met not with compassion but with frustration, as if you were an inconvenience in the realization of their largely non-negotiable plan.

6. They Make You Feel Comfortable

Someone who wants to make sure you're still in their life a week from now will want to confirm ahead of time that you're comfortable with the things they're doing.

They're going to dinner with an old friend you could feel threatened by? You might notice the subtle ways they make it clear that this person is just a friend, or married, or someone they can't wait for you to meet. They don't leave things open to ambiguous interpretation because they don't want anything to jeopardize what's blossoming between you. They also want to avoid any suggestion that they would be comfortable with that kind of ambiguity coming from you.

Crossing the Border
Between Attention and Intention

You might have noticed that the six steps above are arranged in roughly chronological order, from first encounters to conscious connection. In other words, there's a gradient from flirtatious attention to more serious intention that roughly corresponds to the transition from attraction to commitment.

The real danger comes when you start assuming that as attention increases, it's matched on their side with increasing levels of intention. It's easy to mistake intensity of feeling with seriousness of purpose, especially if you feel your own level of commitment growing and just assume that seriousness and intensity go hand in hand for them the same way they do for you.

This is why it's usually safer to take your time, not for any prudish reasons, just because time is the only way to measure the most reliable outward marker of intention: consistency. Inconsistency usually shows up uncomfortably early. But consistency can only be appreciated over time. Going slow gives consistency the time it needs to show up, and it gives actions a chance to catch up to words and feelings.

9

NEVER SATISFIED

ALEXANDER: You're like me, I'm never satisfied.
ANGELICA: Is that right?
ALEXANDER: I have never been satisfied.

—*Hamilton*

Happiness in love can prove maddeningly elusive—not big news to anyone in a relationship with a wonderful person whose feelings are stronger than your own. If you could just scratch together a spark or two of love, it seems like you could have it all. But despite your best efforts, your affection never rises above lukewarm.

Then you meet someone who sets your passions ablaze, inspiring giddy fantasies about your future together. But this time the tables are turned: You only hear from them sporadically, and, never quite sure if they want you, you're pitched into a cycle of euphoria when they call, and high anxiety when they don't. In such a state of "excitement," you find that you can't seem to eat, sleep, or focus on anything at all.

Once you escape that situation, you feel newly ready for someone kind, trustworthy, and dependable, only to find that you're unmoved, understimulated, wondering if you should just hold out for someone who makes you feel alive again. You feel so safe that you can dedicate all your spare time to imagining the life you could be leading with someone else.

Why is it so damn hard to get it right? It's as if at the end of every relationship, we make our wishes looking backward, and fixing one failure only sets us up for a completely different disappointment the next time through. Based on these wild swings, it's easy to conclude that nothing works. Not simply tired of dating, or other people, we become tired of the one thing common to every single failed relationship we've ever been in: ourselves.

Are we the broken one? Are we just wired wrong? Are we condemned to rolling a giant boulder up a mountain, only to watch it roll away from us anytime we catch a glimpse of happiness? According to Albert Camus in *The Myth of Sisyphus*, the gods think there is no more dreadful punishment than futile and hopeless labor. No wonder so many of us give up. But even giving up offers no peace—desire for a shared life of intimacy follows us everywhere, haunting any space we once hoped someone else might fill.

But if we're still not ready to give up, how can we stop ourselves from falling for people who don't treat us with respect, who fail to see in us someone worth holding on to? And how can we summon excitement for the kind of people who actually might treat us better?

Why We Say Yes to People Who Are Bad for Us

Let's begin with the first question: Why do we keep falling for the players, the emotionally unavailable, the ones who make us chase, who don't treat us right? At a certain point, we have to shift our question from "Why are people like this?" to "Why do I keep giving time to someone like this?" Why do we keep swooning over the ones we just said "never again" to, again? Let's explore why *again* will never be a safe word for us.

1. The Scarcity Mindset

You arrive at a party with your friends, hoping to meet the kind of person you've been talking about on the way over. You dance with a few people. Each has something you like, but each is also missing something you need. One is fun, but more of a friend. Another is hot, but you don't connect. The authentic and intriguing one was wearing . . . those shoes. While you keep looking, a funny thing happens: As your group of friends thins out, time starts playing tricks. You spot one making her way to the exit with someone she'd been dancing with, but they look as if they've known each other for ages. Alone and self-conscious, you take out your phone, and it suddenly feels as if you've stepped into another dimension. The friend who just left with someone has put up a photo of their engagement. Another friend you lost track of hours ago has just posted an ecstatic baby announcement. There's even a post from the hot dance partner you failed to connect with earlier. It turns out they left the party and are now honeymooning in Santorini with their new spouse. You can't believe it. "How long have I been here?" The room is nearly empty. The music now sounds less like a beat and more like the second hand on a stopwatch. "Was I too ruthless in dismissing people? The hot stranger seemed wrong, but someone else didn't think so. Did I judge that connection too harshly?" Your breath turns shallow. You stop worrying about finding the perfect partner and instead start looking for someone who can get you out of here before it's too late.

This is the scarcity mindset at work. In painting a catastrophic picture of how desperate our situation is, it urges us to entertain people we shouldn't—often people our loved ones can see are bad news from a mile off. There's the one who proudly states they don't believe in monogamy but is the best sex of your life; the one you have the best time with but who goes quiet any time you talk about wanting more; the one who's been getting around to his divorce for the last five years, but is an amazing father to his kids and offers you the promise of a perfect future.

What they all have in common: You get to *feel* something with them. "And what's so wrong with that?" we ask ourselves. "Life is short. Why *not* choose to feel something along the way?" This kind of logic allows us to justify the highs while ignoring the long-term damage from everything else. At this point, we should pay attention to Irving Rosenfeld, perhaps the best exemplar of the con man in movie history, who, in *American Hustle*, paid homage to the nearly universal tendency for people to con themselves: "We talk ourselves into things, you know, we sell ourselves things we maybe don't even need or want. You know, we're dressing them up. We leave out the risk, we leave out the ugly truth. Pay attention to that, 'cause we're all conning ourselves one way or another, just to get through life."

We condemn those who lie to us, then ignore the lies we tell ourselves—that we are happy, that they can change, that our needs are being met, that we are not risking devastating regrets if we go on living this way. Delusions of this scale are the most dangerous sort of lies. They stop us from leaving people who get in the way of our happiness, and in doing so, they make us co-conspirators in the theft of our own future.

We dress up our delusions in flippant justifications. (I know this person isn't right for me, but I'm just having a bit of fun for now, not taking it all too seriously. Not everything has to have some tidy label. We're just seeing where it goes. Besides, it's a complicated situation.) But "fun" can be the trapdoor to toxic relationships. "For now" is often the benign face of betraying our dreams. We settle for these euphemisms, because they're easier than stating the truth of our scarcity mindset: that when we are afraid that this is all there is (or all we're worth), we stop choosing what's right, and start taking whatever we think we can get. If we ever hope to make the right decisions for our future happiness, we have to overcome this scarcity mindset. But it's not the only thing that's limiting our chances.

2. What We Know

When we repeatedly wind up in damaging situations, there can be an assumption that we keep making these choices due to a lack of self-worth. This may not be wrong, but it can be reductive. A captive dolphin may spin around and jump through literal hoops to get its next meal. But release that dolphin into the ocean, and it's likely to encounter two problems: First, if she keeps associating humans with food, she'll find that she's looking in all the wrong places for survival. Not just wrong, potentially dangerous—approaching boats for food could even be fatal. Second, the tricks she learned in the tank would be useless in the ocean. But that's what the dolphin knows, and that's not her fault. If the dolphin performs because doing so once earned her fish, or if she looks for people because that was once a reliable way to get food, we wouldn't say the dolphin had a self-worth problem—we would acknowledge the sad reality that she currently doesn't know any different, and that what she does know has left her poorly and unfairly equipped for the ocean.

Many people who come to me for coaching hope to build up their sense of self-worth, which is certainly a worthwhile pursuit. But often, in order to do that, they must first retrain their expectations on interpersonal, behavioral, and emotional levels. On the interpersonal level, since people often fall into a specific pattern in one relationship after another, it can be hard to imagine any other kind exists. If we've only ever been with unfaithful sorts, it doesn't matter how many happy faithful couples we're friends with, we still seem to wind up with the wanderers. We only seem to recognize what we're familiar with emotionally. You might finally leave a narcissist, but still feel that sense of dread and continual threat poisoning your outlook even when you connect with someone stable and emotionally generous.

On the behavioral level, we all have tricks we rely on, some of which we developed as kids trying to win our parents' attention. We may resort to traits we picked up in challenging formative romantic connections, and our behavior hasn't caught up to the company we'd like to keep. Maybe you're used to making someone jealous just to get their attention, a behavior that worked with exes who were only in it for the chase (even though these were the same types who got bored with you the moment you expressed any sincere affection). Someone who's trying to engage with you authentically will not be quite sure how to deal with you when your old habits pop back up, which land in a completely different way in this new relationship, where they seem to signal a lack of loyalty and mutual respect. They may just pass you by for someone whose kindness and vulnerability are more accessible.

Still, it's hard to lay down the weapons that have worked in the past. I know men who complain about women who only want them for their money, but they still can't stop going to five-star restaurants on a first date instead of the family-run ramen joint right down the street. I hear women complaining that men only seem to want sex, yet all their social media posts are barely safe for work. To find love, we sometimes have to give up the very thing that gets us attention. This is harder than it sounds, especially when our ego's involved, and we start worrying that if we give up the attention we know how to attract, no one will ever see us again.

On an emotional level too, our nervous system becomes wired to certain kinds of experience. If we're used to wild shifts of erratic behavior, it can be hard to stick with even a healthy relationship that doesn't provide that volatility. A friend of mine, Lucy, had her first real boyfriend in college. He was disrespectful, made her feel small, and was inappropriate with other women right in front of her. When that relationship ended, she met an attractive, funny, but above all, kind guy. Things were easy between them and she knew exactly where she stood with him. Visiting home a few weeks in, her mother asked how it was going. "It's weird, Mum, he's so nice to me," Lucy said, genuinely perplexed.

"That's how it's supposed to be," her mum replied, barely hiding her relief. The kindness of Lucy's new boyfriend first presented as unfamiliar and disorienting. If the same happens to you in such circumstances and things like kindness and patience make you feel disoriented, give yourself grace. It's normal. The poor treatment that was once so familiar may not have made us happy, but we were still used to it. That's why it takes more than just wanting something new. Deprogramming ourselves requires us to actively choose what is unfamiliar over what is known. When we find that something new is possible, it takes courage to sit in the discomfort it creates. That's hard, which is why people get trapped in their unhappiness for so long. But just as we might breathe through the pain in an intense session of bodywork, we have to sit with that discomfort until it releases. If we can do that, what began as intensely uncomfortable can turn into a fresh source of pleasure. If we don't want to be condemned to relive these painful emotions, we have to sit with the new experiences until they turn into something well-known and familiar.

Fortunately for my friend Lucy, this shift occurred in her early twenties. Many of us aren't so lucky, unconsciously repeating the same patterns for years or decades because it's what we know, what our old behaviors attract, and what our nervous system responds to. And every time we return to our old habits, it leaves us with a reduced sense of possibility. It is as though life validates a painful reality as long as we indulge it. Understanding this can help us exercise self-compassion. Simply noticing unfamiliar behavior can be hard. The types we've become wired for in our lives tend to be the stronger signal on our radar. Learning to make more sophisticated distinctions takes time and conscious intervention—a commitment to stop indulging in our old habits and start embracing something new. As anyone who has tried to quit drinking or smoking can attest, this isn't a simple task. It means training ourselves to override a dangerous but natural instinct: the instinct to keep focusing on the one thing we are trying to avoid.

3. Staring at the Wall

When the Formula 1 driver Mario Andretti was asked for his number one tip in race-car driving, he said, "Don't look at the wall. Your car goes where your eyes go." Professional racers are taught to override this instinct. But how many of us can relate to repeatedly steering directly into the very thing we want to avoid?

My father was prone to conflict when I was a child. I remember moments when things escalated quickly between him and other men. At best, I would feel embarrassed and tense in these awkward situations; at worst, I was afraid it would turn violent, as it occasionally did. My adrenaline would spike. Sometimes I would dissociate; other times I'd find it hard to think about anything else for hours afterward. To add to this, I grew up as a young teenager working in my dad's nightclub (yes, yes, not OK, I know), where every night I would witness the awful things drunken people were capable of doing to each other. I learned to hate fights, while simultaneously developing a sixth sense for when they were about to happen. This was one of the factors stoking a hypervigilance that has followed me most of my life, making me monitor my surroundings for threats of conflict and danger way more than is either necessary or useful. As the eldest of three brothers, some of that hypervigilance got channeled into a protective instinct that all too often led me into precisely the kinds of situations I supposedly wanted to avoid.

In a bar called Champion, in Golden Gai, on a trip to Tokyo, we'd befriended the manager, Melody, a woman we'd first gotten to know because she recognized me from my YouTube videos. Golden Gai is a neighborhood with rows of ridiculously small bars like Melody's, seating five or ten, crammed into an intricate network of impossibly narrow streets. Every time we came in, Melody treated us like we'd been regulars our whole lives. On the night in question, my brother Harry was belting out "Hey Ya!" on the karaoke machine—not an easy choice, as you could tell from the number of lines he missed, although that might have been the sake—while Stephen and I watched.

While Harry was busy telling everyone to "Shake it like a Polaroid picture," I began fixating on a fellow Westerner staring at Harry. It bothered me, not just because Harry is my brother, but because despite standing at six foot four, he is just about the sweetest guy you'll ever meet. Imagine a giant, people-loving, fun-seeking puppy, and you have Harry. Nothing about him says trouble. But this guy wouldn't stop looking over at him. I kept looking back to confirm it—as Andretti would say, I couldn't stop looking at *the wall*. And every time I checked, that same disgruntled stare was fixed on Harry.

Before I'd even consciously realized it, I marched over to him, my blood fully up, and asked: "Is everything alright, mate? You keep looking over at my brother. If there is an issue, tell me and we can sort it out."

It didn't sound polite. I had unconsciously summoned my thickest Cockney accent (cheers, Mum and Dad). That's not a good sign. Twenty years of studying human dynamics and positive communication had boiled down to this: me, the YouTube love guy by day, playing Michael Caine as a gangster in a Japanese bar by night. What I wanted more than anything—what I've always wanted more than anything—was simply a peaceful, carefree time with people I love. Yet here I was, picking a fight. Stephen, recognizing the symptoms, grabbed my arm: "What are you doing?" Melody, who no doubt had seen every version of this event before, spotted it too. Fast as any pub landlord in East London, she wedged herself between the man and me, and in that lovely way that no-nonsense people do, said, "Enough," pointing each of us to our respective corners.

I used to wonder how my brothers survived without me around. Then I realized: They didn't find themselves in situations like this. For me, historically, these situations were everywhere; for them, they weren't. Why? Because I was staring at the wall, and they were not (at least, not the wall I kept staring at). And when there was no wall in sight, I still unconsciously scanned for it, for any situation that would validate my ongoing public service announcement to anyone I love: "We are not safe, and we all need to watch out, all the time." What I didn't realize was the extent to which I wasn't just experiencing, but creating, a different reality than the one my brothers were part of.

We each try to control our fear in different ways. My way was to get as close to the wall as possible. For fifteen years, my chosen hobbies have been boxing, Brazilian jiu-jitsu, and a little Muay Thai, all activities that constantly put fighting on my mind, and sometimes in my face. There were days when my director Jameson Jordan would have to delay video shoots because my face was too bruised from sparring. I was drawn to YouTube videos of people fighting that simultaneously spiked my adrenaline and fueled my perception that violence was ever-present (the algorithm was happy to oblige). Whatever wall you're looking for, you'll find it, and sooner or later you'll have spent so much time staring at it that you won't even realize it's a wall anymore; you'll think it's just life. I consciously try to avoid such videos these days—some fixes are simple ones.

When our mind is searching for the wall, it'll even see it where it doesn't exist. I recently had a client who was terrified of getting hurt. The moment she feared she could be, she pushed people away. She'd been newly dating a man who, even by her account, had been a decent partner so far. Then one Saturday, he had a small gathering for a few friends from his work and hadn't invited her. He hadn't covered it up, but it hurt her feelings all the same. It sparked fears that he didn't feel the same as she did, which ignited her even deeper fear that she wasn't enough. By Saturday, her hurt had turned to anger, and she fired off a text: Why didn't you invite me? Realizing it had affected her, he apologized, explaining it was just a group of friends he had been getting around to seeing, and asked if he could call her later that evening. She texted back: Don't bother. But every day that he didn't call her—something she had told him not to do—only confirmed her suspicions that she had been right about her fears. She had a right to be hurt that she hadn't been invited to meet his friends, but her focus on the wall had turned an opportunity to be vulnerable and create intimacy into a reason to prematurely explode the relationship. But as far as she was concerned, she had proven her theory: Everyone would inevitably end up hurting her.

We have to be extremely careful about the "normal" we are creating for ourselves. There are so many different realities, yet our focus and our choices trap us in one we don't want. Don't let your wall become your world.

4. Our Level

We've established a few crucial reasons why we keep saying yes to people and situations that are bad for us: Fear of time and options running out leads us to a scarcity mindset where we believe we have to just take what we can get; our past experiences have shaped what we know; and a dangerous focus on the wall drives us toward what we know, not what we want. We've also talked about how when we try to look away from the wall and toward something new, it can feel intensely uncomfortable, and that instead of sitting in this discomfort, most people return to what is known, even if it makes them unhappy. Part of this discomfort is simply that it's a new experience, and the unfamiliar can be scary. But on a deeper level, there's another challenge. When we experience something new, and it represents more than we've had in the past, we don't just need to get familiar with it, we need to allow ourselves to feel worthy of it.

Our past conditioning hasn't just been responsible for what we know, but also what we think we deserve. To our mind, the past is a reflection of our level in life. We may want more, we may even see that more is possible for other people, but it's hard to believe that more is possible when it comes to *us*. We misinterpret our own experience, falsely believing that if we really had been worthy of more, we would have it already.

Training ourselves to be comfortable with more is hard. In our past, we were told things, or taught to accept things, that lowered our perception of what our worth can be. So we learned to get comfortable with a level where we feel safest. And once we've settled on that level, getting any more can feel alien and make us scared: scared we won't be able to hold on to any gains or improvement in our life; scared that we will get found out for not being worthy of our new position—the essence of impostor syndrome. There is a twisted sense of safety in getting less. Safety is the devil we know. Safety is knowing our way around, even in abject terrain.

Even if we've been asking for more, getting it can make us feel instantly unsafe. Have you ever put your foot down with someone you are used to appeasing? Having taken a stand, or been more honest about your feelings, how long did it take before you started feeling guilty about it? How quickly did you return to the dynamic that made you resentful in the first place?

There's a safety in being the one who is complaining about someone else's selfishness. There's a security in being the one getting taken advantage of. We know how to play that role. But we may never have learned how to play the role of an equal.

Once we realize that getting *more* can actually make us feel more unsafe than less, we begin to understand why we've spent so much of our life with the same complaints. It's easier to complain than to train ourselves to be comfortable at a new level.

We may only feel safe in a relationship when we're doing more for them than we allow them to do for us. After a while, this fundamental inequality can even start to feel like a sense of control. This imbalance is even more common when we've decided someone is desirable, or more desirable than we are: They're especially good-looking, successful, charismatic, charming, or impressive. Our self-worth level tells us it would be too much to just be with someone like this without having to endure some awful side effect as part of the bargain: They cheat, their communication is patchy, they give less than we do, they make us feel uncertain, they are only kind after bouts of emotional abuse. When you find yourself in this situation and you feel psychologically unsafe having a hard conversation for fear of losing them, your *set level* is telling you that you are asking for more than you are worth.

The net effect of this is that we feel comfortable receiving love, but only when love comes with a catch. This catch gives us permission to accept the gift. I once heard comedian Nikki Glaser in an interview describing her relationship with having an orgasm:

> I've always been into being tied up. I'm someone who doesn't feel like I deserve pleasure without having pain. Like, I don't ever celebrate anything—I can only celebrate or relax if I put in so much work that I'm dead. It's really hard for me to enjoy myself in life. I have to punish myself first. And so orgasms—it's hard for me to give myself one, and let myself have that much. It's too much. It's like Christmas. You have to wait a year for Christmas; you can't have Christmas every day. So I like to be tied up and forced to have Christmas.

Some may see in this a shocking description of what she feels she has to go through for the privilege of having an orgasm. I see the way so many of us live our lives. I struggle to believe I'm worthy of moments of joy and peace without first putting myself through a brutal schedule, monitoring my productivity levels down to the minute. Perhaps some people apply this "earn your cookie" mindset in ways that lead to healthy achievements. Not me. Mine is a mutation whereby joy and self-compassion are regularly outlawed by an internal tyrant who decides when I've been flogged enough for one day.

Just when I'm about to collapse, a voice inside says: "OK. Give him half an hour of peace before bed. But make sure he knows we'll start again, bright and early in the morning."

Becoming conscious of patterns like this is an important first step. It helps us exercise self-compassion, recognizing the force pinning us where we are, even once we have begun to sense there is more available to us than what we have allowed ourselves in the past. But instead of letting any lack of worth persuade us that more is for other people, not for us, we have to begin re-educating ourselves on what our worth is. It's a kind of reparenting, where we unlearn deeply wired old associations that were wrong, and teach ourselves new associations, maybe for the first time, such as: Love shouldn't come with a catch that makes us suffer; it's OK to have needs and to voice them without shame or guilt; we deserve the same respect, decency, and kindness as anyone else—there's no special reason we deserve worse treatment, regardless of how we've learned to think of ourselves as bad or undeserving; it doesn't matter how outwardly impressive anyone appears to be, because at their core they are just another person like us.

Most of us have been living life waiting for other people to educate us on what our worth is. But it's time to start living by a different truth: While there will occasionally be special people in life who uniquely see our worth, it is actually our job to educate *others* on what our worth is, not the other way around.

These things are hard to learn. It's like learning to walk all over again. But just like a child learning to walk, we will need patience, kindness, and encouragement as we stumble clumsily into a new way of moving through the world.

5. It Feels Good

Any exploration of the reasons why we keep gravitating to what is bad for us would be incomplete without reviewing our behavior through the lens of addiction. So many facets of dating are addictive: sex; honeymoon periods; charismatic, affectionate people, and the surging oxytocin we feel in their embrace; the dopamine hit when someone's name reappears on our phone. Even the cycle of highs and lows from dating a person who makes us feel loved, and then anxious, and then loved again is addictive. It has a name in psychology: the trauma bond. The chemicals involved in love and dating are so addictive that many of us will do or accept anything to keep getting our fix.

We look for our fix on the path of least resistance: going back to people who aren't progressing rather than going through the effort of finding someone new. We return to an unhealthy dynamic because it offers a familiar high when it gets good again. We settle for any connection in the short term, no matter how low-grade, rather than experience solitude and extended periods of being single.

What all drugs do is offer a quick fix for painful emotions. But the quick fixes don't last—a chain of events that can easily convince some people that there's no long-term fix for their love lives. This is a kind of crescendo to the scarcity mindset—the complete loss of hope. When there is no hope, what starts as a quick fix can turn into a way of life. This comment left on my YouTube channel serves as an important reality check:

> When you started listing off reasons we might justify dating the wrong people, I was like YUP that's me! But honestly, it's better than nothing. I've lived many, many incredibly lonely years with nothing due to the fact that I was always wanting to find the right person and not waste time on casual partners. Meanwhile I just kept getting older and never found him, so I had to settle for the norm, which is casual. If I didn't date the wrong guys, I would still be single. At least it's more fun this way, rather than enduring complete and utter loneliness.
>
> —Sarah, YouTube Subscriber

How can one not sympathize with Sarah? Who couldn't understand why she might simply resolve to enjoy what comes her way, instead of whittling down the years of her life waiting for a theoretical committed and loving relationship that never shows signs of materializing? Her candor forces us to confront the question: Is having nothing really better than having the wrong thing? It's not lost on me that when I describe the four levels of importance in a relationship (admiration, mutual attraction, commitment, compatibility), a meaningful percentage of the crowd initially stares at me with their arms folded, because their experience is that even mutual attraction is nowhere to be found. Why bother worrying about long-term compatibility in that case? For someone who's had no one for years, mutual attraction, no matter how flawed, feels like a life raft, or at least a fun time.

But is this just another low-confidence sleight of hand, with a lack of self-worth posing as a kind of existential fatalism? Is it just another way to let ourselves off the hook, a cop-out that convinces us to settle for less, distracting us from something greater that life has in store for us if we could only break our own cycle? And what does breaking this cycle look like in practice? How can we attract the kind of relationship we may have begun to doubt the existence of? How do we ensure we actually get excited about something that is better for us, instead of yearning for what hurts us? And how do we make sure we feel worthy of it once we have it? These questions hold the key to finding satisfaction in love. To find this satisfaction, we need to take the job of creating a new reality in our love life seriously. We need to consciously recalibrate the default settings that have been governing our choices so far. Whether we are twenty or sixty, perennially single or serially dating the wrong people, we need to start taking daily steps and making decisions that, once and for all, rewire our brain in love. While this isn't easy, I promise you it can be done, and the road map is more practical than you might think.

10

HOW TO
REWIRE YOUR BRAIN

We all have patterns that have been automatically directing the course of our lives for a long time: a pattern of anxious thinking that has us sabotaging any good thing that comes our way, fearing deep down we are not enough to hold on to it; allowing jealousy and insecurity to take over and destroy our experience of a relationship; repeatedly chasing after emotionally unavailable people; falling into codependent patterns with unhealthy and even abusive partners; overinvesting and consequently scaring healthy relationships away the moment we like someone; finding flaws and running away every time the honeymoon period ends and a relationship gets real because deep down we don't know how to receive healthy love.

It isn't easy to disconnect from these kinds of painful patterns. Patterns become habits, which can turn into automatic behaviors that finally feel so natural we may even wind up embracing them as part of our identity. These fundamental beliefs about what and who we are can continue to cause us harm. While they are difficult to change, we have the ability to short-circuit what seems automatic and become, instead, intentional. Once we identify the stubborn patterns that are causing us harm—something we tried to do in the previous chapter—we begin to consciously rewire our brain for a love life that will leave us more at peace and, hopefully, more satisfied.

The five steps that follow are less about steps to take when you're out in the world and meeting new people, and more about the conditions of your mind, your outlook, and your expectations before you do. They deal with taking on our most worn-in behavioral grooves, so it's important to calculate progress with compassion and remember that small changes add up.

Step 1: Make Change Necessary

The beginning of change is not belief, it's necessity. Once we've learned from experience that we can't keep doing what we're doing now, doing something new and different becomes necessary. As Plato put it, "Our need will be the real creator." Unfortunately, a clear grasp of such need only comes when we connect to the true pain, and ultimate cost, of continuing to do what we are doing now.

What's the pattern that's causing us intolerable pain? Ruining any good relationship that comes our way and ending up alone and feeling like we're broken? Continuously chasing after people we know are bad news and getting betrayed? Dating emotionally unavailable people who waste years of our lives? Being so anxiously attached (or avoidant) we can never relax and end up sabotaging every relationship? Never being able to advocate for what we want in the relationship and being taken advantage of? Or maybe the pain doesn't come from dating, but from avoiding connections altogether: denying any part of ourselves that wants to find love; dividing time between work and dinners with married friends, insisting that "dating apps don't work for me," but taking no steps to meet people in real life either. And then self-loathing (from doing nothing to change our situation) kicks in, amplifying our loneliness.

One day the pain will reach a crescendo when we realize the costs: of losing our shot at a biological family (if this is meaningful to us), of wasting years on someone who never deserved our focus, of never taking an honest shot at finding love. To grasp this, we only need to see where our current trajectory will land, an exercise that has less to do with time travel, or psychic powers, and more to do with common sense.

With some patterns, like returning to an abusive partner, the cost is obvious. With others, like keeping in touch with exes who don't meet our needs, it's more insidious. I call that impulse "microdosing in love." We tell ourselves we're only seeing them until someone better comes along, but then that casual arrangement winds up being the reason we never have the urge to run into someone better. Every interaction, whether it's texts, calls, or sex, reasserts their psychological imprint in our life. The intimacy is never enough to satisfy, but it's enough to distract us from anyone else. We neither get them, nor get over them.

Thanks to microdosing, there are unavailable people everywhere who aren't actually taken, passing by potential partners with complete indifference because they're semi-absorbed in a phantom relationship. The upside of heartbreak is that it passes eventually. But microdosing is like an old vinyl record with a scratch where the needle keeps skipping: heartache on a loop.

Microdosing is only one of the patterns that keep us from finding love. Whatever your situation, if it isn't working, connect with that pain. Decide that the future cost of that pattern is not one you are willing to pay. That decision makes change necessary and inevitable, because once you say "No more," you are confronted with the next question: "What now?" The answer to that question requires you to make another decision: "What's most important to me in this next chapter of my life?"

Step 2: Choose What's Most Important

Deciding what we stand for in our love life is crucial to deciphering what's worth our time and what's not. It's practically the opposite, from a priority standpoint, of an ideal-partner checklist—we have to choose what's most important *to us* first, our highest criteria for choosing a partner. These criteria become the map that orients us as we navigate through dating.

Which way do you go? Toward someone who creates peace in your life, or the hottest person you think you can get? Someone who's willing to plan a future together, or someone impulsive? Someone committed to self-growth, or someone six feet tall? Many of us choose as though we're casting for a cameo, not looking for a partner in life. Take the heartbroken Natalie, in the movie *Up in the Air*, explaining what she loved about her ex, who's still the kind of guy she dreams of ending up with:

> He really fit the bill, you know. White-collar, six foot one, college grad, loves dogs, likes funny movies, brown hair, kind eyes, works

in finance but is outdoorsy. I always imagined he'd have a single-syllable name like Matt or John or Dave. In a perfect world, he drives a 4Runner and the only thing he loves more than me is his golden lab. And a nice smile.

Natalie's checklist reads like a casting call in one of the trades; there's barely anything there that would make someone a good partner. Real life requires two people to play many parts in a range of crises, not just put on a dazzling performance for a sizzle reel. Whenever I'm helping a person get over someone, I ask them what they loved about that person, knowing how rarely their answers will have anything to do with what might have made them a great partner. One time, in defending her continued investment in a man who'd been messing her around for months, a woman said to me, with no hint of irony, "He's incredibly educated, philanthropic, takes charge, and had a big exit from his company." None of those traits related to how he treated her or made her feel. It can be shocking to see what a minimal impact the things we've had our heart set on actually have on the quality of our relationship.

One sign that we're successfully reorienting ourselves: The items on our original casting description start to disappear. I once spoke with a happily married man who told me that while he'd always chased after dancers, his wife is one of the least-coordinated people he's ever known. He laughed when I asked if this bothered him. "What percentage of my life am I on a dance floor? My wife is the best person I've ever met, she's an amazing mother, and we adore each other's company. These things affect my life every single day."

While reviewing the qualities that really matter, consider how much ego, and not future happiness, has been the determining force. One of my private clients, Lisa, is one of the most successful career women I've ever known and she deeply wanted to find love. But when we met, it soon became clear that her ego, and not her well-being, was driving her choices:

I get fixated on men who are desirable to lots of women. I find my-self looking for someone who's more desired by women than I am desired by men. It's like when a guy is the man of the moment, and I overhear other women talking about how amazing he is, I become preoccupied. This is especially true if I think he's more intelligent than me, or if he's doing something impressive in his career or business. I simultaneously want him and become terrified of his rejection.

Despite her elevated status, Lisa lived with a deep feeling of unworthiness that showed up in her relationships with men. This unworthiness motivated her to prove that she could attract somebody others found highly eligible, a personal accomplishment that would finally help her feel like she had arrived. But when these men treated her poorly, it didn't convince her that such guys might not be a good candidate for her investment; it only confirmed her fear that she wasn't good enough for someone like that. That made her try even harder to win their approval, regardless of how much she suffered—a vicious circle of self-abuse, and one that made her a target for bad types. With her insecurity leading the way, she had become disconnected from her own experience, looking not for someone who could make her feel happy, but for someone who could make her feel *enough*.

What our ego wants, and what our heart needs, are often two very different things. The word *ego* is often associated only with an inflated sense of self-importance, but ego can just as easily arise from the insecurity that makes us desire that importance in the first place. The same ego that says "I'm amazing" is the very voice that can be saying "I'm worthless" a day later. These are simply two sides of the same coin. It's all ego. There are entire books on this subject, and mentors like Eckhart Tolle are wonderful teachers of it. All we need to know for our purposes here is that our ego is always trying to reinforce and validate itself. When we believe our stock is high, ego makes us think other people aren't good enough for us. When we are questioning our own value, ego makes us think other people are too good for us. Letting our ego make decisions is a bad strategy for happiness in love. Your ego might want a hot, tall, self-made entrepreneur who lives in a penthouse in the city—the guy all your friends validate you for finding. But your heart may be lit up by someone you can be yourself around who makes you feel accepted.

If you ever notice that someone's lack of effort is making them more interesting to you, ego is driving. We see our ability to "get" this person as the way that we will validate our own worth. "If they are so valuable and they don't think I'm good enough, then I must not be enough," we think. And if such a person appears desirable to others, we are liable to fall into the memetic trap of basing their value on what others think is valuable. This is the problem with listening to our ego over the internal voice that tells us what we need. Ego lands us in the trap of prizing whatever the crowd is going after. But as my wife, Audrey (my fiancée when I started writing this book!), once said to me: "No one is more valuable because the spotlight is on them."

When we listen to the nuances of what makes us happy—which are, by definition, specific to us—our interest becomes its own spotlight. The more we tune in to what matters to us, the less we care about what matters to other people. We're not trying to find someone who's right for everyone else; we want someone who's right for us.

To find out what's important to you, ask yourself this question: "When I was at my most miserable with someone (whether or not I was desperately trying to hold on to them), what was missing that made me unhappy?" Put another way: "Before I even consider what I want in a person, what do I need in a relationship in order to be happy? What do I need to feel from someone to experience peace? What values do I need someone to share with me before anything else even matters?"

Here are some possibilities: full commitment, equal investment in the relationship, open communication, kindness, consistency, stability, reliability, dependability, loyalty, integrity, accountability, being a team, making you laugh, feeling seen, being understood and accepted, feeling safe to be yourself without judgment or shaming, knowing they acknowledge and care about your feelings, quality time, their presence, feeling secure in the relationship, prizing a shared outcome (for example, getting married or having children).

In the past we may have clung to someone with charm, charisma, looks, or status, but when a crucial need went unmet, the things we thought we really wanted turned out to be worthless. We kept trying to convince ourselves that these were things we couldn't afford to lose, but what was missing made it impossible to stay—certainly to stay and be happy. What qualities has life made you realize you can't live without? This doesn't just extend to someone's values, but what they want in life—their outcome. What kind of commitments do they need to be open to for you to be happy with them? The right person is both right and ready.

Remember the wall and the way you could start seeing them everywhere, even where they didn't exist? In rewiring the brain, we have to start disconnecting from the idea that we always meet one type of person, or land in one kind of relationship, and start connecting to the opposite idea: There are people out there who are unlike the ones we've been drawn to in the past.

One sign that rewiring our brain is starting to work comes when things we used to hunger for start to appear not just unnecessary, but unattractive. A friend of mine was always drawn to charismatic, life-of-the-party types—so drawn that she repeatedly ignored deeper character flaws. They cheated on her, and, even worse, she never felt accepted for who she was. Whenever she relaxed and behaved like the kind and deeply emotional person she really was, they told her she was "too sensitive." Their reflexive need to command the room left barely any space for her feelings. After years of pain in these relationships, she reorganized her hierarchy for what was important to her, starting with finding someone who appreciated her emotional intelligence for the gift it was. She was surprised to discover herself becoming less impressed with, and even turned off by, the kind of charm that once had dazzled her, a trait that now started to register as insecure and self-seeking. She developed a new appreciation for people with a deeper, quieter confidence, and paid particular attention to conversations that were authentic and reciprocal with people who made her feel comfortable being herself. Her husband is someone her younger self would never have imagined herself ending up with, she says, and she joyfully states that she's never been happier.

Determining what's most important to us creates a model for our happiness in love that is both achievable and tailor-made for our needs. It disconnects us from the superfluous, sometimes ego-driven demands of our former selves, and wires us into the essential ingredients for our long-term happiness, clearing the way for us to make decisions about who to give our time and energy to. The next step is to orient our lives around this path, sticking to it even when our feelings threaten to derail us.

Step 3: Follow Your Path, Not Your Feelings

If we are serious about the path we've chosen—and we should be, since we already know where the previous paths went wrong—we will say no to things that only provide short-term comfort or excitement. Here the old adage applies: *If you want a hard life, do easy things, but if you want an easy life, do hard things.* Every time we make a choice that's in line with our new path, we affirm our intentions, sending ourselves (and anyone else who notices) unambiguous signals about what we value.

Unfortunately, our love life is an arena where there's always somebody telling you to follow your feelings. Judging from the dilemmas that people come to me with, following your feelings seems like the textbook example of the easy thing that creates the hard life. I remember a breakup that took me months to work up the nerve to commit to—as well as my mum's confusion seeing me suffer in the aftermath. When she reached her limit watching this sad spectacle, she said, "Oh, darling, if it hurts this much, can't you just go back?" As much as I appreciated her mixture of frustration and concern, even then I knew that if I'd followed her advice, I'd only confuse what might feel good and bring me relief in the moment with what would make me happier in the long run.

This same dilemma occurs at the beginning of relationships too. After an exhilarating first date, you may want to shoot off a text that communicates your excitement, like: Hey, I know we just met, but I think I love you. It seems clear to me that we should get married and begin our life together. Thoughts? Mercifully, there seems to be a natural breaker switch that keeps us from hitting send, an emotional pause button that lets us set aside our feelings and ask: "Will this serve the path I want to be on?" This question, which might be instinctive in situations like this, is one we tend not to ask nearly enough in others; yet it's a question we need to start asking consciously and often as we're rewiring our brain and reshaping our behaviors.

I was interviewed once by someone in a T-shirt that read: "Your feelings are valid." I didn't say then what I'm writing here now: I don't think all my feelings *are* valid. If feelings are based on thoughts, consider how many invalid thoughts we have a day that arise from irrational anxiety, fear, or stress, all leading to feelings that are utterly divorced from reality. It can be like the blind leading the blind inside our brains.

Following my feelings all the time is usually a bad idea. If I did that, I'd probably go to the gym seven more times in my entire life. Instead of putting my in-the-moment feelings in charge, I always ask myself this question: "Is this a thing, that once it's over, makes me say, 'I'm glad I did that'?" With the gym, the answer is almost always yes. For situations like this in my life, regardless of the resistance I feel before them, I know they are actions I need to push through that resistance and do anyway. This, of course, also works in the negative. There are things we might really want to do in the moment that invariably make us feel worse after having done them. For those, we can ask: "What, if I refrain from doing it, makes me say afterward: 'I'm so glad I didn't do that'?" Like having so many drinks that we hate life the next day. One of the side effects of applying this kind of intentionality to our dating lives is that it earns the respect of others. When people see that we have standards for who we let in, even when our heart is racing, it shows integrity. It's evidence that we value ourselves, and in doing so it raises our value to them. It also shows we need more than an in-the-moment feeling; we need something that's going to feel good afterward too.

In the early stages of dating Audrey, she found herself face-to-face with the kind of guy you've been told to avoid at various points in this book (the horror!) I had met her in England, and we had had some truly amazing dates and had built a connection already. But having returned to my home in Los Angeles, there was now an ocean and a continent between us. While I started strong, over the following weeks, my communication grew more sparse. Phone calls became texts. Texts became texts only every few days. Then at one point, having not spoken in days, I sent a message telling her I missed her. It must have seemed both out of the blue and out of sync with the temperature of our dynamic at the time, because a few hours later, I got a reply that felt like a gut punch: Hey, I hope you're good. If I'm being completely honest, I haven't felt like we've been that close for a while, and that message (rightly or wrongly) came across like a bid for attention.

Ouch. I'm not kidding when I say that was like a gut punch. I felt called out, naked. I *was* looking for attention. I liked Audrey; a lot, in fact. But

I wasn't in the market for a long-distance relationship. And even that was still an excuse. I wasn't in the market for any kind of real relationship, and she could sense it. Audrey will happily tell you that she liked me a lot when I left London, but the more she saw that our paths weren't aligned, the less interested she became in giving me any more of her energy. It's worth sharing that although Audrey and I are now happily married, this text didn't create any immediate result from my side. We went our separate ways for a while after that. But when we did eventually reconnect, I knew exactly who I was dealing with, and what would be expected of me. In the meantime, she hadn't wasted a minute of her time on someone who couldn't meet her where she was.

Intentionality on that level takes reorienting our focus from giving in to our feelings to sticking to our path. This is one of the most loving things we can do for ourselves. Our path, which we landed on at some cost, becomes reflected in our everyday decisions, conversations, and actions. And when it is, it can be revelatory to see how seriously other people begin to take us, and how willing they can become to merge their path with ours.

Step 4: Communicate Your Path Unashamedly

In rewiring our brain, we have to go a step further than just living in accordance with our path: We have to be bold enough to share it with others too. Doing so serves as an invitation for them to reciprocate, which will help both parties see if their paths have a chance to align. It lets someone know the prerequisites, and it helps avoid wasting time with anyone unwilling to meet them.

My friend Tanya Rad used to produce my radio show *Love Life* before it became the *Love Life* podcast. Since the day I met her about ten years ago, she's been in the market for a serious long-term partner, so she took every word I said on that show to heart. One remark from a live seminar stuck with her: "Out of one hundred single people, there's probably only one or two who are actually right for you, so if you're only meeting one new person a month, you'll need to live at least another hundred years to guarantee a positive result." After that, she treated dating with the intensity of a second job; she was not going to wind up single because she hadn't met enough men. Even so, years passed without her finding the committed relationship she wanted.

Nearly ten years later, Tanya is now the cohost, with Ryan Seacrest, of one of the biggest radio shows in America. And somewhere between then and now, she also found the relationship she'd been looking for and become engaged. I invited Tanya to tell her story to my Love Life Club members, hoping she could tell us all about the one thing she'd been missing all those years.

We started talking about dating and intimacy, where she kept running into one idea that always made her uncomfortable:

> I think there's this messaging, especially with women, of "Sow your oats! We can be like men too! Get all the one-night stands out." And I was like, I'm not that person. I was just never wired that way. And if you are that person, good on you, I respect that, but that was never me. I could never have unattached sex. So I said, "OK, from this point on, I'm not having sex outside of a committed relationship." And when I said committed relationship, I meant boyfriend-girlfriend—this person is committed to me. And well, that really weeded them out real quick.

This was a different Tanya than I remembered. The idea of weeding out showed something crucial: the willingness to take a tactical loss for the sake of a significant long-term win. Tanya was able to do this because she had arrived at the point of necessity we talked about, the first step for rewiring our brain. She'd assessed the pain and the cost of her old pattern. As a result, it was clear to her what was important: finding someone as intentional about their search for love as she was. Once she started on that path, she was no longer trying to appease people or give in to what felt exciting in the moment.

That led her to the missing ingredient: Since her goal was no longer a private one, she was actually willing to communicate her path, regardless of the consequences. She explained what this openness looked like in action:

I remember I met this guy at a restaurant and gave him my number at happy hour. He asked if he could take me on a date, and I said sure. This was a Monday or Tuesday, and we were supposed to go out that weekend. He called me just to chat, and I thought, "Oh my gosh, nobody does this anymore." It seemed really cool. Then as we were chatting he made a sex joke; I don't remember exactly what it was. It wasn't crude or anything like that, but it became my way in, and I just laid it out there. I said, "Oh ha ha ha, well, I don't have sex outside of a committed relationship." And he goes, "Neither do I." I said, "Oh, that's so cool." But even though he said that, I still got player vibes from him. We finished our chat that night and he never followed up on the date. I think he thought, "I'm not gonna get what I want," and just didn't follow up, which is fine.

Conversation, she saw, provided plenty of openings for her to communicate her path. Some guys would make a joke about it; others didn't think it was a big deal. But they all understood her, and because she was sure about her decision, she was at peace with whatever reaction she got. Her behavior in the moment wasn't without nuance: For her, sex meant penetration, so other things were on the table if she felt comfortable. And I think it's worth pointing out that months into dating her fiancé, she slept with him, before they were in a committed relationship. Here's what she told me about that:

That was really hard on me because it was just the heat of the moment. And I think I knew really early on with him specifically, that he was it for me, and so I just let myself kind of feel safe in that space and [by that point] it was something he didn't take lightly either. I was the one who took things there, so he never pressured me. It actually kind of brought us closer because we were able to have that serious conversation about it right after. And I said, "I made this promise to myself, and I feel like I let myself down. I don't regret it. I'm really happy, and I'm happy with where everything's going, but I don't want to do this anymore until we're in a committed relationship."

She owned it, which is inherently attractive. Despite openly being sad at what she perceived as having let herself down, she was also open with him about not regretting it. And she didn't toss everything out the window simply because she had deviated once. In fact, breaking her own rule became an opportunity to reinforce it. The two of them returned to not sleeping together until they were committed. A month later, they were. Nobody has to be perfect. But Tanya remained conscious of her behavior, even when her actions took her outside the lines.

She was just as straightforward with him about her desire for marriage and children—which couldn't have been easy given that he was both divorced and already a father of two. "We talked about our experiences," she told me. "And I said to him, 'I know that you've been married and have kids. That's something I really desire in life. I'm excited about getting married one day and getting to be a mom. I'm excited for that season of life.'"

If Tanya had anxiously blurted out, "I want to get married!" we could forgive a guy for wanting to skip out. Someone we barely know shouldn't get the impression that we have them penciled in for a position they haven't remotely earned. But Tanya was mentioning something she was excited about for herself. It really had nothing to do with him (except for the fact that he'd been through it himself). But the subtext was there: If you don't want those things again, let's just chalk this up to a lovely meal.

I asked Tanya how she pulled this off at times when she didn't have a "divorced-dad" opening, and she gave an equally practical answer:

> I would approach it in almost a career-spinoff type of way, saying, "I've accomplished a lot in my career, but there's still a lot I want to do in my personal life. I did not give myself the chance to be in a serious committed relationship when I was focusing on my career for so long. That's something I really desire. I have a lot of friends who are married, who have wonderful marriages around me. That's something I really look forward to. And kids also in that same respect. I always felt like I was working too much to even think about having a baby."

She never expressed an urgency about these things (even if she felt it), which wouldn't have been appropriate to pass on to someone she'd just met—a common mistake that reads as anxiety and feels like pressure. Instead she simply framed her path in terms of her own excitement. The message was all positive.

"How easy for Tanya! Good for her!" we might be tempted to think anytime we hear a story like this. But hers, like most, was not an overnight "success." She had to go through multiple men, failed dates, and "situationships" to land on someone who was receptive to her standards. She didn't change one day, and then the next day run into a man she liked who just happened to be ready to go all in. She dated for a decade, got to know herself a whole lot better—what she wanted, and didn't want—solidified her path, and eventually found someone who aligned with that vision. One of the greatest causes of impatience in people's love lives are stories that go something like: "I did xyz and then out of nowhere the right person just showed up!" Growth in real life is slower, but the results are much more real. As in so many areas of life, the battle in people's love lives is usually won long before they have anyone to show for it.

Let's summarize what we've learned so far about rewiring our brain:

- Necessity is the beginning of change. Like Tanya, we have to be honest about the present pain and the future cost of our approach up to now. This honest assessment leaves us no choice but to do things differently.
- The next step is to decide what's most important to us now: our new path.
- We must follow this new path, instead of impulsively giving in to our feelings in the moment. Fortunately, the more connected we get to why our path is important to us, the less excited we'll feel about situations that are wrong for us.
- We communicate our intentions without shame, knowing that it's OK to lose people, no matter how attractive they are. No one has a free pass to our path.
- We should communicate where we're heading in a positive frame of mind, since we're excited and certain, not anxious or unsure. It's not about them, it's about us.

If you do these things, you'll avoid 99 percent of the suffering that exists in other people's love lives, and pave the way for a healthy relationship in your own. But what about the elephant in the room: that feeling deep down, even when we're doing everything right by saying no to people and experiences that are not aligned with our path, that we'll still never find someone who makes us feel the way we've felt before with someone else, or what we've been told we *should* feel with the person we end up with? What about chemistry?

Step 5: Don't Comparison Shop for Chemistry

Let's imagine (or maybe you don't need to) you've found someone who treats you well, is keen, and wants the same things. But they're not someone you're attracted to, and it's making you increasingly anxious. How long do you wait before you decide it's not right? Should you continue searching for someone you're excited about, or stick it out because they tick so many other boxes?

The short and emphatic answer: no. Not only should you not have to give up on attraction, but I strongly advise against it. Sexual chemistry is the essential factor separating friendship from romantic relationships. If you can't bring yourself to imagine or enjoy your partner sexually, it's going to be a long road. It's worth asking: Is the level of chemistry I feel with this person something I can live with for the rest of my life? If the answer is no, it's time to move on. Don't try to force it; attraction doesn't respond well to coercion.

However, we will find more people we're attracted to if we remove some of the barriers we've put up. One such barrier is being too strict on our "door policy" in dating. Today more than ever, we turn people down at breakneck speed. Nowhere is this more apparent than on dating apps, where we maintain an artificially high standard that's far more ruthless than anything we stick to in real life, where our lens has a softer focus. The digital buffet makes people appear cheap and disposable compared to an actual person standing in front of us, saying surprising things. The great danger of technology is that we unknowingly reject people we might have actually had real chemistry with, and we do so with ease, knowing somebody else is right behind them.

Who hasn't discovered sexual attraction with someone they wouldn't have picked out of a dating profile lineup? Maybe you even married one! That's because sexual attraction isn't a picture, it's a play—an evolving plotline that either comes to life or is lost in person. Even superficially, so much of attraction comes from animation, that is to say, how someone moves, smiles, stands, or walks. We might find ourselves attracted to someone simply by the way they are nodding their head to some music. This truth can be discovered in all directions. We might see a picture of someone we believe to be objectively gorgeous, only to find ourselves strangely unmoved when they show up. We may feel animalistically attracted to someone we've just met for the first time in person, only to discover, to our bemusement, that pictures of them online "don't do them justice." Ever had a friend pull up a profile of her hot date from the night before, and you quietly thought to yourself, "Really?" The difference wasn't necessarily just taste. She was there, you weren't. This isn't about easing up on your need for chemistry; it's about realizing that chemistry is far from simple, so it might be worth easing up on a door policy that's stopping you from ever finding out if you have it.

And chemistry doesn't just require more than a picture; sometimes it requires more than one context. Have you ever developed a crush on someone you barely noticed before that? One day they did something endearing, or popped up in an outfit that made you see them in a new way, or they showed you how compelling they are in their element. And just like that, you felt something. This is why we have to be careful about pronouncements like "I never meet anyone I'm attracted to." Attraction is more than a meeting, in the same way that a beach is more than a bucket of sand and a bottle of salt water.

We also have to be wary of ego's role in interfering with chemistry. Ego says: "They don't dress like other people I've dated" or "They aren't the outdoorsy type" or "My friends and family won't think they're attractive." Criteria like that are backward-looking and judgmental and they constrict our ability to exercise real choice, putting too much value on external factors like good looks and style over qualities we may only find sexually attractive once we're present and involved. Sexual attraction is personal, often unpredictable, and it can be felt intensely with someone who wouldn't have fit into preconceived notions of our "type."

Ego doesn't just shut out potential chemistry, it falsely identifies it. It turns someone who is elusive and hard to get into someone valuable and desirable.

Why chase an unavailable person? The unexpected highs and whipsaw lows become confused with feelings of chemistry—a complete non sequitur. Be careful not to confuse a cycle of anxiety and temporary relief with chemistry.

When this turns into a habit (even an addiction), it can lead to some contorted outcomes. One of my members, Meg, once asked me: "I've been hurt badly in my past relationships, and yet I find it hard to have the same attraction when dating other men. What should I do? I'm also afraid of being hurt again. What qualities should I look for?" Meg has summed up the strange catch-22 of so many of our love lives: How do I find another person just like the one who just hurt me—without getting hurt again?

But when Meg and I started to unpack that relationship, it became clear that her partner didn't hurt her only when he broke up with her. Even when the two of them were supposedly in the relationship, she never felt safe and at peace. And that's true in so many relationships: We never really feel like we have the person. When that's the case, the chase never ends. We white-knuckle through it, holding on for dear life. Since security never comes, the emotional turbulence of early dating never ends. This was Meg's situation, and it set up a nearly impossible situation for her new partners, who had to make her feel the same level of desire she felt for her ex—except that it had always been a desire that was predicated on making her feel uneasy. But you can never feel safe with someone who remains out of reach. Remember, in any real relationship, you fall in love with someone's presence, not their absence.

Also be wary when peak chemistry grows out of conditions you can't easily reproduce: the vacation romance; the thrill of an affair; the two-month fling that takes on outsized importance only after it ends abruptly. We all love fireworks, but to arrest our attention they need two primary conditions: the dark romance of nighttime, and the knowledge that they will be over shortly. Take either factor away and all those fireworks become pedestrian. How many experiences that we consider high points were brief to begin with and are now distorted by the hazy lens of memory? What if your lover from the tropics had flown home with you? What if your two-month fling suddenly texted you to pick up their prescription? You can't compare the fast-twitch chemistry of a romantic sprint to the stamina required in a long-running engagement. At the very least, we have to temper whatever romance we feel about a situation like this with the reality that we really have no idea what it would have been like to be with that person long term.

The bottom line is this: Chemistry is crucial, but it's not the only quality to look for in a long-term partnership. True, it's extremely important in the startup phase, but if we're picking based on chemistry, why aren't we also looking for the kindest person or the most supportive or the one who understands us best—qualities that are just as important, if not more so, as chemistry in making us happy in the long run?

None of this is to suggest you start filling your diary with people who hold zero physical appeal for you, or continue going on dates with people you originally felt nothing for. It's simply an invitation: not to form snap judgments about chemistry and sexual attraction, which need a degree of exposure and openness to be achieved; to stop putting the feelings we've had in the past—feelings that, by definition, never had to stand the test of time—on a pedestal; and to put chemistry at an appropriate level of importance, but not on a higher plane than other qualities necessary for a happy relationship. Lastly, we have to resist the urge to make constant comparisons. When we are serious about finding a full-spectrum relationship, chemistry is a vital component, but it's not a competition that a new person has to win.

PATTERNS LIKE THE ONES WE'VE discussed in these last two chapters can become second nature to us without us even realizing it, which is why we can't rely on the hope that one day we will simply wake up and start feeling better or making better choices. Change won't happen to us here; it needs to come from us, which requires more than a single epiphany. Epiphanies (maybe you had a couple reading this) only light the way. Intentional action is what reorders our way of being—it is a war of attrition against our old ways. When something's not working for us, we need to laser in on that thing like a sentry guarding the gates to our happiness, and having identified it, resolve to stop doing, or inviting in, that thing and start doing what will be better for us going forward. Pay attention to things that make you feel better about yourself. Align yourself with something higher, like the values you've come to appreciate at this stage in life. Decide ahead of time what's important to you in a person. Know what kind of energy you want to be around, and what qualities bring you peace in life and in relationships. Orient every part of your life around these qualities: the way you spend your time, the energy you put into the world, the kinds of people you invest in, even as friends. Saturate your life with the energy you want to attract. It's not an overnight fix, but it's more powerful than you might think. The more you do it, the more you will notice, and be visible to, other people with these qualities.

None of this is easy. It's far easier to go for things that make us feel better in the moment than to do the things that will make us feel good long term, having faith that they will at some point attract the right person into our life. The latter requires sacrifice, patience, and commitment. It requires us to keep training our focus every day on our new target—our peace and happiness. It's a discipline, requiring us to take ourselves and our well-being seriously.

The right thing may not appear as shiny at first, and it's essential in moments of temptation to keep connecting to why the old ways never worked. But soon, if we keep going, we will gradually find ourselves in a healthier place, one of calm and objectivity. We will have taken ourselves out of the frenetic currents of anxiety and trauma bonding, and into the calmer waters of mindful dating, where it will become far clearer to us what healthy attraction is, and what it isn't. The wrong people will start to recede in importance, or even become undesirable. The kind of person who could enter your life before and destroy your peace suddenly seems completely unappealing and out of sync with the rhythm of your new life.

Having freed ourselves from the addiction cycle in love, we may start finding a more serene, but no less rewarding, form of chemistry with new people we might never have previously considered. You won't magically start finding everyone attractive, but you might start seeing people you never did before, and in doing so find that your pool has expanded. This creates hope. The pain that instigated these changes in you subsides, and makes way for the realization that new things are possible: Not only are people we never knew existed out there, but they are in our midst. It becomes clear that our younger self was not in fact the expert they claimed to be on what we needed to be happy. With some distance, we may even find ourselves enjoying a new kind of closure that is available to us: the ability to joyfully, and lovingly, laugh at our previous confusions.

11

THE QUESTION
OF HAVING A CHILD

In the years I've been sharing ideas and philosophies around the subject of confidence and self-worth with women, there has, for many, been a hidden fear that affected their ability to maintain the standards they set while we worked together. The group I'm speaking on behalf of here are those who felt they had a limited time in which to consider having children.

I have little cause to be comfortable or confident weighing in on this subject. But my discomfort isn't the point; the point is the conversation. Many of my clients have known they've wanted to be mothers since they were children. They may not always have voiced it in adulthood for fear of being thought regressive among other women, or being considered too intense around men, but for many of them, having a family has always been their biggest life goal. Even one of my most successful female friends confessed recently that despite her success—which makes her the envy of many—her biggest dream was, and still is, to have a family, and that this was even bigger than any career dream she'd had, despite how hard she'd worked.

For others, wanting to have children seemed to sneak up on them. Years of putting their focus elsewhere in their life, on careers, travel, friendships, had suddenly, and without warning, given way to an intense and overwhelming urge to satisfy something that suddenly felt instinctive. Despite enjoying their own life, they started to feel the pressure. Such pressure needn't be explicit. They may never have suffered family pressure, presumptuous friends, or even thought of kids as something they wanted, and yet find themselves inflicting that pressure on themselves nonetheless. Whether the message quietly crept in from the outside, or subtly emerged as a voice from the inside, it had grown louder.

Certainly not all women feel this urge. I've coached my share of women who have had to end a relationship because their partner wanted children and they didn't. For others, the family, societal, and cultural pressure that mounts with age leaves them confused as to whether their anxiety is simply the result of societal or cultural pressure or derives from something they really want.

There's also the common anguish of the person who, while feeling no gravitational pull of maternity, is inclined to have a child as a kind of insurance policy against the future regret of not taking that path. This internal misalignment leaves them feeling isolated and exhausted as they battle with the shame and fear of having to cajole themselves into something that is "supposed" to feel like one of the greatest experiences there is, but for them feels akin to a disconnected risk-aversion strategy.

Nonetheless, for those who feel it, the deep desire to have children is an urge that, as time goes on, can dominate their focus. It can rob them of their confidence, and simultaneously fuel an anxiety and even panic that can lead to damaging and sometimes disastrous relationship decisions.

What is this fear? It is the fear that this essential life process that some deeply want to experience, and feel is fundamental to their happiness and sense of completion in life, might not happen. This isn't just true for those who find themselves perpetually single, or who bounce from one relationship to the next until it's too late; it's also true for many who have a willing and excited partner, only to find that achieving a successful pregnancy is more complicated than they ever imagined (due to difficulties on either side, or both), or altogether impossible.

I worked with a couple who, even with access to the best doctors and several rounds of embryo freezing over multiple years, could not reach the stage of a successful embryo implantation. Another woman, with her partner, has been on a fertility journey for nine years, having done IVF many times (and remortgaged her house to do so), still to no avail. Life isn't as simple as: "If I don't meet my person on time, I'm not going to be able to have children."

Having biological children is not guaranteed either way. To have children within the traditional structure, culture tells you that you must find someone you want to have them with, biology demands that you and your partner must conceive within the time frame of fertility, you must be compatibly fertile, and finally, you must carry a pregnancy to full—or at least viable—term. No wonder this life goal has so many people feeling out of control. There are so many variables along the way that can thwart it.

My first introduction to the challenges that arise from the desire to be a parent was not an education on the science, but rather a crash course in the pain it wreaks: not only in the form of anxiety or panic when the alarm goes off, but through the compounding pain caused by the bad decisions that are made from these states. It has sometimes felt like my sole job has been to lower people's dating temperature amid an unstoppable global warming taking place inside their mind as their yearning for a family intensifies. While I'm encouraging slowing down and not overinvesting too quickly, this counterforce is telling them to speed up, ignore red flags, and come to the negotiating table as someone in need of a lifeline. A fertility doctor may have deep a knowledge of what this process is doing to women's bodies, but I came to a deep understanding of what it is doing to their lives.

I don't profess to fully understand the deep currents of fear and isolation that take hold as some women experience the shortening of a time frame for something that feels fundamental to their being. But I know the nauseating terror of feeling out of control with something that feels like your life depends on it. It can be paralyzing. Many women I coach continue to function in their everyday lives by fracturing themselves—separating from that longing voice inside through the distractions of work obsession, daily obligations, and unconscious dating.

But this voice never stays as far from the surface as we might hope—there remains the deep yearning for something that somehow already seems to be a part of them, even though it hasn't arrived. I know, because the slightest hint that we are going to talk about this difficult issue can reduce many in an audience to tears in an instant. It can become a chronic, unspoken anxiety people feel plagued by: a desperate feeling for what now appears singularly to hold the key to their happiness.

If you happen to be in the camp where it's no longer possible for you to have your own biological children, you may find yourself in a state of unresolved grief, or feel condemned to the feeling that something is missing in your life. Though it may seem as if much of this chapter is geared toward people at an earlier stage, my hope is that this chapter will create a sense of relief for you, too.

The closer I got to this subject, the more I understood and felt the inequity of it all. Many men believe there is no hurry since they can, at least in theory, impregnate a woman until they die. A women's biology says otherwise. Men have their own biology to contend with: There's plenty of overestimation when it comes to how viable men, or their sperm, remain for the process of having children in later years; and this overestimation only exaggerates the biological asymmetry between men and women. Men have used this asymmetry to justify making flippant and often cruel jokes about women being "too intense," or "crazy," simply because women demand some kind of clarity in an area where they pretend to not relate. Meanwhile, these guys act with all the ease of someone who believes they have plenty of time to spare (regardless of whether it's true). I've often wondered what kind of visible desperation we would see from these men if they were told that their life's greatest dream, be it having kids, starting a company, or becoming a millionaire, was only available for the next three to five years (and relied on another person to make it happen!), after which it would never be available again no matter what they did.

Given this imbalance, and being a recovering control freak myself, I couldn't help but think of the terrible resentment I might feel at the idea of having to wait around for my partner to agree to sign off on one of my most important goals in life. This instinct was backed up when I was walking down the street many years ago with the editor of this very book, Karen Rinaldi, and I asked her what her view on the whole thing was, to which she didn't miss a beat: "Why on earth would you rely on a man for that?" It turned out, despite eventually having children within a relationship—one that, not insignificantly, she's no longer in—Karen had already made up her mind to have children on her own even if she never met a life partner to do it with. This wasn't just a hard line from an ardent feminist, which she is; it was a reflection of how important the whole deal was to her.

While I may not have been ready to tell women to give up on men altogether—I myself still wanted to find a girlfriend after all—I started to become impatient, even to the point of anger, when I saw women wasting time with men who neither cared about nor shared their goals. *This is your life's dream that's at stake! Don't you realize that? This guy doesn't care one bit about your timeline, or the regret you will feel later on if you run out the clock on having a family while you flit off to some faraway location with him . . . and yet you're handing over responsibility for these things!* I didn't always say this (though sometimes I did, as you can see in my YouTube videos), but it was always there when I was barely masking my frustration at the situation where a woman kept highlighting what a great connection she had with someone while muttering under her breath that he had openly told her he wasn't ready for a relationship. Sometimes I feel like it gave me a reputation of being a kind of love-life Scrooge, a romance killer, incessantly bah-humbugging the stories I was hearing. But I am a romantic. It just triggered anger in me about how our culture has brainwashed women to abdicate their spot in the driver's seat when it comes to their own future. Not anger at them, but anger at how we are predisposed to judge women for their needs and give a pass to men who refuse to get it.

I'd watched women settle for abusive relationships because they came with the possibility of having the child they'd always wanted. I'd coached women on the other side of that dynamic, struggling to raise children with someone who set out to plague their existence and poison their children against them at every opportunity. I'd seen women who kept sabotaging themselves in early dating because their anxiety about running out of time was getting in the way of them being themselves.

I will never forget the woman at one of my retreats who crawled under a table during a breakout session and wept uncontrollably because she had stayed married to a man who she'd always hoped would "come around" to the idea of having children, while her window for doing so gradually closed, only to have him break up their marriage at the end of it all anyway. I sat with her as she grieved the child she never had.

The profound level of pain I have witnessed in this area has led me to two conclusions: The first is that any advice designed to empower women in their late twenties, thirties, and early forties is incomplete if it does not include a conversation about this subject. The second is that I will never avoid initiating this hard conversation (which, it turns out, is one of the hardest) out of fear of getting it wrong. Avoiding it might be the easier option, given that I'm clearly the other elephant in the room outside of the conversation itself. But we can agree to the impossibility that I can feel this issue the way a woman does, and instead trust that I have been witness to the pain. I ask that you allow me, as others have in the past, any clumsiness I demonstrate as I stubbornly address a subject that I've come to believe isn't being discussed nearly enough, and for multiple reasons.

The fear women have of coming off as desperate and unattractive is potent. So is the embarrassment they can feel, even among well-meaning friends with children, in sharing the deeply vulnerable admission: *I so badly want what you have, but I feel I'm getting old and running out of time.* It's as though women have been shamed into thinking it's not OK, cool, or attractive to have this conversation; meanwhile, vast numbers of men don't even feel the need to have it because they think they have all the time in the world.

I wrote this chapter so that we might meet this conversation head-on. Together we can strip it all back and talk about it with no shame. As with all hard conversations, before we have it out loud with someone out there in the world, we must be brave enough to have it with ourselves. This means a conscious, thorough examination of what we want, and what our options are in making it happen, so that we can be better equipped to make the right decisions for ourselves.

Where do we begin in this conversation? Well, we've already started, inasmuch as if you've gotten this far, you're already embracing a kind of acceptance that having children is anything but guaranteed, no matter your circumstances. This feeling is undeniably greater if you haven't got a partner. But beyond that, it's time for a radical acceptance of your own time frame from where you stand now, and at what point it is safe to assume it will no longer be possible to have children in the original way you'd hoped.

This isn't defeatist. This kind of acceptance is precisely the point from which you can honestly assess your options and put a plan in place. This plan is a key to taking back your personal power in this area.

How Important Is It to You?

Before we make a plan, consider this:

Just how important is it to you to have children? And why?

Knowing the answer to these two questions informs every other decision. They may seem deceptively simple, but your answers are profoundly important. It forces you to ask: Just how real is this desire? Where does it come from? What need am I trying to fulfill?

Let's deal with the first of the two. *How important is it?* No matter your answer to this question, the answer helps with decisions about what to do going forward. If the answer is that *there's nothing more important*, then that should determine who and what situations you give your time to. Why date someone who doesn't share your vision for having kids when it's a fundamental life goal for you?

If, on the other hand, you're not sure you want children, that's a different kind of clarity. You might take action that buys you time while you look to develop stronger feelings about what you want.

When it comes to *why* you want children, I've always found answers to this question surprisingly wide-ranging when asked to an audience. Some say they want someone who will love them no matter what; others say they want someone they can feel unconditional love for. Some want to give someone a better life than the one they had. Some say they want to biologically experience being a mother, while others say they want to feel like they can be a mother to someone (a vital distinction when it comes to assessing the options). Some want someone to take care of them when they're old. Some say they want a piece of themselves to carry on after they're gone.

It's fun to play around with assumptions about what having kids will give them. It can offer a little dark humor in an otherwise heavy conversation. I remind people that there's no guarantee your kid will love you no matter what, or take care of you when you're old . . . you can't even guarantee that they'll return your phone calls or texts. As for wanting a piece of us to carry on after we're gone, I always like pointing out that this feels like a very human streak of narcissism: "I must carry on ME!" Of course, I realize this is a common instinct, and it doesn't come from a bad place, but I'm also not entirely joking.

Other reasons are harder to joke about: wanting to give a better life to someone than you had, or the desire to *be* a mother. Yet even then, sometimes when I listen to the reasons people give for wanting children, there's a flexibility inherent in their answer itself that they haven't acknowledged. One woman, Andrea, told me that her desire came from trying "to save the child in me that no one was there to save." When she spoke in front of the audience, she said she was confused about whether she wanted to give birth to her own biological child or adopt. I wanted her to realize that her answer had left room for her to be happy in both outcomes, and that therefore her uncertainty was actually a positive sign. Her confusion about what she should do actually meant freedom about what she *could* do. It's not a freedom everyone allows themselves. They become attached to the idea that they will only be happy if they have a child that is biologically their own within a traditional family unit. I've seen the maternal instinct directed to make an impact in stunning ways over the course of my career. I have come to see that there are many extraordinary mothers in this world, and not all of them have given birth.

Your Criteria

The more we concretize our concept of what our future contentment looks like, the more we stifle the wide-ranging possibilities for our happiness. We become a prisoner to a path that can end up holding our happiness hostage. When this happens, first we panic, then comes resignation, then comes depression.

Exploring other options, like adoption, or having a child alone, can feel like changing religion. It can mean rejecting everything you've been told. But we have to invite a freedom of thought that doesn't blindly conform to societal or familial expectations, but one that is tailor-made for us. Connecting to what is uniquely right for us and our future requires us to step back from other voices and listen to our own. Andrea's confusion actually put her one step ahead of most people. It meant she was exploring what felt right to *her*.

ULTIMATELY, THERE IS A LESSON in all of this that I have always found to be one of the most important lessons in life: Anything we have that we value meets some kind of need, or at least we believe it will once we get it. One of the most powerful ways to take back control of our happiness is to realize that the very idea that this very specific thing or experience is the only way to meet that need is nothing but a story we've been telling ourselves. With a little imagination, and perhaps experience, we realize our need can be met in more ways than we ever gave life credit for. There's no one way to live a fulfilled life. Instead, we each have a set of criteria for what we need to be happy, and there are myriad creative ways to meet those criteria. Many believe that having children will meet some of their most fundamental criteria, and maybe they are right, but what they don't realize by clinging to their unchangeable blueprints for their future is how many other ways they could achieve the same thing.

None of this is to say we shouldn't have a Plan A and pursue it seriously. Being honest with ourselves about just how important Plan A is to us informs our decisions, big and small. If we want to meet someone and have a child with them, then we need to do everything we can to add to the inevitability of that, including saying no to things that make it less likely to happen: like spending years in a relationship with someone who has no interest in the same future we do (regardless of how much chemistry we feel with them). Knowing what our number one option is tells us what to value and what not to value. In my years of coaching, I have worked with so many women who are only entertaining a certain kind of man—the playboy, the success junkie, the commitmentphobe, the guy who has no family future in mind—because they haven't truly decided, or been honest with themselves, about what they value the most.

Plan A, when looked at through this lens of "criteria," shows us that there's more than one path capable of satisfying these criteria. We can look to Plan B, C, D, E, or even F—all options we can be happy with if they get us the end result we desire. Being flexible about getting there helps us to reach that goal.

Ignoring what we would do if our original plan didn't happen is just another way to bury our heads in the sand and avoid a hard conversation with ourselves and the people who would support us. It strikes me as interesting that most adults' association with the term "Plan B" is a little pill you take when you don't want to be pregnant (at least in the United States, where the emergency contraceptive pill goes by that brand name). But in my experience, there are far too many who don't know their Plan B for if they do want to get pregnant. If something is a must, then it's important enough to know how it will be achieved if our ideal scenario doesn't happen. This is the essence of resilience and adaptability—the knowledge that everything in our world can shift and change, and we can still find our footing, and our happiness, in a new place. That's a superpower.

The irony is that the abundant mindset this thinking and planning creates allows us to relax and begin taking more confident swings in our love life (in all of life, really), which actually makes it more likely that Plan A will happen—if Plan A is having a child with a partner and it is what you want. Making peace with Plan B, or C, or D might be one of the greatest secrets to bringing about Plan A. It can feel unromantic to plan for something unfamiliar or as yet unknown, but strangely, planning for other options can actually help us to become romantic and present in our love lives again.

None of this is intended to be flippant about how difficult any of the alternatives are. I don't pretend for one second to know the lived challenges of adoption, or of being a single mother raising a family. But I know people do it and manage. And I know that there's life after these scenarios, and that these people often go on to find love, because I've helped them do exactly that. This isn't to say you should adopt or opt to be a single mother—these are necessarily intensely personal calculations every individual has to make. Christopher Hitchens once said that, in life: "You have to choose your future regrets." Regret is an inevitability in life. Everyone has them (and if they don't, I can't see how they've ever managed to learn or experience anything). When you look at your future, what will create the greatest regret? Waiting for your traditional nuclear family to occur until it's no longer an option for you to have a child of your own? Or raising a child as a single parent? This isn't intended to be a leading question at all. For some, being a single parent may not be something they ever feel is right for them. Others learn that they will struggle to forgive themselves if they wait on a man until they're forty and still haven't taken it into their own hands. What's right for other people isn't important. What is important is that we have these conversations with ourselves and our trusted confidants, so we can make informed decisions without unconsciously sleepwalking into our worst fear.

Importantly, it's worth remembering that we tend to be much more likely to take action when we are trying to get out of pain, not when we are comfortable. So if thinking about these things is painful for you, that's likely a positive—by bringing the pain forward, we are also bringing the decisions forward, decisions that might otherwise have been left until a time when there would be far fewer options on the table to choose from.

Embracing Your Options

To know your options, you have to start with clear information about your own situation. Getting one's fertility checked is yet another potentially hard conversation people avoid. *What if I get an answer I don't like?* Remember, information is power. Learning you produce fewer eggs than you thought can create urgency, in the positive sense. This urgency might make you step up a timeline you would have neglected otherwise. A disappointing answer now can hold the key to a happy future, because it informs your next steps. So does being a realist about general fertility rates: knowing that there is a pronounced drop in fertility in most women in their mid- to late thirties, and a significant decline in their forties, with an increased chance of complications. Then it's important to do an honest self-assessment in light of the health and lifestyle factors that contribute to fertility. For all of my male readers, I urge you to do the same. We bear the responsibility just as much as the women in our lives for educating ourselves on timelines, our own fertility as well as theirs, and making decisions as a team. If having children is something we want "one day" then ignoring or endlessly deferring the conversation is an abdication of that responsibility, and simply forces the women we care about to shoulder the thoughts and attendant anxieties alone.

From here you may decide that, having not met anyone yet, you need to give yourself the longest timeline possible for becoming pregnant. Egg freezing can be a viable route for doing this. Setting aside the medical issues, which are admittedly both complex and costly, freezing eggs gives some peace of mind and a sense of independence, and can help you avoid being dependent on someone else or staying in a situation that's less than ideal—or even actively dangerous. I've heard many stories by this point of people freezing their eggs as an immediate Plan B—even if it's one that feels unlikely they'll ever need, one that will prove necessary only in a remote future—and seeing an immediate effect on their confidence. It gave them the leverage to set their own terms, to walk away from something without feeling they were jeopardizing their future.

When I talked about the merits of egg freezing on a recent podcast, I got a lengthy reply from a longtime listener, Elizabeth, a registered nurse, who'd frozen her eggs. As someone who still hoped to have a family and a child through the traditional means, Elizabeth nevertheless made the financial and emotional calculation, and decided to go ahead with the procedure. Even though she was a medical professional and was fully informed, she still ran into a number of difficulties, which she detailed in her letter. Given those difficulties, which she thought I'd underestimated by concentrating on this message of confidence, she thought my perception of the procedure was overly optimistic—maybe even blithe to the point of being flippant.

Thanks to Elizabeth's letter, which I appreciated tremendously, I did another podcast, to read her letter and to take the time to really assess what a difficult decision it is. First, she wanted to remind people (me, especially) that freezing your eggs is not the magical solution that it sometimes seems. She stressed the financial burden, which is repeated with every round of egg collection, because many people need more than one to feel like they're giving themselves enough eggs to work with. And even when the procedure (which is more involved, and for some more painful, than people usually acknowledge) is successful, that still doesn't guarantee that you will be able to bring a healthy child to term when you do decide to go ahead with a pregnancy years later. At that later stage, all the same expenses and complications of in vitro fertilization apply. In between those two stages, the initial harvesting and fertilization years later, you have to pay storage fees for the eggs you freeze. It's a lot of time, energy, and expense to take on single-handedly, she said. She found the cost-benefit analysis to be razor thin, but she went ahead anyway.

In the second part of her letter, she called me out for suggesting that freezing eggs somehow put men and women on equal footing, by removing the biological clock from the equation, which was part of a calculation she saw as an inherent and valuable attribute of being a woman. She saw a flaw in the whole concept: When it comes to the formation of family, it's not women who should have to do painful and expensive things to their bodies simply so they can enjoy the same freedom as men, but men who should think in a mature way about family formation, and not simply come to the idea magically when they're ready, at age thirty-five or fifty-five or never. "It's reasonable for adult women to expect adult men to know where they stand on this issue and to be able to talk about it without men misunderstanding it as pressure on them."

She then had her own modest proposal: "I think that instead of saying that in an ideal world, all women should freeze their eggs at twenty-one, we should say that all men should have reversible vasectomies at fifteen, a far, far less invasive procedure, to be reversed when they are ready to be parents. If that sounds ridiculous to you, then you know how ridiculous it sounds to me when you say I should just freeze my eggs." I loved that. It *is* ridiculous that on top of the time frame women have to contend with as a fact of their biology, there should now be a practical pressure on them to fix the problems of delaying childbearing. Why should women have to face an invasive, painful, and costly procedure on their own, all because men can't get their shit together or say anything more enlightening than "We'll see what happens" when it comes to this fundamental issue of existence? And men can do so while smiling smugly, because they know that pushing the question further might be taken as pressure and scare them off.

I do think that in addition to what Elizabeth is saying, there are women who come to this issue with their own ambivalence about having children (as the people in the comment section online were quick to point out). But if I were coaching, say, someone wanting to make progress in her career but still have the option to have a family, I don't think debating the politics would be of any practical help. The questions would be what they almost always are when I'm coaching someone: "What solutions do we have on hand today to help you reach your goals?" It's in that spirit that I talk about the possibility of freezing eggs, because we'd be dealing with the same cost-benefit analysis that Elizabeth looked at when she decided to do it herself. Egg freezing doesn't guarantee peace of mind, and only you know if stacking the odds in your favor in this way will give you a sense of control, or at the very least a sense that you've done all you can.

Thanks to Elizabeth's eloquent letter, I felt inspired to go further with this conversation, so I followed up with another podcast, this time inviting to the table two doctors. Serena H. Chen, a fertility doctor and founding partner at the Institute for Reproductive Medicine and Science, and Ioana Baiu, a surgery resident at Stanford, came on to talk about their professional and personal perspectives on the subject. Dr. Chen pointed out that fertility treatments should not be an elective procedure, but should be universally covered, since they serve such a vital purpose. Dr. Baiu spoke personally, as a woman in her thirties in a high-pressure profession, who had elected to undergo two rounds of treatment to freeze her eggs. With limited time for dating, Dr. Baiu wanted the option to start a family later in life, when the unavoidable pressures that are part of surgical training had let up enough to allow her to start a family. She spoke in detail about the unanticipated difficulties she encountered. Even as a surgeon who's very familiar with complex medical procedures, she still found it daunting when she got home with all the hundreds of syringes and medications she had to mix to the microgram and procedures to perform at all hours of the day that had to be timed precisely. There were hormone levels that had to be adjusted from one cycle to the next and, unexpectedly, a period of hormone imbalance and fatigue after the retrieval that took her weeks to recover from.

When I asked Dr. Baiu if she still felt that it was ultimately worth it despite these difficulties, she said that it had been, that it took the pressure off, and that she now worried less about whether she could someday have a family. Knowing that the health of the eggs generally declines with age, she feels better with the healthy eggs she now has in storage, ready if or when she decides she's ready.

I can't pretend to cover the topic in these pages with the thoroughness it deserves. Anyone seriously considering the procedure should seek professional guidance. I was struck by how sympathetic both doctors were, and how they took pains to frame their discussion in the broadest possible terms, knowing what a wide range of motivations people have for looking into the subject.

That was easy to see in the reactions online, which elicited a ton of comments. A thirty-four-year-old woman from France wrote that she'd just started the process of freezing her eggs (which is free for all women there) and hoped that the US would follow suit in universal coverage. Another woman had traveled to Barbados to have the procedure done in a comparable medical setting where the costs were significantly less. A woman who was herself adopted by a single mom said she'd adopt too if she doesn't meet someone by forty. A woman who'd "had kids young" wanted people to know it was OK not to have it all together before starting a family. A forty-four-year-old who hadn't "met my husband yet" was starting IVF with donor sperm and praying it wasn't too late. A woman who'd been to a party at her CrossFit gym mentioned that four of the five women she'd met there, ages thirty-two to forty, had frozen their eggs. A woman who'd stopped dating at forty and then had a child (who was now ten) on her own, using a donor, was happy to be dating again now, without the pressure of having to find a father.

It's very moving to see so many people considering the procedure and expanding their options, taking their fate into their own hands, despite the pain it can entail or the disappointments they'd been through. It is clearly not for everybody. It remains prohibitively expensive for far too many. Others will not pursue it for religious reasons. It is simply not available or practical in many parts of the world. And even those who do undergo the treatment do not always use their eggs, or if they do, the procedure to fertilize them years later is unsuccessful, or the circumstances for having a child prove impossible when the time comes.

It's an imperfect solution to a real source of heartache for so many, but it remains a very empowering option, freeing many from a chronic stressor in an already busy life. I am always in favor of creating choices that potentially lead to greater freedom and fewer anxieties.

To me, the important part isn't an emphasis on egg freezing (or in some cases, embryo freezing). It's understanding that Plan B is tied into other bigger acceptances one may make that provide freedom and calm. Someone may decide that Plan A is to meet someone and fall in love today, while freezing her eggs as an insurance plan. Plan B is to meet someone in the not-too-distant future and use her viable eggs from the freezing process if it's not possible naturally at that point. Plan C might be to decide an age by which she will use donor sperm and have a child regardless, even if it means being a single parent. Plan D is to adopt if this doesn't work out. Plan E is to mentor children in other ways, or love her nieces and nephews as if they were her own.

Freedom comes from knowing that at any time, you are prepared to make Plan B, C, D, or E the new Plan A. This is about settling *on*, as opposed to *for* something. Plan B is not a consolation prize. In fact, once we know Plan B is the path we are taking, we resolve to make it extraordinary. It almost becomes an act of rebellion, one where you tell yourself: If Plan A can't happen, then I'm going to make Plan B so amazing that I never look back, and it winds up being the greatest gift of my life that it happened this way. Plan B can't happen? OK, then I'm going to turn Plan C into the best thing I could have imagined, so much so that I'm truly grateful Plan B never happened. No plan ever remains the "backup plan." The moment you settle on Plan C, it immediately becomes the new Plan A, and makes the new Plan A so beautiful that you never look back.

This, to me, is what practical adaptability looks like, both in this area and in life in general. It's not a magic fix. It's a conscious formula that can bring you back to a place of acceptance about where you are right now. You give yourself all the confidence of someone who can be happy no matter what. That doesn't mean there isn't grieving to be done at times in our life where we have to say goodbye to a once-cherished idea of how our life would be, and that grieving may be necessary before we can arrive happily in a new place. Figuring out how to go on after a life-changing disappointment can at first feel very isolating, as if you've been left behind after the life you wanted or counted on slipped away. But what's startling to find out is how common these isolating experiences are. Losing a job, ending a relationship, being unmarried, finding you've wasted years of your life with a narcissist—the list of isolating disappointments is extensive. One of the simplest and most comforting realizations in these circumstances is to see how common, how deeply human, the experience of painful alienation really is. When that sinks in, when you can shake free or slow down and see how many people share a version of this hurt with you, it can even be a comfort.

In the upcoming chapters (especially in "Core Confidence"), we will look at this crucial step in greater depth. It's a process of reframing that nearly everyone goes through, to see these inevitable disappointments in a new light. What's amazing to me is how literally nothing in life needs to change circumstantially to feel better. You can sit where you are sitting right now and change your entire experience and the emotions that threaten to overwhelm you by rewriting your story. Not that rewriting is simple, but in doing so, you take back your power and become the author of a *better* story.

12

HOW TO LEAVE
WHEN YOU CAN'T
SEEM TO LEAVE

Sometimes the differences between people draw them together, and the unpredictability of the attraction can be exhilarating, certainly in the beginning. The old saying "Opposites attract" has staying power for a reason. Exploring the territory between our nature and theirs, we can feel the boundaries of our identity shift and expand. It's the same reason people recommend traveling—we come into contact with new ways of living and thinking, and our sense of possibility expands in ways that stay with us long after we return home.

But sometimes we can get out there on the edge of the known universe and invite in a force that's not just foreign to us but truly alien—a force that we can never truly coexist with because it operates according to different laws than the ones we live by.

Last week, I was ambushed by a video on my timeline that started innocently enough, with a bunch of crocodiles lying around together in a zoo. Lying around is probably a crocodile's number one occupation, and initially the entire scene looked pretty chill to me. Then a zookeeper tossed in some meat, and as the crocodiles began to stir, one of them chomped another in the leg, spun into a death roll, twisted his mate's foot clean off, and swallowed the bloody hunk in a single gulp. There were shrieks from behind the camera. After the event, both crocodiles went right back to lying around as if nothing had happened. There are many animals I can find myself relating to, but having seen this video, I can safely say a crocodile will never be one of them.

Some people are as dangerous to relate to as those crocodiles. They can't be reasoned with on normal terms. Their actions are indecipherable, and so are their reactions when you confront them—because, let's face it, like crocodiles, these people do not have the same sense of personal accountability that we do. They think you should accept the unimaginable and get over it. ("It was just a snack!" they say.) Since they don't seem to feel standard human empathy, they can't understand what you're going on about. They may even get angry, because as long as you're upset, they can't get what *they* want—love, adulation, or just you getting off their case so they can go back to chilling.

These kinds of people carry various labels depending on who you talk to—egomaniacs, narcissists, sociopaths; whatever conclusion you come to, they all describe an animal fundamentally different from ourselves.

Here's a sobering test for realizing what kind of animal you're dealing with: Try to recall something they did to hurt you, or something they did carelessly or maliciously to create destruction in your life. Was that something you would ever do, not just to them, but to anyone?

Why is it that you could never do that? You have a conscience. Knowing you hurt them would hurt you, which is the appropriate reaction to inflicting pain on someone you love. Now, knowing how much *you* would suffer if you'd done to them what they just did to you, think of what they actually did do. When you forgave them and moved on, did they struggle to forgive themselves the way you would? Did they redouble their efforts to make sure you felt safe and loved? Or did they just go back to chilling, like a crocodile floating in a mangrove swamp?

Usually after someone like that wreaks havoc in your life, they just want everything to go back to normal as quickly as possible. This might mean underplaying what they did, gaslighting you about how big a deal you're making over it, making you believe it is somehow your fault, or turning the attack back on you and your flaws. If none of this works, they might adopt a different tactic, like getting upset, groveling, or showing you the most loving version of themselves you've ever seen in an effort to recapture your affection.

But remember, whatever they do to try to win you back isn't motivated by remorse, but by their own personal fear of loss at the prospect of you walking away.

This doesn't mean they're not hurting. And of course, seeing them cry creates heartache in us. It can be especially confusing when, in an effort to understand their behavior, we've spent a lot of time convincing ourselves that they're cold and devoid of empathy. Seeing them in pain makes us doubt our analysis of them. If they really can hurt this much, maybe we've got them wrong after all.

It may be tempting to convince yourself that they're just crocodile tears, but it's neither entirely accurate nor necessary. They are sincere in their way. But no matter how genuine they may seem, it's not the same kind of sadness—born out of regret, empathy, and guilt—that you'd be feeling if you were in their shoes. They're not hurting because *you* are hurting, they're hurting because *they* are hurting. It's a selfish shade of pain, like a child crying when his favorite toy is taken away in a time-out. Don't get tricked by tears that may be *over* you but are never tears *for* you.

Coming to terms with this is a difficult step. If you find yourself in a long-term relationship with a semiaquatic reptile, it can take years to take that step, at great cost to yourself. Often it's your own admirable emotional instincts that hold you back—because you're projecting that same mix of regret, empathy, and guilt that would motivate you if the situation were reversed. Your functional emotional register, which can get a big, albeit one-sided, workout in this relationship, keeps you from leaving somebody who has proven that they can be hurtful (again and again) and show no remorse.

Out in the world, even the most enlightened of us are guarded. Sure, the Dalai Lama smiles everywhere he goes, but when he's out on the streets of New York City, he's surrounded by big guys in suits saying, "Ma'am, back up, please, you can't be here." That's exhausting. With people we know, we want to drop all that and be our full and loving self. It's why we like dogs so much. We come home and they're always excited to see us. They can barely contain their affection. (In fact, dogs are missing a gene that some people are missing too; people with this condition, Williams-Beuren syndrome, have to be trained, for their own safety, not to hug complete strangers.) But *crocodiles are not dogs*. Amazingly, people in love make that mistake all the time. A word of warning: If it looks like a dog, but it moves like a crocodile and it bites like a crocodile, stop trying to understand it. You won't. Just head for the exit. This chapter will help you stop fooling yourself and know when it's time to go.

Don't Be Distracted

In Tokyo, every tall building has red lights on the rooftop corners, warning helicopters and low-flying airplanes as they navigate through the darkness. But down on the street level, where dizzying displays of neon signs flash up and down the sides of the buildings, a distraction at every step, it's impossible to spot the gentle regular pulse of those warning lights. That's what happens when we get deeper into a relationship: All the red lights you can easily spot from the bird's-eye view get lost in constant assaults of pedestrian life.

Some relationships are so high drama, so filled with dizzying highs and impossible lows, so wild and unstable, so painful and exhausting, that to be in them is to be completely monopolized by the experience: It takes all our time, our energy, our every thought. And when a person dominates our every waking minute for so long, life no longer feels recognizable without them in it. We can become so dependent on them that we even grow suspicious of our own independent instincts in the rare moments when we have a chance to sit alone for a few minutes and think.

I'm not talking here about those inevitable moments in a relationship where we've grown momentarily tired of somebody, despite them being a generally solid partner; those idle spots where you find yourself fantasizing about leaving, but you're too scared of the unknown and too unfamiliar now with the kind of person you used to be back when you lived on your own. I'm not talking about ennui. I'm speaking of a partner who has failed the fundamental test of being a force for good in your life, someone whose presence in your life has become poison to your mental health, who has convinced you that somehow your mind or your needs are the problem as opposed to the impossibility of living with them.

Earlier in this book, I warned you about joining a cult of two. But cults are tricky, and you don't always know you're in one until after you've been swept away and signed over your life savings and the deed to your house. Many people who've gotten safely out of a cult talk about those moments of elation at the beginning when it seemed as if they were in the one place on earth where they were truly seen and understood. Does this ring a bell? If you're reading this with unwavering attention and the occasional flash of recognition, this just might be you.

Being in a cult takes a lot of work. Somebody has to be constantly brainwashing you (subtly at first, and then less and less so), cutting you off from anybody who can talk sense to you, stealing your independence, and warping your reality until it feels sometimes like the two of you are living on a planet all your own.

In order to justify staying in a situation like this, you can find yourself clinging to the good times you've had together. You live for them, both the memory of them in the past, and the hope of more in the near future. And these good times feel even more exquisite when they arrive on the back of the lowest lows—highs that are artificially enhanced because of their contrast with the discomforts of the rest of your waking hours.

There are psychologists whose entire careers are devoted to understanding the motivations that keep us tied to a person like this. In a way, it doesn't matter what fraction of these behaviors you recognize in your own situation. What matters is what you do after you realize that one or another of them, alone or in combination, is keeping you from living a life of peace and happiness as long as you stay with this person.

In the next few pages, we're taking a practical approach, looking first at the necessary steps in the process of separation. These steps are meant to help you find the strength to act, avoid second thoughts (and third and fourth ones too), and steel yourself against the unavoidable anguish of following through. The steps below are numbered, because they build on each other, and because, over years of coaching, I've seen the importance of taking each one in sequence. Don't leapfrog over any of them. Getting through them quickly is less important than seeing them through to a definitive end.

1. Assume This Person Will Never Change

Being a coach means I have to believe people can change, because otherwise, what's the point? But with someone who has mistreated you in countless ways, sometimes over years, assuming they will never change is an essential act of self-preservation. There are three good reasons to conclude they won't change:

They Don't Want to

I don't know if you've ever been to therapy. If you've read this far, I'd guess you're the kind of person who has at least considered it. From my own experience, it takes quite a lot of effort just to show up—and it's not a jolly activity once you're there. Whenever I tell a joke, the therapist assumes I'm hiding something. Progress is often measured in tears. And that's the good part!

If you've ever pleaded with someone in your life who you know needs it—a mother, brother, or best friend—you'll know it's even harder to get them to go than it was for you. They first have to be willing to admit that they're repeating harmful patterns, then they have to want to change those patterns, and finally, they have to commit to the slow and often painful process of changing them. That's a lot to ask when someone is unselfish and well-intentioned. If instead the person is unmotivated, selfish, uncaring, entitled, and/or narcissistic, it quickly looks like a lost cause.

What gets people to reassess their own life and make changes? Suffering. That's what motivated me to go to therapy in my late twenties. I wasn't trying to implement some beautiful life design; I wanted to be out of pain. It was like breaking a bone: I had to fix it fast.

Is that how your partner feels? Before you answer, avoid the trap of saying, "Yes, Matthew, *I* know deep down they're suffering." If they're ever going to take steps to change, they need to not only be conscious of their "apparent" suffering *and* the suffering they're inflicting on you, but also be motivated to change it.

Let's start with the fact that they are highly unlikely to be motivated to change it if they've never really felt in danger of losing you. Yes, you may have at times said enough is enough and threatened to leave, but did you? Have they ever really learned that their behavior has consequences to them? If they haven't, it's likely they've never had this extrinsic motivation to do something about their behavior.

Now let's look at whether your suffering is genuinely a motivation for them to change. When you or I realize we are consistently causing harm to someone we love, there's a natural reaction: "I better change this. It's hurting them, and that makes me sick to my stomach." Compare that to someone without empathy who instead responds: "God, this is such a pain. Why do you have to be so emotional all the time?" Even when compassion is driving our desire to change, change still isn't easy for us. So imagine how minuscule the chance of change is when someone is devoid of compassion.

Remember, if the only thing invoking their desire to change is us being on their back, then there's nothing in their actual character that wants to make a change, or will support it long term.

Even with expert help and plenty of motivation, changing things about myself has been messy; I stumbled, I've put in a lot of time, and it's ongoing. The battles I have won were hard ones, and many require constant upkeep and vigilance. I have little doubt it's been the same for you. Why then would change come easy to them? As Jacob M. Braude said: "Consider how hard it is to change yourself and you'll understand what little chance you have in trying to change others."

The Changes Are Too Big

Even a one percent shift in our behavior is hard, and maintaining that change isn't easy either. Those who do summon the strength to change tend to do so slowly and in small amounts. When the changes needed are fundamental—when they involve personality traits and basic values—it takes even greater will and commitment. If this chapter seems to speak directly to you, the changes your partner needs to make are probably drastic. The clients of mine who have changed often do so in subtle ways that make a profound difference in their life. But they don't get a personality transplant.

Here's a thought experiment put forth by Dr. Ramani Durvasula,* the leading expert in narcissism, in my conversations with her. I'm going to take

---

* Dr. Ramani Durvasula, *It's Not You* (The Open Field, 2024).

a wild guess and assume that you, dear reader (at least you dearest of readers who have read this far!), share certain characteristics with the majority of people who have come to our in-person events, which means you're an empathetic, nurturing individual who thinks of others and goes out of your way to help people be happy. Now what would it take for you to stop caring, and start lying, manipulating, and acting solely out of self-interest, even when it hurts someone you love? Could you do it? I'd bet my life savings on that being practically impossible no matter how hard you tried. It's utterly implausible that you could change that much from your fundamental nature—even with a gun to your head.

Seeing how hard it would be to change your nature, and knowing just how different their nature is from yours, can you now see that it is as unlikely that your partner would be able to become like you as you would be able to become like them? Apply this rule: If it would require a complete personality transplant for someone to behave the way you want them to, assume it will never happen.

These Aren't Just Behavioral Differences, They're Character Differences

We often make the mistake of identifying so intensely with the person we're closest to that we simply assume they're doing the same thing too. But closeness and dependence are not always reciprocal, and they don't automatically create or reflect shared values. In fact, all too often, sharing a daily routine can blind us to just how little we have in common. But still our identification with our partner continues to grow by the sheer force of our closeness. After a while, this blind identification becomes a necessary element of the relationship, especially if we're in a position of dependence, either for something as pragmatic as our finances, or for something as fundamental as our identity. Too often, this one-sided connection leads to fantasies about how life will unfold—fantasies that become so elaborate and familiar that they can begin to feel inseparable from your own identity. To sustain this fantasy, you have to believe that your partner is, at their core, like you, and will come through for you in ways you need them to when you need them the most. The alternative to that fantasy is a version of hell, one where we realize we are emotionally wed to an alien—a person from another planet altogether whom we just cannot relate to. Unfortunately, this is exactly what happens to so many people who realize just before the divorce that they've been lying to themselves for years, completely making up a shared moral and emotional universe that their partner had never actually set foot in.

But before you reach that breaking point, you still expect them to be like you. If you're kind, you can't fathom their callous reaction to something that hurt you. If you are conscientious, you can't understand how they could make key decisions (major investments, job relocations) without so much as consulting you. If you value being a teammate to someone, it's genuinely shocking to find out that despite all of the ways you have supported them over the years, when it's their turn to come through for you, they appear utterly disinterested.

If your version of loving someone is based on care, empathy, compassion, conscientiousness, and kindness, and theirs is based on having someone around full-time to cater to their needs at their convenience, not only will you wind up dreadfully unhappy, you'll be exhausted from living in a world you cannot make sense of. How they "love" is not the same as how you love, and there is no comparison.

That doesn't mean you and the person you end up with have to be the same. Part of the charm of relationships that work comes from the differences and distinct perspectives we offer each other, that pleasant friction of surprise and challenge that comes when two strong and independent people navigate through life together. But if we can't agree on basics—such as the necessity for honesty, loyalty, or accountability when we're wrong—then we are doomed to rely on moments of joy that come only from those moments when our common needs intersect by chance. Such moments are never long enough to establish trust; they're brief interludes like the two times a day when a broken clock looks like a working one. Please don't endow those two coincidental overlaps with any special meaning. You have every right to be loved in those 1,438 other minutes in a day too.

2. Don't Let Your Empathy Become Your Enemy

Empathy is a beautiful thing. It helps us see others as they are, and lets us share in their pain and setbacks, joys and triumphs. It piques our curiosity, excites our kindness, mutes our prejudice, softens our judgment, engages our compassion. On the simplest level, it helps us know someone, both strangers and our closest friends. And the more we know, the easier it becomes to reach out, to do the straightforward things that help the people we know in big or small ways.

But empathy can mutate into something extremely dangerous. The more empathetic we tend to be, the more resourceful we become in identifying and forgiving our partner's worst behaviors. And the more we know our partner, the more context we have to rationalize even their most painful behaviors. It can even become a badge we wear. ("I know them better than anyone. It may look crazy to you, but it doesn't from here.") We're proud to be their confidant and emergency contact, the only one in the special position to forgive them, even when most of the things they need forgiveness for are what they keep doing to us.

Too often that's the problem with this level of empathy: All our capacity for understanding doesn't help them change. We're still the first person to suffer from the way they are. We may be the only one who knows why they're hurting us so badly, but that doesn't change the fact that they continue to do so, sometimes so often and so easily that it can even seem that it's our capacity to empathize that makes them hurt us.

Here's the second problem: Simply having this expansive capacity for empathy makes us vulnerable to those who would prey upon it. And preying on our empathy serves several purposes. If they "let us in" on some difficult childhood experience that seems like the key to all their pain, not only does this pass for intimacy ("Sweetheart, you know I'm not a monster"); it also transforms them from the perpetrator of pain here and now into the victim of some deep, buried trauma from long ago.

This is one of the ways a person like this can weaponize your empathy. Every time you gloss over their most recent awful behavior and instead sympathize with them and the hurt they have carried for so long, they reward you for "getting them." ("No one else does!") This is both validating (you win the prize) and isolating (you are the only other inhabitant of this island). It also sets a terrible precedent. You are giving them so much license now, they will feel wronged any time in the future when you don't. ("I just can't believe after all you know about me, my life, my suffering, you still don't understand why I am the way I am. I thought you knew me.")

This is how our empathy can be transformed from a loving instinct into a compulsion fueling codependence. Beth Macy, the author of *Raising Lazarus*, a book on overcoming opioid addiction, says there's a misconception that there is a rock bottom for people, and that once someone hits that horrific level of pain, they will ricochet back up to a normal life. Instead, she explains, it turns out that rock bottom has a basement, and that basement has a trapdoor, and on and on. It is entirely possible, in other words, to find oneself falling farther than one ever conceived possible in their wildest nightmares. I have discovered this to be no less true when a bottomless capacity for empathy meets an unrelenting willingness to take advantage. With enough empathy there's really nothing you can't justify:

They compulsively lie to me: Well, their parents never allowed them to do anything, and the only way they learned to actually live life was to lie about what they were up to.

They keep cheating on me: It's an addiction they don't know how to stop, and it really does hurt them too because they're wracked with guilt all the time because they love me so much. Anyway, how were they ever supposed to have a normal relationship with sex given the upbringing they had?

They never consider me in major business and financial decisions that affect our life, and just act without consulting me: Anyway, that's something they know more about than me, and while it hurts that they don't consider me at all, I know deep down they're just trying to do what's best for us as a family.

Like an opioid addiction, our empathy has no bottom. There's no limit to the horrors we'll endure before we'll call it quits: financial devastation, isolation from family and friends, obliteration of our confidence and any sense of self, even life-threatening situations. There's no way out until we change the rules of our empathy.

Changing the rules of our empathy doesn't mean changing who we are. We can still exercise our understanding, but we must trade our tolerance for distant compassion. We may choose to pity someone from afar, even somebody capable of the most despicable things, but we can't have them in our lives. Our empathy is defective if we can only apply it in one direction. We can't allow our compassion for one person to turn into regular torture inflicted on somebody else, especially when that person is us! That's not empathy anymore. It's something far deeper and more destructive that we're using our empathy to disguise.

3. Don't Allow Your Empathy to Become Your Cover for Your Fear

With a partner or family member, it can feel acceptable, even noble, to make allowances out of our love for them. In a sleight of hand that can even fool ourselves, we use our overachieving capacity for empathy—one of our best qualities—to justify persisting in the relationship, when in truth, a huge part of staying is rooted in our own fears:

I'm terrified of losing this person.

I can't bear the thought of being alone again.

I'll never find a connection like this again. No one will ever love me like they do.

I'll never love anyone else like this again.

I'll have to start all over.

I've wasted years of my life.

I won't know how to get by on my own.

When we do confront these fears, they quickly take on existential implications: "If I lose this person I have given so much of my life to, what does my life so far even mean? If I've been with someone most of my life, how can I possibly admit who they really are without invalidating my entire adult life? Who am I without them? Who will I be in the eyes of others?" It's no surprise then that instead of addressing these fears head-on, we revert to more palatable, even righteous reasons to stay. It's easy to tell friends that only you really understand this person, or that there's something unique and complicated about the situation. It's harder to admit that you don't know who you are, what you're worth, or how you'll ever cope on your own.

Remember, you may be a kind, loyal, caring, conscientious, empathetic person, but don't let your ease in playing that role mask the true reality of what's keeping you in a damaging (or even dangerous) relationship. In order to break free to a better life, you have to see through your own empathy mask, shed that disguise, and face your existential fears.

4. You Have to Be Willing to Light the Fuse That Blows Up Your Own Life

Sometimes a relationship blows up without our having any say in the matter. It's horrible—like an emotional car crash—but whether it hit you out of nowhere or you could practically see it all happening in slow motion, if someone didn't give you a choice, you never had the feeling of being at the wheel of the decision. In situations like this, we say it happened to us, as if we were the helpless victim. Whether your ex broke up with you with no warning, or left you after a series of small betrayals built up to a complete break, it feels like it ended before you even had a chance.

But what about the other kind of breakup, the one where you have to be the one lighting the fuse that blows up your life? That requires agency and resolution. You can't just wait around for it to expire of natural causes. You have to set everything in motion and follow through. For this you need a powerful form of bravery: total acceptance. Not the kind of acceptance where you acknowledge your limitations ("I'll never run a marathon") but the kind where you recognize the reality of a difficult situation. ("That will not be the last time. It probably won't be the last time this week.") It takes total acceptance of the fact that your needs are not being met, that this relationship (as well as perhaps the life conditions it creates) is untenable, that you are deeply unhappy, and that nothing will change until you admit that your fantasy version of the relationship is nothing like your actual lived experience.

To take the wheel, you have to admit how unhappy you are now and have been for a long time, and how unhappy you will always be if you stay. You have to take a deep breath and admit:

I'm not in a functional relationship/marriage, and this relationship/marriage is over.

I have no future with this person if I ever hope to be at peace.

This person will no longer be in my life.

I'm going to miss this person, even though they caused me tremendous pain. I will first have to go through a painful withdrawal, grief, and the initial loneliness that will take its place.

I am [insert age here] and I am going to be single again.

All the time I invested in this relationship didn't make it a success like I'd hoped. It simply made it clear that nothing will change it.

I'm not where my [friends/family/coworkers/community] think I am. I'm in more pain than I have let on, and I don't have the relationship they all think I do.

That will come as a shock to some, and I will feel shame, especially if I actively maintained a false image of a happy relationship with the people around me.

This step is the hardest. It takes radical acceptance of your situation, courage, and the ability to adapt and reinvent yourself. But this comes with a tremendous gift—the rejection of a false identity and the gift of real confidence. This analogy helps explain what I mean:

Say you've told all your friends that you have $100,000 in the bank when you're actually $20,000 in debt. Every time you bring up that $100,000, it starts to feel more real to you. The validation you get makes it feel real to you, and it becomes part of your identity with your friends. Now imagine you worked overtime, trimmed your expenses, and cut your debt to $10,000. That's huge, halfway to even. But you can't celebrate because everybody thinks you have that $100,000! You'd have to give up all that validation (and deal with the fallout from all that pretending) before anyone could be happy for you.

We should take a tremendous amount of pride in our real accomplishments. But we'll never be able to pull that off until we're honest with ourselves about our real position. Only when we accept the fact that we'll never find peace and happiness if we stay—our actual starting point—can we find the courage to light the fuse that blows up the broken part of our old life. It may feel like taking fifty steps back, but it only takes one honest step forward to start feeling alive and proud again.

5. When the Reality of This Tough Choice Sets in, Your Mind Will Trick You Into Thinking That This Person, and Your Life Together, Aren't So Bad After All

The closer we get to acting—taking that decisive step out of our old life and into the unknown—our fears and demons reach out to undermine our resolve. It's a subtle form of bargaining we do with ourselves when we're facing painful change. It summons our greatest fears: being alone, not knowing how to get by in the world, having to rediscover our identity ("I don't even know who I am anymore without this person"), acknowledging and grieving the end of a life that will never be.

This new voice says to us: "This is madness. You're really going to go through all of this just because you had a fight with this person last week?" It accuses us of having an over-the-top reaction to what has happened. Think about all the things that voice tries to say to you at this turning point:

Underneath it all, they love you so much, you know they do.

They do so much for you, for your children, for your family. Remember when they helped your brother out that month when he needed money? Remember when they took you on that expensive trip to Italy? Remember how they paid the school fees for the kids?

On their good days, they can be so wonderful. Do you really want to lose that?

Despite everything, they mean well. Yes, they're complex. Maybe the relationship has its challenges. But what relationship doesn't?

You've had such wonderful times together. You have history. That all has to count for something. Do you really want to throw all of that away?

Real love is unconditional. If you want someone to love you unconditionally, shouldn't you do the same for them?

You are going to be alone . . . you do realize that?

This is all self-inflicted misdirection, saying, "Look here at everything you're losing, and not at the mountain of pain that got you to this point." It's the first of many tests to see whether you are finally serious about ending this suffering in your life. You've been here before and turned back, only to find the same pain and suffering waiting for you. How many times have these voices convinced you to go back? They're good at what they do, making you doubt if you should listen to your exhaustion, anguish, anger, your utter inability or unwillingness to endure it anymore, or if you should just give in to the voices telling you to stick it out.

Remember: You want a relationship. You have wanted this relationship, which hasn't been easy to end or you would have done it already, not just once, but a hundred times. You don't need any help staying. But somehow, despite every instinct of your being, you've still ended up in a place you can no longer stand. How bad does something you desperately want have to be for you to no longer want it?

The answer to this reveals the bottom line: It would take an intolerable amount of pain to make you turn on something you deeply want. And so: An intolerable amount of pain is what you have.

In this part of the process, you'll find that each time you finish with one demon, another pops up. You may find yourself comparing your relationship to another where the abuse is more obvious or extreme to justify it not being "that bad"; or, on the other end of the spectrum, one that's so "boring" you couldn't imagine trading places. And if you can dismiss those, a final voice will come crawling out, the one who knows that if the other voices can't succeed in convincing you that your situation is good, it can at least make you feel bad:

> You think you're perfect? Look at the things you've done wrong over the years. And you're not off the hook for everything they've done wrong. Half the time it was your behavior that drove them to act that way. Hey, at least they want you. Who else ever will? Think about it. Maybe this is as good as you're going to get. You're no bed of roses either. At least this person loves you and wants to be with you, despite all that.

Every message of resistance inside your head is intended to distract you from the only truth that matters in this situation:

6. If You Stay Where You Are, You Will Never Be Happy and You Will Never Be at Peace

The antidote to all the doubts in Step 5, the answer to all those demons is, strictly speaking, a non-answer. You don't have to tell yourself you've done nothing wrong in your relationship (even if it's true), you don't have to pretend you have nothing to work on, you don't even have to believe you'll find someone else. The only thing you have to tell yourself (sometimes a hundred times a day) is that no matter what else may be true, you cannot stay here.

When experience has taught you that someone will devastate you or bring chaos into your life—reliably and predictably—staying will not only inevitably lead to more pain, but an amount of pain that makes you feel physically sick when you imagine having to go through it. There is no more hope for all the hopes you once had for the relationship. Earlier I spoke of Pandora, and how she shut the box before hope could escape. I can't help but see how this myth applies to the kind of relationships we've been talking about here. Upon opening the lid on a relationship like this, we can be completely blindsided by all the cruelties that fly out of that box.

But maybe the worst and most dangerous of all is hope. Hope can make you stay when there's no reason to anymore. Hope may start out looking like a positive—giving you the strength to believe in someone's better self—but it quickly turns into a kind of denial that allows you to block out reality. In the end, hope can take away your sense of agency, your ability to act, and it can even rob you of your most basic instinct for self-preservation. As long as you can take some consolation in hope, you will stay, passively, submitting to things no one should put up with. What is terrifying is how different it feels to you and what it looks like from the outside. Hope can turn this passive state you've been reduced to into heroism. From the outside, though, that behavior seems indistinguishable from addiction.

This is why, as unnatural as it sounds, we must kill that hope to save ourselves. When we extinguish hope, we make way for something more active, assertive, more in control. Only after we have set hope aside and admitted that, yes, our situation is untenable, can we have the clarity to take the necessary steps to protect ourselves and make a change. Never mind not being strong enough or worthy of something better; once we see that the future we wanted will never be found here, we will find the strength to do what's needed. It's not unusual, when something is absolutely necessary, to discover hidden reserves of power, like the twenty-two-year-old Virginia woman who lifted a BMW 525i off her father and then gave him CPR. Necessity is a wonderful antidote to both hope and self-doubt.

7. Just Because It Hurts Doesn't Mean It's Wrong

Here comes the final test: the ultimate pain of loss.

Once you do leave, your mind will play new tricks on you. When the lonely nights begin—no matter how many friends you have or how close your family is—the moment comes when you feel the gravel in your stomach and an ache in your heart. When you reach that point, it won't take much of an argument to convince you that you have done something terribly wrong.

But pain is not a reliable indicator of a bad choice. If you make that mistake—if you turn around at the first sharp stab of pain—you can wind up sentencing yourself to a life of comfortable unhappiness. You can psych yourself back into something that feels comfortable, or at least more comfortable than the loneliness that feels like all you'll ever have. But comfort is not happiness. What is comfortable can be hell (it was before). And pain is often a precursor to happiness.

By starting from "It hurts so bad" and jumping to "and therefore maybe I did the wrong thing by leaving," we've created a non sequitur. There's really no connection between the pain we're in and the assumption that we could only feel this much pain if the love we just left was somehow special and important. This logic has sent too many people racing straight back to someone who will only break their heart and poison their life all over again.

But let's stop evaluating intensity of pain as an indicator of love. When an addict is trying to quit drinking, heroin, porn, or obsessive phone use, they will experience significant emotional (and in the case of some of the above, physical) pain in the process. But that doesn't mean that heroin was therefore special and they should never have quit it. Nobody at rehab says, "Look how bad they feel; maybe they should never have given up drinking after all." Instead, we look at the intensity of the pain they're in as a measure of the severity of their addiction, not the importance of the thing they just cut out of their lives.

When I started Brazilian jiu-jitsu, I was warned that it would feel like I got hit by a train after my first roll (rolling is to jiu-jitsu what sparring is to boxing; you face off with another person). And it did. One telltale sign of the beginner: You can't control your breathing once you start rolling. Nerves are high, there's ego involved, you're scrambling around trying frantically to get the upper hand, and within a minute or so of tensing every muscle and forgetting to breathe, you feel like you're drowning. I quickly confirmed this with my own experience.

At this point, my jiu-jitsu coach told me that in his training with other black belts, he'll sometimes set a timer for sixty minutes, and then proceed to continuously roll for that amount of time! When he saw my shock, he said, "When you have to roll for a whole hour, you know it's going to be hard, so strangely, you stop panicking because you know it won't be over soon. So instead of trying to get out of it, you decide to control your breath, and with a greater sense of calm, and more oxygen in the tank, you just settle in for the ride." I've since learned that when you do that, it no longer feels like you're drowning. It may still feel like a marathon, but knowing and accepting that helps you realize how you're actually going to run it.

Severing these relationships is the same. It may feel like it's breaking you for weeks, months, or even longer, but when you're desperate to get out of the pain and there's no immediate end in sight, panic sets in. If instead you just accept that this part of life will hurt for a while, you can stop holding your breath—for minutes, for months—and just surrender to the process of moving through your pain.

It's important to remember that while this path hurts, the other one is worse. At this point, you can only regain your happiness by going forward into the unknown, and not back into a situation that always made you unhappy. Neither of those paths is easy, for different reasons. If you pick staying, you're renewing a contract that will guarantee you'll be mistreated, your needs won't be met, and you'll have no chance of finding peace or improving your life. If you decide to leave for good, you're venturing into the unknown, setting yourself up to miss your ex, and to experience grief—not just the grief of the relationship having ended, but the profound and exquisite grief of the absolute, terminal acceptance that they will never change. In the second of these two paths, you will ultimately learn to be OK on your own. Both choices will guarantee pain. But only one leads out of the darkness.

13

IDENTITY CONFIDENCE

We talked earlier in the book about how the most dangerous stage of attraction arrives the moment you decide you like someone. That's when you're most liable to throw standards out the window, be distracted at work, cancel your Tuesday yoga session, or skip taco night with friends so you can spend every waking minute with your new obsession, as though there was no life before them. (It's too easy to fall into the trap of thinking, "This new person has all my needs covered!") Even if you're studiously avoiding these pitfalls—rationing communication, refraining from low-level social media stalking, etc.—you can still run into trouble if you're spending your free time imagining a future with a person you've only been on two dates with. Because even if these fantasies remain unknown to the object of your attraction, your private fascination still has a way of showing up when you meet again. Instead of just hanging out, now you're worrying about not getting hurt. You can see the little signs that you're already way ahead of things, a source of frustration that leaves you wincing instead of just enjoying the outdoor movie the two of you decided on for a fifth date.

You could make the case that it's not entirely your fault, since heady romance is the water we all swim in. So much of mass entertainment—movies, music, paperbacks, advertisements—underscores the idea that true happiness is impossible without love. This onslaught can leave us feeling worthless any time we have to face the world without the validation that comes from being in a relationship.

In chapter 8, we looked over some techniques to prevent us from getting overinvested in early dates while you're still trying to spot the difference between attention and intention. But even when what we have in front of us shows real intention on their part, there's still the danger that we will lose sight of everything else that's important in our own life. A useful rule of life is this: We tend to value what we invest in. So if we stop investing in anything that doesn't have to do with them, the importance of our life outside of the relationship will shrink, and our reliance on them for our happiness will grow. The more we are connected to the other grounding aspects of our life, the harder it is for someone who hasn't texted us back for three hours to overthrow our equilibrium.

It may seem counterintuitive, but the moment we think we've found our dream person is precisely the time to do anything else but feed that obsession. It's time to double down on the other sources of meaning in our life: our hobbies, our family, the books we're dying to read, the activities that leave us feeling refreshed and fulfilled, anything that connects us with ourselves and our sense of purpose. You want to concentrate on activities that are most likely to result in the conviction that, as nice as it would be for this new person in your life to reciprocate the feelings that have been bubbling up, your own life, just as it is, with all you've put into it, is enough for you.

I often frame that advice in practical terms, telling people that the best thing to do before a date that you deem important is to have a busy week. That's a pretty fail-safe short-term strategy. It takes your mind off your anxieties, cuts short the opportunities to exaggerate expectations, and, ideally, leaves you so preoccupied with the things you love to do (or need to finish, or just took up, or put off starting) that there's no bandwidth to anxiously fret about your upcoming date. Thanks to all this activity, you smoothly transition into a fun time with someone you haven't had time to overthink. And you have plenty to share as a result of how much living you've done since the last time you saw them.

You've probably heard the term "F-U money." It's the amount of money you need to be able to say no to anything you don't want to do—to say no to jobs, bosses, and working with people who make you unhappy.

What if we could achieve such an effect in the domain of inner confidence instead of money? Picture your confidence as a tabletop, with all the sturdiness that comes from the legs that are holding it up. The various supports of your life give that tabletop the stability it needs. If the tabletop is your confidence, each one of those legs is a different part of your life that gives you strength, meaning, purpose, love.

There's nothing wrong with admitting how important finding a life partner is to you. But by investing in the other legs under our table, when a potential partner does come along, we don't immediately rely on that person to stay sturdy. "F-U confidence" comes from having that kind of sturdy support in your life already.

The instinct to forget everything you've got grows more tempting when someone comes along who's particularly good-looking, charismatic, or impressive. But none of those traits makes your world less important. So what if they're "better-looking"? So what if they're smoother in a roomful of people? So what if they're thought of as important by everyone around them? None of those attributes diminish the size and intrinsic value of your life and all that's in it.

In *A Man for All Seasons*, Sir Thomas More is giving advice to an ambitious Richard Rich, who feels he won't be worth anything unless he achieves his grand ambitions. More wants him to know that there are more profound ways to achieve a sense of significance:

More: Why not be a teacher? You'd be a fine teacher, perhaps a great one.
Rich: If I was, who would know it?
More: You; your pupils; your friends; God. Not a bad public, that.

Whenever we date someone with an exciting life, it's tempting to devalue our own, as if it had somehow been made insignificant by an overshadowing presence. But even the most seemingly normal life can be of profound importance. Who's to say that the life of a care worker who spends their time tending to a handful of dementia patients is any smaller than one who manages one hundred employees in a tech company? Stay connected to what is rich in your world, to the difference you make in your immediate circle, with your family and friends, in the work you do, the hobbies you love, the practices you keep. If you do, nobody who comes along can intimidate you. No one can make you feel you have to work overtime to get their attention, as if they have something you don't. And when people see that you are deeply connected to the value you create and/or the love you have in your own world, you already have what everybody longs for and wants to be close to: love, meaning, and fulfillment. Even the largest life can't guarantee those things.

Differences between people are great for relationships. But if someone can't conceive of you as their equal—keep moving. It's a good thing to look for early on: How soon does this hot stranger recognize you as their equal? "Right away" is probably the best answer here. No matter how attractive your potential counterpart may be, that's an essential test; no relationship can last for long or provide real happiness unless it's a relationship of equals.

The Identity Matrix

There is an exercise I've conducted for years on my retreats called "The Identity Matrix," which has always been a highly practical tool for understanding what might need to change in our lives for us to develop this F-U confidence we've been talking about.

I first ask my audience to make a list of the various aspects of their life that they derive a sense of confidence from: their friendships, the position they've earned in their career, being able to play an instrument or speak a second language, their treasured hobby, the financial security they've created for themselves. Anything that gives us a feeling of pride, attractiveness, or significance, a sense that we are interesting, or a reason to feel secure in our lives, are all items that tend to make the list, especially if they're something we draw on frequently for our sense of worth or identity. For someone who has fought for citizenship in a new country, their shiny new passport may make the list. Another might list the home they've poured years of love into. For someone else, it could be how well-read they are, or how much they've traveled abroad to experience other cultures. Whatever makes an individual's list is a direct reflection of the identity they've constructed for themselves in their lives up until now.

Then I ask each member of the audience to draw a square, with smaller squares inside it, evenly spaced like a tic-tac-toe box but bigger. I have them dedicate each square inside this box to a different item on their list. What they end up with is a matrix of squares that make up what I call their "Identity Confidence."

However, I go on to point out that in reality, the size of these boxes in our life is anything but uniform. I ask them to draw their matrix again, but this time I have them resize the boxes so each shape roughly reflects how important the item in the square is to their identity. Usually, one or two of the boxes are way bigger than the rest, because we all have things we derive a disproportionate amount of our validation from. For a lot of people, it's their career. For many others, the dominant square is their relationship. The matrix, as one attendee from our retreat wrote, stops looking like a bingo card and starts looking more like a Mondrian painting, with one or two big squares surrounded by smaller ones.

Making up an identity matrix isn't always a comfortable exercise. If you're honest with yourself, you might look at your matrix and see that you've been giving some areas of your life more emphasis than you'd like and others less than they deserve. Some people even come to find there's not much they can think of to put in their matrix at all. If that's you, don't worry, you'll likely have more ideas as to what makes up yours as you read on.

One of the key things to understand about our matrix is that the size of our squares tends to be a reflection of what we identify with the most. We tend to identify with aspects of our lives we have come to rely on for validation and significance. The person who was rewarded in childhood for always being helpful is told as an adult that they are a "star" employee for staying late, for never complaining about an unmanageable workload, and for sacrificing their life and health for work. The person who receives disproportionate attention for their looks obsesses over the maintenance of them later in life, believing them to be their primary value. In many ways, the stage gets set early on for what our identity matrix will later look like based on what we learned "worked for us" in our early years. It's not easy to tell if our identity matrix reflects certain intrinsic aspects of our personality that would have always inevitably emerged, or if we've simply followed the breadcrumbs of validation along the path of least resistance, until at some point our identity turned into what we think of as *us*. It's probably a little bit of both. We are all trying to get certain needs met—security, significance, a means of identifying ourselves in the world; our matrix just reflects our best attempts at doing so. But the identity matrix we write down today is never a final portrait; it's more of a snapshot, showing us the muscles we've been using the most leading up to this period of our life.

Maybe it's easier to see on the page than to picture in your head. So, here are two sample versions of an identity matrix; the first one is my matrix at twenty-one, and the one on the following page is me now, at thirty-six. There are more squares I could have added into these, but I've narrowed it down to the most obvious ones for the sake of illustration. (I did them both in the same week, so there's a chance I misrepresented some elements of my younger self, although I doubt it!)

Age 21

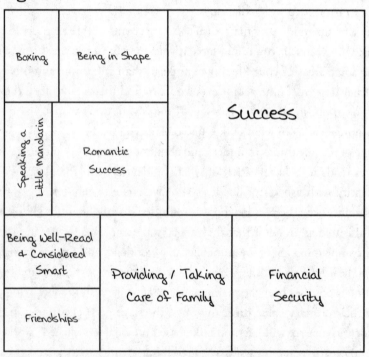

You can see that at twenty-one, I placed a large part of my worth in how successful I thought I was externally, and the idea that I was financially in a sound position. I also provided for my family, which, although rooted in generosity and a sense of duty, also made me feel good about myself and became part of my identity. Romance was a pretty big deal, but it was less about finding love and more about feeling like I was, egoically and heroically, successful at dating and attracting women. I boxed, and that added to my confidence.

I didn't put a lot of emphasis on my friendships; I was too focused on my ambitions, but they played a small part in my matrix nonetheless. Having spent a couple of months working in Shanghai, I had a little Mandarin under my belt, which became something I felt made me more interesting. Being in shape was important, but that was tied into the whole "being wanted" thing. I enjoyed the notion that I was well-read (regardless of how well-read I actually was), and that people thought I was smart when they talked to me. Suffice it to say, I was running on a healthy dose of insecurity in most of the things that were driving my decisions about where to put my time and energy, and what gave me a sense of significance.

Age 36

Living in America		
Jiu-Jitsu	Sense of Purpose	Marriage
Internal Growth	Success	
Being in Shape	Financial Stability	Close Connected Relationships
Being Healthy	Life Experiences	
Being Well-Read & Considered Smart	Public Speaking	Writing Ability

Now to my matrix at thirty-six. There's no denying my career still occupies a major part of it. But it's not as simple as external success. A part of it is still success—I'd be lying if I said I'd eradicated all trace of ambition (you wouldn't believe me if I said I had anyway)—but I take much more significance these days from having a sense of purpose, even if it means my career doesn't grow as quickly. My internal growth is something I am more proud of than ever, so that's a significant square these days. When I was twenty-one, internal growth was only important if it got me more external success, which was the thing I really wanted back then.

Being in shape is still important to me—I'm not above vanity—but equally important these days is the feeling of actually being healthy. A new prominent box is "life experiences," which reflects the fact that these days a far greater part of my confidence and identity comes from living and not just working. In my identity matrix now, you'll see I don't have a large square dedicated to "taking care of family." Now it's just "close connected relationships." I still look to be there for my family, as they do for me, but doing things for family is no longer where I'm trying to get my significance. Instead of obligation, I now choose love and reciprocity as the basis of those relationships—I feel the rewards of being truly connected in those relationships, not feeling important or valuable because of what I might be able to do for people. I now take confidence from the strength of my marriage, not how many people might find me attractive.

Relationships in general play a greater role in my life today, and are much bigger squares in my matrix as a result. I've never been so grateful for the love in my life, love that, without realizing it, I took for granted at a younger age. I used to believe that the relationships in my life—friendships or familial—kind of stayed where they were, like prehistoric insects frozen in amber, preserved forever somehow without my investing in them. Now I'm much more focused on how I can show up for them. More than ever, I'm aware that the size of my "close connected relationships" square is a direct reflection of how much energy I put into it—because I'm so much more grateful for that love, that energy has increased exponentially. This is how self-fulfilling cycles occur in our matrix—the more grateful we are for something in our lives, the more we respect and invest in it; the more we invest in it, the bigger the square becomes.

Filling out an identity matrix is a straightforward way to be honest about where your priorities are, and what you might need to shift to become happier and more confident. This doesn't require months or years of therapy. There's an organic quality to it, and, especially if you take the trouble to draw one up with some regularity, it can't help but reveal how your priorities shift and change. With this visual readout in hand, you're less likely to feel that circumstances are dictating your direction, and more like you're steering the ship. You can see where you're vulnerable, and where you're overinvested, and you can redirect your energy accordingly. Don't overthink it when you draw your own; it's inevitably a crude and imperfect exercise. Just try to roughly draw what you think yours looks like today, and then make some decisions about what needs to change for you to have a more robust matrix.

You can see that, at thirty-six, not only does my matrix have more squares, but my overall matrix itself is bigger. It's like I've added a penthouse level! That's because my identity has expanded over the years, and the sources of my confidence and where I derive a sense of my identity have become more numerous. This is as much a reflection of where I put my focus as it is how I spend my time. If the size of your overall identity matrix was all related to time spent on things, it would always be a zero-sum game between competing aspects of your personality and your life that give you a sense of confidence. For me, the ability to live and work in America is a significant part of my identity confidence, but it doesn't "take up time" like my hobby of Brazilian jiu-jitsu in recent years does; it just exists as something I'm proud of that gives me a sense of security. The same goes for my public speaking ability, which, despite not appearing in my younger self's matrix, doesn't actually reflect an increase in time allocated to it (I was doing a lot of it at twenty-one too). It reflects the fact that I'm now much more consciously connected to how wonderful it is to have that skill set. I especially like this square in my matrix because it's something that would remain even if I had zero cents to my name. This is also true of my ability to write, which I consider a core skill that I would still have even if I lost everything in my business. When I give renewed focus to how fortunate I am to have these skills, the size of my matrix increases just through what I'm choosing to be grateful for.

Still, most of the things that give us a sense of confidence do take up time, so naturally, a good part of what the matrix reveals is how or where we spend our time and our focus, and that gives us the chance to consider if we're dividing that finite resource in ways that support our long-term goals and lasting values.

Beware Your Mutations and Diversify

For better or worse, we tend to form what we think of as our "identity" based on the squares in our matrix. In life, we fight to maintain our identity, because it gives us a sense of security—it's "what we know." We may not even enjoy our work, but the title, status, and money that come with it have become part of our identity, and that can feel indispensable to us. We can come to feel like losing it would be tantamount to losing a limb. The danger here is that we come to rely so much on our primary sources of validation that they turn into our mutations. If we're not careful, these muscles become the only ones we know how to use. Little by little, these mutations transform into our greatest vulnerability. If losing all that validation would be devastating to our sense of who we are, we can easily become a prisoner to those one or two overdeveloped squares in our matrix. If you were struggling earlier with trying to figure out what the biggest square in your matrix was, you need only ask yourself one question: "What would have the biggest effect on my confidence if it were taken away?"

For some people, you can literally see the mutation: the guy at the gym with massive arms, the TikTok influencer who wears elaborate red-carpet makeup to pop into the deli. Some are less obvious but still apparent, like the workaholic dad who started as ambitious, but years later can't bring himself to switch off while on vacation with his family; or married people who make each other their only focus and risk losing the spark of otherness that keeps desire alive. Christopher Hitchens, probably the greatest debater of his generation, confessed to being very wary of using his outsized skills at home with his family, since there are clearly some arguments it's good to lose and other times when silence is the smartest option. We all know people pleasers who wound up overwhelmed and burned out, or parents who smothered their kids with so much attention that the kids would do almost anything to get away. There are so many ways we can overindex.

A good question for all of us to ask: "Who would I be without the biggest square in my matrix?" Show me your answer to that question, and I'll show you how vulnerable you are to failure, crisis, or tragedy. There is no question that relying too much on the confidence that arises out of any single element in our identity matrix is a precarious proposition. That's partly because nearly all these things that give us confidence are susceptible to change. People close to us die, relationships end, we lose a job, we get injured, we age or grow critically ill. The skills we have carefully acquired erode if we fail to practice them (sometimes they erode even when we practice all the time!) and we can easily lose access to the places where they can be exercised or the equipment they require.

There are some who see the things we strongly identify with as a sort of armor, as if our matrix itself (as well as all the confidence that comes from it) is in some sense a crutch, maybe even one of the central impediments to a full-spectrum human experience. They're not wrong. It's an observation that would be quick to be pointed out in mindfulness circles. There is definitely a deeper and more unshakable level of confidence that you can access, core confidence, which we'll explore in greater detail in an upcoming chapter. But we are all people living flawed everyday lives, facing out to meet the world at least as much as (and probably way more than) we face inward to meet ourselves.

One of the best moves we can make to hedge against the downside risks of our chief character assets is to ensure that our life isn't all about one thing. There are three ways to diversify our matrix: 1) Put more effort into one of the boxes you haven't allocated much time or attention to, so that it grows with increased investment. 2) Develop a newfound appreciation for some-thing you already have—do this and you'll discover sources of confidence you already have access to, like I did with the skills of writing and public speaking. 3) Add a completely new box, starting in with something you've never tried before. I'm sure you can think of squares in your matrix that, if you go back far enough, didn't exist before. For me, it's jiu-jitsu, something I took up when injuries cut into my ability to box. Now I try to roll at least three times a week, no matter what else I've got going on. I've become preoc-cupied with my progress there, and I often find myself thinking of the lessons I've learned from doing so.

Unlike simply focusing on a newfound gratitude for something you al-ready have, the problem with adding a square or devoting more effort to a teeny square you'd like to enlarge is that, to the extent that life is a zero-sum game, it can take away from areas where you have your greatest strengths.

That's not always a bad thing. I have a friend who is a master of sarcasm, which she uses to make everybody laugh, to control the conversation, to keep things light and moving. Sometimes this means she nukes whole topics of interest before anyone can say a word, and it often means there's almost always no room for vulnerability or curiosity while she's holding court, both of which require space and sincerity and sometimes silence in place of wise-cracks and uproariousness.

I've gotten exactly nowhere trying to get her to ease up, and that's surely because she would fare a lot worse in social settings if she took my advice. She'd almost certainly feel less powerful, less interesting, less comfortable, less confident, at least for a time. It would feel like a step backward, even if from the perspective of her identity matrix, it would be a step forward, toward strength and diversity, away from overreliance on a skill that's quite clearly becoming a kind of dodge. Who wants to be an awkward student again, which can be an intensely humbling experience, especially when we know there are better places we could be, and things we could be better at doing?

My friend and publisher, Karen Rinaldi, wrote a book that might as well be an ode to diversifying your matrix, called (It's Great to) Suck at Something. Karen likes to surf even though, as she tells everybody, she sucks at it. It didn't stop her from buying a place in Costa Rica where she could get away and spend hours on the waves, wiping out, getting back on her board, and paddling right back out to take her place in the lineup. She wrote a piece in the New York Times about some of what she'd learned from failing with such regularity. ("Failing is OK. Better still, isn't it a relief?") To go along with the piece, she posted a video of herself surfing, and a colleague stopped by her office to say, "So, you really do suck at surfing!"

"You thought I was being modest?"

Her colleague mentioned the image she'd imagined of cool Karen, off in Costa Rica, and she said, "It wasn't what I saw in that video you posted . . . You really do suck!"

"And?"

"It makes me happy to know you really do suck at it!"

As Rinaldi points out, cool (and the self-protective attitude it often dis-guises) can be an enemy—of trying new things, of the joy you can find in learning, of the resilience that comes from not caring how good you look doing something you never mastered, and maybe have no hope of mastering, ever. There's a reward in trying new things. It loosens the hold of perfectionism and makes room for the beginner's aptitude for play and awe. Maybe someday you even do reach a point where you feel skillful, but the benefits are far more wide-ranging than that. By taking up something new, you've loosened the hold of the things you were overreliant on before. And thanks to that one little bit of daylight, you're far less vulnerable to collapse if circumstances in life rob you of something in yourself you'd always counted on.

Unique Pairings

There's another reason to diversify that goes beyond these internal rewards. When our confidence comes from multiple sources, it offers the wonderful bonus of making us more attractive in the eyes of others. This leads to what I call unique pairings, two or more characteristics in a person that are attractive qualities on their own, but in combination create something much more potent. Why? Because they're unexpected. They make us realize, almost immediately, that we don't have this person figured out, that they're an enigma, unpredictable. They make us think not just "What else don't I know about this person?" but also "Where in the world could I ever meet someone like this again?" One trait grabs your attention; the second one makes them irresistible.

As Rinaldi (publisher/surfer) proved, you don't necessarily have to be good at both of your pairings. But you do have to be passionate about them. The two distinct poles create a kind of energetic field where anything seems possible. It's easy to find examples among people who are already famous for one thing, like the actor Seth Rogen and his obsession with the pottery he makes. And ex-President George W. Bush may have retroactively won a few votes when he started devoting himself to painting sensitive portraits of veterans and immigrants.

I have a friend, Jesse Itzler, who's a successful entrepreneur with a passion for feats of endurance. One of them he does in his own backyard, an impossibly steep hill that he invites people to climb one hundred times in succession. He calls it "Hell on the Hill," and I can verify that it's the kind of devious challenge that only someone who's completed an Ultraman (6.2-mile swim, 261.4-mile bike ride, 52.4-mile run) could come up with. One year he invited me to try it (it was the hardest physical challenge of my life), and when I got the invite the next year, I asked if my fiancée, Audrey, could come along too.

Bring her! She'll love it! Itzler texted back. It was the year we got engaged, so maybe part of me thought it was worth finding out how she'd respond to the hill before I seriously went through with this. (Don't tell her I said that.)

She'd seen videos of me finishing dead last the year before, supported by two friends who helped me up the final climb, and I think she'd decided that it had just been a bad day for me, and it probably wasn't all that hard. I kept telling her, "No, it was truly horrific," and despite my protestations that she not skip training for it, she casually missed multiple sessions with me, convinced it was all just a ploy for me to have company during those lonely hours at the gym.

When we got to Jesse's house in Connecticut at the end of summer, there was a buffet table of bananas and the kind of energy gels and electrolyte concoctions that are usually zipped up in the pockets of people climbing El Capitan. Once the Hell started, and the first twenty or so hills went by, Audrey was still being Audrey, grabbing us both waters and a slice of orange at the start of every climb. But by the fortieth climb, around hour two, it was clear to her that not only was this as intense as I'd said, but we now needed to go even harder in the second half to have any hope of finishing. By seventy climbs in, at the three-hour mark, Audrey's thoughtful water ritual was gone. By eighty, I could see the quiet anger, and she was mute. Music was blasting, people were yelling affirmations to each other, but Audrey was neither making eye contact nor saying a word.

This was unprecedented in my experience. Audrey is the most effortlessly thoughtful person I know, kind and compassionate. She not only notices what other people are feeling, she works out what she can do to make them feel better. But at this point she was directing all those resources toward herself. Up at the top of the hill, Jesse yelled, "We didn't come this far to only come this far!" which I vaguely recognized at the time was a pretty good mantra for life. Then seeing us falter, he put down his megaphone and said,

"Yo, Huss, Audrey, let me give you a tip. Each time you finish a lap"—he pointed to a barrel of ice water—"put your hands and arms in there for ten seconds then dunk your head in. Trust me." We took his word and followed his advice and it seemed to work well enough to get us through the next climb, so we repeated the procedure on every climb from then on. (After we finished, he would reveal that this "ice dunk trick" was something he completely made up on the spot.)

Four hours had passed, and my extra training that year was paying off. I was feeling better than the year before, so much so that at the end of the ninety-ninth lap, I turned to Audrey and said, "Hey, Babe, why don't we run the last lap and have fun with it?" Audrey did not miss a beat, responding with an unmistakably non-negotiable "No," between steady and heaving breaths.

We both finished. Audrey rang the bell at the finish line, more to signify the end of the torture than to celebrate any great victory. Someone hung a "Finisher" medal around her neck, and she collapsed on the grass in tears. Every few seconds, out of embarrassment, she'd say, "I don't know why I'm crying." But I did. It was exactly what had happened to me the year before.

I knew before the climb that I loved Audrey, and I think my attraction to her was pretty clear from the first time I said "Hi." But I'd never been so in awe of her. Back when we were training, she'd often been the one arguing to stay in and order pizza instead of hitting the gym. Then on the hillside, the warrior emerged. I knew from seeing that determination up close that this was the kind of teammate I needed in hard times. I knew she was tough, but she had a gear I'd never suspected, and I knew that I would be a fool to ever doubt her. Unique pairing.

This is what unique pairings do. You see two parts of a person you never expected to find together in this same person. But you also sense a whole third thing too, everything between those two sides of the person that you don't see, the entire valley under the clouds that you still have to explore.

14

SURVIVING
A BREAKUP

There are two types of breakups: the ones that happen to us and the ones we make happen. These two experiences can seem so distinct that it's hard to imagine any advice or life strategy that would apply in both situations. But the aftermaths in both situations are not as different as you think. Both leave a void in our lives that, like any vacuum, presents a real danger. Both can leave us with lingering regrets, even a profound sense of shame. Both take time to recover from. (And this is true even if we jump right into our next relationship.)

"Forward ever, backward never" is a pretty good breakup mantra for both of them. This is especially true when we've just emerged from a toxic or abusive situation. But it's also true when someone broke up with us: We can't romanticize the love we only thought we were getting from a partner who was never really there for us. No matter how the breakup started, there are practical things we can do to move forward—to keep ourselves from getting stuck in place, or worse, running back to the troubled relationship we just left. Every breakup can feel painfully individual—it happened to you and no one else—but there are steps we can take that can help lead us back to life. The six strategies that follow are presented in no particular order, because heartbreak is like that: You can go weeks or months feeling fine, and then some tsunami of emotion rolls in and suddenly you feel like you're back at day one. So, use them liberally, and repeat as necessary.

Connect with a
Newfound Sense of Peace

In your current circumstances, this may sound like telling you to make a surfboard out of spaghetti, but every day I coach people whose lives have been improved by their breakup. Yes, the person we relied on is gone, and the emotional toll of that absence may be devastating. It feels next to impossible not to think about them, expecting them to appear around the next street corner, just as they were when things were good. But while we're obsessing over bygones, we often fail to notice all the ways our life has objectively improved now that we're on our own.

You can see the improvement in two distinct ways. The first one might be hard to spot because of all the negative emotions that come with any breakup—but don't let that blind you to all the negative emotions you have just been liberated from. Recognizing that unburdening can help you now. Remember all the situations when something they did (or didn't do) made you sad, anxious, or angry, or robbed you of your joy. Maybe your ex behaved badly at dinners with your family, perhaps they never took an interest in the things that mattered to you, maybe they diminished the work you do, maybe they kept you constantly on edge. Maybe they made you late for every trip you ever took together, so at the start of every supposedly relaxing getaway, you had to board the plane stressed-out, out of breath, and embarrassed, looking away from row after row of angry passengers.

Courtney was part of my Love Life Club, an online group made up of people all over the world we coach on an ongoing basis. She'd just been through a rough breakup, having discovered that not only had her husband been cheating on her for years, but he'd also landed their family in serious debt. It was a double disaster: She and her two children had to start a new life on their own, and she had to find some way to dig them out of financial peril.

But despite the family's sudden disarray, and the very real threat to their lifelong security, when she got on our coaching calls, she could only fixate on her heartbreak. In this situation, I have one mission: to reorient her focus away from the pain of losing him, and onto the newfound peace she had access to now that he was no longer around. I wanted her to see the contrast. There were no more days she spent sick with anxiety over something he wasn't telling her, no nights waiting at home while he was out with another woman. There were no more weeks she had to spend feeling completely invisible to the man who shared her home, while he evaded both her and the reality of the debt that was mounting around them. When I pointed these things out, she said: "Yes, Matthew, but in spite of all that, back then I still had someone there with me. It's so hard now to be away from him."

Then we looked closer at how often he actually was there, and the truth came out. All the weeknights he worked late or didn't come home at all because it was "easier to get a hotel," all the weekends he shut himself in his office with his laptop. She'd felt terrified of living without him but had failed to notice how long she'd been doing just that. When we did the math, there was scarcely any measurable difference between the old days and the way she lived now. She'd been surviving on her own for a long time; the thing she was afraid of doing was something she'd already learned to do. In ways she hadn't connected with yet, her life had gotten easier.

That's the second way life improves after a breakup: Your life gains value in positive ways. Now instead of idling at home all weekend like a white-collar criminal with an ankle bracelet, she was off spending time with friends. Instead of telling people she couldn't see them because she didn't want to leave him "by himself," she was now deepening long-neglected relationships, spending entire weekends with family or friends. Her heartbreak lessened as soon as she stopped fixating on the fantasy of what she had lost. She began to realize she was losing far less than she believed and gaining far more than she credited. She was free now to say yes to things that enriched her life, and that led to more connection and more adventures. She was rediscovering herself.

I know what you're saying: "Matthew, maybe this works when your ex was a pilfering narcissist and abusive cheat, but my ex was wonderful in every way except for wanting to be with me anymore. How am I supposed to get over that?"

There are instances where somebody we are happy with breaks up with us seemingly out of the blue. Breakups like this feel devastating both to our self-esteem, and to our ability to trust our judgment in future relationships. But when someone who has pretended to be perfectly happy suddenly pulls the rug out from under you, it can be useful to look for the red flags along the way that showed their character wasn't everything you'd allowed yourself to believe. Retroactively uncovering red flags—ways they lied, acted unexplainably, or negative things other people said about them you chose to ignore at the time—can prove invaluable in taking your feelings for them off a pedestal, instead of allowing them to be preserved in a peak state of love. Peace can come from realizing you didn't lose the person you thought you'd lost.

But maybe you can't find any such red flags from your time with your ex. Maybe they were just awesome, you were happy, and then they broke up with you. Even if the above is all true, never forget the fundamental, deeper truth: the love of your life can only ever be the person who chooses you for their life. It can never be the person who doesn't choose you. So no matter how happy you were for a time, it wasn't your dream relationship because, by definition, your dream relationship is one that lasts. Moving on gets easier when we realize we lost something that only simulated the real thing temporarily, but in fundamental ways, wasn't even close to the real thing.

But let's backtrack for a moment—were you really as happy as your heartbreak is telling you? Did you always feel happy in their presence (or their absence), or was your happiness marred by a constant feeling of unease? Someone doesn't need to be a bad person for you to feel bad when you're with them. One reason we feel that way is that we sense that the love and investment in the relationship isn't equal, something that happens when our partner begins to have doubts about us. Even if they have said nothing and continue to fulfill the functions of a partner (up to and including having meaningful sex), it's rare for our intuition not to pick up on the fact that they have, in some way we can't quite place, checked out of the relationship (or were just never in it with the same level of commitment that we were).

Except for complete sociopaths, people don't break up with someone on a whim, on the same day they tell you it's over. It's an internal process that can last weeks, months, or years, until the day they finally decide to let us in on their decision, at the time of their choosing. That disjunction—between what they've been thinking in private and how they've been acting whenever we're around—is one of the principal reasons the breakup can feel like such a betrayal. They've been hiding their inner world, letting us believe we're in one kind of relationship (the one we fill with such commitment and intensity) while they're in an entirely different one (the one they have filled with doubt and dissimulation).

Realizing that we've been living in a fantasy relationship with a person who was never all there can be humiliating. The emotional weight of all the landmark occasions of the past months and years disappears in an instant. The rich life you thought you were leading turns out to have been a hologram. This also explains why they can move on so quickly: Maybe we just got the news today, but they've been living with it (perhaps even looking elsewhere) for months before they said a word.

Our intuition can sense that something's off long before we put all the facts in order. And the longer we live with this disparity, where our feelings don't jibe with the events of our daily life, the more we internalize our anxiety, telling ourselves *we're* doing something wrong, *we're* the crazy one, and shaming ourselves for our unexplainable anxiety. This quickly turns into its own gaslit hell, where we feel increasingly unsafe with the one person everyone else considers our perfect match.

In a typical breakup, there's an instinct to demonize, to catalog all their secret misdeeds and betrayals, as if that could make it easier to move on. It's healthier and easier to focus instead on how they made us feel. And I don't mean how we felt about them—all the ways we admired or loved them. I'm talking about how we felt day-to-day in their company, when nothing else was being said: Did we ever feel secure, happy, loved? Were we loved enough? Or could we never quite shake the feeling that something was missing, that our happiness was a shaky stage set that we filled with pretending?

The wrong person for you isn't limited to someone who's "toxic." It's also someone with whom you cannot achieve peace. And you will never achieve peace with someone who doesn't choose you.

When we lose someone like that, we may suffer at first, thinking we've lost the one thing we wanted more than anything. But if we allow ourselves, we can actually connect with a newfound sense of peace. Now we're free from constant anxiety, free from feeling like we weren't enough, free from trying to hold on to something that wasn't meant to be. Whatever you were experiencing in the relationship, it wasn't happiness, which only grows richer the more you put into it, like an organic garden. And even though you may not have found love again yet, you'll see that your new sense of peace feels solid and substantial, not imaginary at all. When you do find the right kind of love, it'll feel like a continuation of that peace, not a departure from it.

Realize You Will Need to Repeat the Story, a Lot, and That's OK

No single conversation with someone, no matter how good, is going to permanently solve our pain. It may shift the heartbreak a couple of degrees, and those degrees certainly matter. That's just the slice of daylight that can mean the difference between getting out of bed and staying there all day. But within hours of any one conversation, the hurt tries to reassert itself. Hearing the right things, navigating around the pain, is something that needs to happen many times a day. It takes massive amounts of repetition, especially in the early stages when we are slowly trying to write a different, more positive story about what this all means. Make lots of plans with friends you can be yourself around. And tell them the truth about what's happened. Sometimes when we don't want something to be real—especially at the end of a marriage that has become the keystone of our identity—we abstain from telling the people who love us the most. But letting them in on what's happened is not only a vital step for acceptance; it also gives our friends the gift of being able to show up for us.

It's worth noting that many months or even years after a breakup, there may be ways we are still silently hurting. If we feel that we have passed some invisible boundary where it's no longer socially acceptable to talk about our breakup anymore, we run the risk of experiencing a second wave of isolation. Therapists and coaches can be useful to have around at this stage, if for no other reason than paying for someone's time can give us license to repeat ourselves a hundred times without being self-conscious, or worrying about who among our closest friends and loved ones has had enough of hearing it.

Remove What Reminds You of Them
(So Long as It Doesn't Affect
Your Quality of Life)

This is simple but important: Remove the things that remind you of them. We must draw a line between processing the breakup and ruminating over the breakup. Processing is proactive and helps us move on. Ruminating is reactive and quickly becomes compulsive. Processing can be done with a therapist, a coach, a healing conversation with a friend, or just by taking some time to connect with the sadness and disappointment of it all when you're alone. It's like a workout—you go to the gym to get the health results you want, but you don't want to be in there all day. Go do the work, then get on with the rest of life for the next twenty-three hours.

But what about rumination? These are the hours we lose when we're blind-sided by a stray memory. We're especially vulnerable to this if we fail to take control of our mind and the things that trigger it. After a breakup, we have to be as unsentimental as a triage doctor cleaning a wound, eliminating every particle that could trigger a potential reinfection. Trash anything that makes us think of our ex, wherever they pop up, on our desk (that framed sunset over Tahiti), in our bedroom (the booklight they never turned off), the top shelf of our fridge (the moldy rhubarb jam), our phone (why track the weather in Tahiti anymore?) Change their name in your phone so that you don't experience that Pavlovian pang every time your phone lights up with it. (I once had a client change a person's name in her phone to "Done," knowing that instead of evoking painful hope it would create an immediate sense of finality and empowerment.) Clean the medicine cabinet and under the passenger seat of your car. Edit the everything drawer in the kitchen, the top shelf in the hall closet, the bin of broken electronics. If there's anything left to remind us of our ex, we are sleeping on the job.

We have to be systematic if we want to move on. After doing a full sweep of your house, bagging up the snapshots, sweatshirts, and novelty socks that remind you of them, get it off the premises. If it's possible, get away from where you live for a few days. Stay at a friend's, take a hike, visit a town or a local landmark you always wanted to go to. At the very least, go to parts of your city—restaurants, bars, coffee shops—that you don't associate with them. Think of it as an excuse to try new places and get to know parts of your city you've never been to before.

Simultaneously, do a full social media purge. It goes without saying that you should stop visiting their profile, even when you think you're starting to feel better—you do not need to know what they are up to and it can only serve to take you backward. But go a step further than making a rule not to seek them out. Make sure the algorithm doesn't bring them to you. Unfollow or mute your ex so they no longer come up on your feed, and do the same for friends of theirs, even mutual friends: anyone who could post something that reactivates the pain of the breakup. Remember, the game here isn't worrying about precisely whom you might offend; it's self-preservation. You can always call mutual friends and say to them: "Hey, just so you know, I muted you on social media, not because you've done anything wrong or I don't want to be close, but because seeing pictures and stories of my ex really hurts and sets me back." When you do see them in person to catch up, feel free to say: "It would really help me if we don't talk about my ex. I don't need to hear any news or updates about them. I'd love for us to talk about absolutely anything else. It would really help me to move on."

But some long-term relationships become so interwoven with every facet of our day-to-day life—our social circle, our living space, our geography— that to remove every association with them would be tantamount to self-banishment. So what do we do when the reminders of them are everywhere? We can't simply cede every part of our world to our ex (especially the parts that originally belonged to us). You lived in Chicago together? Chicago is their territory now. You obsessed over finding great sushi together? Sushi is theirs now. You used to adore listening to classic rock together? Sorry, now they own rock.

This is why I added the caveat in the title of this section: Remove what reminds you of your ex, as long as it doesn't affect your quality of life. If you lived in a city together for ten years, a lot of that city is going to remind you of them. Do you really want to give up your favorite city? If removing all reminders of them ends up shrinking your life in unacceptable ways, there is a different strategy you can pursue. This is where your inner Navy SEAL has to do the job of retaking the territory you want to keep, not just scanning for and eliminating the things you don't. How can we do this when these things have become inextricably and emotionally linked with our ex?

Change the Meaning of the Things You Don't Want to Lose

One of the reasons that breakups are so oppressive is that they short-circuit the reasonable part of your brain and attack the emotions, which can be overwhelming and hard to change. There are so many things we once shared with our ex that can plunge us into a state of emotional turmoil without warning. You spot a pair of colorful sneakers, you smell paella, you hear a snippet of the theme song of a show you used to watch together, and you are immediately face-to-face with all the powerful specific feelings of the intimacy you no longer have access to.

Smells are particularly strong emotional triggers, since the synaptic circuitry that transmits the initial stimuli—the smell of onions and olive oil, or cocoa butter, or low tide—to the brain's limbic system, including the amygdala and the hippocampus, the regions related to emotion and memory, is the most direct pathway for any of the senses, just one or two cellular links from start to finish. I was once asked to run a coaching session for all the employees on the beauty floor from Harrods and Selfridges, two famous London department stores. One person had the job of spraying cologne for people who came to the counter. She always felt cheerful about this part of her duties, until one woman who walked into that scent began crying, instantly, because it was her late husband's favorite fragrance.

Knowing how powerful emotions can be, I try to get people to consciously construct triggers to engage the positive emotions. I call them emotional buttons—a stimulus we can use reliably to summon the emotion we want. When I'm getting ready to get up onstage to speak to people, sometimes for hours at a stretch, and I want to summon the passion and enthusiasm people can respond to, I revisit some of my emotional buttons: It might be a few minutes of Steve Irwin, Crocodile Hunter—there's this one clip of him perched behind a log having watched an army of crocodiles devour a hippo carcass saying: "Unbelievable! This has been the most fun I've ever had in my entire life." I watch it and two minutes later I feel reconnected to the passion I want to embody in my own work; it's like downing a passion shot right before I meet the audience. I spend a lot of time at my retreats explaining how emotional buttons work, because I want people to be able to have a practical way of consciously programming the emotions they want to feel on a consistent basis.

Heartbreak, however, can tear down all our carefully constructed defenses, precisely because it creates so many negative emotional buttons—stimuli that reliably summon emotions we *don't* want. Negative emotional buttons can seem almost comical, if they weren't so pernicious. One woman I coached couldn't pass a Victoria's Secret in a mall without getting furious, because she stumbled on some lingerie in her husband's closet and none of it was anywhere near her size. Another woman suddenly hated an entire country ("Fuck France!") just because her ex had a French accent. That's a poignant example of the exaggerated importance an ex takes on in a breakup: One bad apple can spoil 67.7 million others.

Guy Winch,* a psychologist and advocate of emotional first aid, suggests that people should cleanse favorite people and places of unwanted associations with their ex and reclaim them by visiting them under different circumstances that create new associations. This is one way to reverse a negative emotional button. For example, you don't have to avoid your favorite restaurants—return to them, multiple times, perhaps with friends who make you belly laugh until the fresh experiences rewrite your feelings about the old haunts. He had one rule: You're not allowed to talk about your ex while you're there.

Another way to disentangle our ex from any association with something important to us is to reconnect with a sense of scale. A client at my retreat had just had her heart broken at the unexpected end of her relationship with a well-known writer. She'd loved reading before she met him, and books were one of her positive emotional buttons—that is, books held positive associations that immediately put her in a good mood and positive frame of mind. And all those positive associations—the smell of libraries, browsing for new books in her favorite bookstore, the exquisite feeling a great book could

---

* Guy Winch, *How to Fix a Broken Heart* (Simon & Schuster, 2018).

summon, allowing her to disappear into a world she'd never have gained access to otherwise—connected her and her ex from the beginning. But the worst heartbreak of her life had reversed that polarity and books had suddenly taken on a painful association. One of her favorite things in the world had become a negative emotional button. Bookstores made her think of their hushed conversations in the fiction section. It was hard for her to go to libraries now, where she often had to confront his books on display tables of recommended reading. She'd see a new book she'd heard great things about only to find his name listed among the blurbs on the back of the book jacket. Suddenly books had gone the way of their other habits, their Sunday reading tradition, their routine of reading in bed holding hands.

But books didn't belong to him. Her lifelong love of books started long before their relationship. How many people—who are nothing like her ex and have nothing to do with him—have their own relationship with books too? By how many years have books predated him? To books, he was simply another person in a long line of people who liked something that was much bigger than he was and lied about how much he reads. By connecting with this sense of scale, she was able to start reclaiming books as a positive emotional button once again.

Defiance can be a useful thing here. There are activities that no one can take away from you, and you have to make that declaration: *They do not get my passions in the breakup*, they do not get my love for old movies, trees, or morning hikes . . . they do not get pizza!

While we are putting things in their proper scale, it's worth reminding ourselves how much bigger the world is than our ex. In the immediate aftermath of a breakup, it can feel as if our ex and the world are the same thing. But while your ex may feel like the entire world to you right now, there are roughly 8 billion people who aren't even aware of their existence. I remember hearing someone I care deeply about repeating the story of her divorce for about the fiftieth time. It had been bad: Her ex-husband was having an affair, and when confronted with that fact, he abruptly ended the marriage and moved in with his new lover without even a pretense of kindness or regret. Naturally, she told this to anyone who would listen. At first it was necessary, but lately it had threatened to become her only topic of conversation. Apart from the social liability, it had the effect of disempowering her. Every time she repeated it, he seemed to loom larger in her life, not smaller.

One day I said, "You do realize no one living in Paris right now even knows who your ex is? In fact, all of Europe is getting on fine without him. Your ex was one drop off a single wave in the entire ocean. He's even just a drop in your own private ocean, if you can lift up your head for a minute, because your future holds many new stories in it, more than you could ever possibly experience. But you can't get to any of them until you let go of this one."

One of the ways to deal with a negative emotional button is to change the meaning of it. Let's say there's a certain street that reminds you of a special moment you had with your ex, and now every time you have to walk down that street, you get a sick feeling in your stomach. Let's take something beautiful in your life that you can learn to newly associate with that street. Perhaps since your breakup, one of the things you've become most grateful for is the deep bonds you've formed with people you lost touch with in the haze of that relationship. Maybe you feel like these friendships saved you, and your heart swells whenever you think of them and the profound meaning they bring into your life. Now it's time to make the connection. Each time you walk down that street, call one of these friends, or send them a text, either having a beautiful conversation with them or simply expressing this gratitude. Do it over and over again every time you walk that street, until that street becomes a beautiful symbol of the love and friendship in your life . . . love and friendship that you only found or deepened as a result of this breakup. This is another example of how to take what has become a negative emotional button and turn it into a positive emotional button that reminds you of how grateful you are for the breakup.

The Notes app on my phone is filled with files of emotional buttons that I use daily. I take this seriously. If I suspect something has become a negative emotional button for me, I set about finding ways to turn it into a positive emotional button. One of the ways I do this is by writing down the thought that is triggering negative emotions, and writing down a new empowering truth that changes its meaning. For this process to work, I have to genuinely believe in the validity of the new truth that is taking its place. It has to actually really make me feel something, or else I'm just superficially attempting to mask my pain with hollow positive talk. Whenever I alight on a truth that works, whether it

184 | LOVE LIFE

be because of a seemingly random thought that suddenly made me feel better, something I heard, or someone said to me, I write it down.

A few years ago, I found myself in one of the most difficult chapters of my life. I was going through multiple losses all at the same time, any one of which had the potential to knock me on my ass on its own, but instead all landed together like a tsunami in my life. My life at the time seemed to be a cockpit where every button around me was negative. But they all triggered some version of the same thought:

I wish this hadn't happened to me. I can't take how hard this is . . .

Around that time, I called my boxing trainer, Martin Snow, and expressed this sentiment to him. He didn't miss a beat. In his perfect, gravelly voice, thick with Brooklyn from another era, he said:

"It has to be this hard. If it wasn't, there would be nothing heroic about getting through it. You have to go through this or you won't be able to show other people how to get back on their feet later on when they need it. People are going to need the version of you who gets through this. Keep going, kid, we got fucking work to do."

I felt my chest rising as Martin was speaking. Something in it had landed. And it had landed as something I immediately internalized as a sturdy logic I could fall back on. So much positive talk in hard times goes right over our heads. Something about it just doesn't connect with us where we are. But what Martin said had. Because no matter how hard things got, they only reinforced in my mind what he said to me that day . . . *the harder this gets, the deeper I'll have to dig to get through it, and the deeper I dig, the more I'll have to give at the end of it.* This became an instant positive emotional button for transmuting my pain around that time. I suddenly saw the pain as a necessary part of me becoming who I needed to be in order to become more helpful to other people, or to a future version of myself who was encountering some new challenge. Martin was right, as it turned out. Without the various pains of my life, I couldn't have written this book; the depths I've gone to here wouldn't have been possible without them. Without that pain, there is no true *Love Life*.

A quick note: Your emotional buttons don't have to mean anything to a single other person on this planet. Often they won't. They'll be too weird, specific, or embarrassing to even want to share them. I read that emotional button to my wife and she said to me: "That wouldn't work on me; I don't care about being heroic" (that made me laugh as I wrote it). We're so different. But that's the point! These things are intensely personal. That's why *you* have to pay attention in your life—you never know when you'll think or hear a truth that has the potential to be your new prized possession as a positive emotional button. At my lowest, emotional buttons have saved me. If our house was burning down, it would be all the devices that contained my emotional buttons that I'd run out the door with. And my wife. Obviously. It would be the heroic thing to do.

Most of my buttons live on my phone and my laptop, because when they are always at my fingertips, I don't have to wait to feel better, whether it's through perspective, gratitude, excitement, or calm. They are the operating manual for my emotions, a way of taking control of my thoughts and my emotions in real time, so they're no good to me if they are buried in a notebook somewhere.

So how might we use emotional buttons for heartbreak? Like I said, I can't write your emotional buttons for you, because they probably wouldn't mean anything to you. But here are some examples of how you might turn a negative button into a positive one during that time. First you'll see the negative button, and then the truth I have offered as an example to transform it into a new positive emotional button for the breakup.

NEGATIVE EMOTIONAL BUTTON: I feel worthless. If I was good enough, they wouldn't have messaged that other person.

POSITIVE EMOTIONAL BUTTON: People do damaging things all the time that have nothing to do with their partner's true value. If I'm worthless, then so is every other incredible human being who has ever been cheated on. Their lack of integrity is not a reflection of my worth. It's a reflection of their standards.

NEGATIVE EMOTIONAL BUTTON: I've lost more than I can bear to lose . . .

POSITIVE EMOTIONAL BUTTON: My world has gotten bigger as a result of this breakup, not smaller. I have connected with friends and family in a way that I never had before. I have experienced exquisite love and kindness from those who have stayed close in this painful time. I've learned who is really there for me, which has been a valuable reminder of the important people I was neglecting, and a signal for who to invest more of my time, energy, and love into. I have developed a new appreciation for nature, for stillness, for the fundamentals of life. I did not see the gifts that were all around me until I was forced to by this loss. It has turned me on to the abundance I have in my life that is priceless. This breakup is allowing me to build up my world in ways that no one can take away.

NEGATIVE EMOTIONAL BUTTON: They made me so happy and now that's gone.

POSITIVE EMOTIONAL BUTTON: They didn't make me as happy as I keep telling myself. Think of all the times I didn't feel seen, or like I was a priority. How often I felt anxious. Never forget that a huge part of why that relationship worked for as long as it did was my ability to overlook all the ways this person didn't meet my needs.

NEGATIVE EMOTIONAL BUTTON: I have lost the person who is right for me.

POSITIVE EMOTIONAL BUTTON: No one can be right for me who doesn't choose me. Period. The love of my life is the person who chooses me for their life.

NEGATIVE EMOTIONAL BUTTON: I'll never feel this way about someone again.

POSITIVE EMOTIONAL BUTTON: I have had this exact same thought about other things or people in the past, and yet I have gotten over them, and moved on to something better. Just like with those things, one day I will look back at this and feel warmth for myself at how silly it was that once upon a time I thought this was the end of the world.

These are just examples. Start a file of your own personal emotional buttons on your phone or computer today. Like me, and the thousands of people I've personally taught this strategy to, it'll not only help you survive whatever terrible things come your way, but beyond that, it might even turn those terrible setbacks into occurrences that, miraculously, you become grateful for.

Do Things You Wouldn't or Couldn't Do While You Were in That Relationship

No matter how close you were with your ex, or how long you were together, there was likely a list of things you used to do before the two of you met that you could never do while you were with them. There was also probably another list of things you always wanted to do and stopped yourself from taking on as long as you stayed together (not to mention things you forced yourself to be into when you weren't: what a relief to get back to yourself!) Perhaps it was something small, like wearing a specific fragrance. (They couldn't stand Tobacco Vanille? Spray away!) Maybe it was a minor pleasure they could never share. (They hated musicals? You can now hit every show on Broadway.) Perhaps it was some hobby you didn't have the time to try out while you were spending so much time with them. (Go sign up for that painting class.) Maybe you just knew they wouldn't be comfortable with you taking a pole-dancing class with your best friend. Or maybe you never felt right just sitting alone for hours on end reading with a cup of tea. Whether these prohibitions were explicit or the kind of thing you denied yourself on your own, there is nothing to hold you back now. Make progress on a project that has deep meaning to you. The wrong relationships make our lives smaller, contract our personalities, and stifle our growth. At this instant in your life, the whole world is in front of you.

It can seem cruel to tell someone in pain to look on the bright side, to think of a sunnier tomorrow. This is not that. This is about starting a project, whether it begins as a small, private, supportive gesture on behalf of your future self or a ridiculously ambitious commitment that will require rearranging your life. You know how, when you're in a new relationship, you feel a burst of excitement the first time the person you're with uses the future tense? This is that moment for your relationship with yourself. Celebrate the landmarks of that relationship as these positive gestures of the faith you have in yourself become a familiar part of your daily life—welcome reminders of the distance you've traveled, the sadness you once felt, and all the beautiful things you've made out of it since.

Resist the Rebound If You Can

None of us would wish heartbreak on someone we care about. It's a terrible pain. And yet, I wouldn't want to deny anyone I love the experience either, as I happen to believe it to be one of the most valuable experiences we can go through. For us to extract this value, we have to deeply feel it, which is why rebound relationships are often worth avoiding. They rob us of the ability to be present with our emotions, to rediscover ourselves, and to see how strong we can be, perhaps even learning to enjoy our own company more than we ever realized, which is one of life's most beautiful and underrated experiences. If nothing else, there is a superpower that comes when you know from experience that you can get through a weekend and be OK.

Shockingly, since it's so painful when we are in it, we may even look back on a breakup after the heartache has subsided and come to realize there is something we long for about that period. I was checking up on a friend about a year or so after his breakup to see how he was doing, and he said, "You know, I actually miss the feeling I had six months ago. I was so motivated and driven to do new things. And that energy has subsided now." He did look healthier in his current state, but he said there was a real value to the fuel he felt he had right after his breakup.

Until I had my own worst breakup, I always immediately rebounded. But the time I really got my heart broken, I was almost repulsed by the possibility. I couldn't bear to hurt someone the way I'd just been hurt. But it was more than that. It was a visceral feeling, a side effect of my heartbroken status, that I was weirdly proud of. In small ways, the wholesome things I caught myself doing, both for myself and for other people, made me feel better and improved my outlook. I felt connected to how truly shitty a person can feel sometimes, and it made me compassionate. I liked that feeling, that tender, wounded quality that made me more aware and open to the world. It was like the ache I was feeling wasn't mine alone, and I would meet people who could share that feeling with me. I didn't want to muddy that perception of the world by immediately jumping into something new.

A Final Word on Heartbreak

At the end of the day, remember, this is your life we are talking about, not your ex's. Breakups only remain devastating if you continue to make them the star of the movie you're watching about your own life. It's normal to make our ex too important. We either glorify them and turn them into an angel in our mind, or because of the pain they've caused us, we hate them and turn them into a demon. Either way, they are being given way too much power.

We are conditioned from an early age to cast someone in the role of "love of our life." It's like our brain is looking for a target to project a lifetime of ideas about love onto. Often when we find someone who represents even 50 percent of what we've been looking for, our hopes and imagination do the work of creating the other 50 percent through this projection. Then we mourn the loss of this person we've told ourselves was perfect for us, not realizing that our mind would have simply found a different target had we not encountered that person in our lives. Far from being a cynical thought, it's an optimistic one . . . it means you can, and will, feel this way again, so long as you are willing to part ways with the previously fixed story you'd been telling yourself about what the old person represented. So let's take them off the pedestal and start putting them in their proper place—a mortal in our past, not a supernatural or haunting presence to take with us into our future.

In truth, the moment the breakup happened, their life, their choices, their successes, the romance or love they find, are utterly irrelevant to you. Now that you're no longer with them, who they are dating, or what they are up to, is no more important than who a random barista is dating in a coffee shop you don't even go to. They are just another person living their life. You're the hero of this story, and there's no better time to be heroic than when things are at their worst. We love the character Rocky Balboa not because he was a winner, but because he was a fighter. So fight. FIGHT.

15

CORE CONFIDENCE

Early in my career, I noticed that people have all sorts of definitions for confidence—one moment it's a look, sometimes it's a way of acting, other times it seems to be a feeling we carry inside. But if we can't quite pinpoint what confidence is, how can we go about achieving it? Without first agreeing on the target, there's no way to create the road map.

Often when we talk about confidence, we're referring to something remarkable, even inspiring, in the way someone walks, talks, looks, or acts. I call this the *surface layer of confidence*, and much of it grows out of the physical cues that signal an inner confidence: the ease in your posture, the grace in your movement, the dynamics of your voice. Paying attention to these cues has helped me come across powerfully onstage, on camera, in a room. I got my first lessons in this from reading *How to Win Friends and Influence People* at eleven years old. I even went on to teach the finer points in a program called Impact, which focuses on these physical cues that determine how we are perceived. Even though I'm calling it surface-layer confidence, it's not superficial. Warren Buffett says the most valuable thing he ever did for his future success was taking a public speaking program when he was twenty-one.

Still, there are limits to the effect that focusing on these changes can have. If our physical confidence is not underpinned by something deeper, it will crumble at the first sign of resistance from another strong presence, or just from the impersonal forces of life. Taking the next step requires a deeper level of confidence, what I called *identity confidence* in the previous chapter. Identity confidence gives a foundation to the confidence we project on the surface level. We strengthen that layer through intentional experience, by putting more time and energy into the existing squares of our identity matrix, or by diversifying our matrix by investing in new squares altogether. According to the *Oxford English Dictionary*, the hallmark of this style of confidence is:

> The feeling of self-assurance arising from an appreciation of one's own abilities or qualities.

But here too, there's a built-in fragility: Our physique breaks down, the stock market tanks, our partner leaves, our abilities come into question. Relying too much on our identity matrix for confidence leaves us vulnerable to shifts of fortune. If our confidence is dependent on everything going well, we'll inevitably find ourselves in a fragile position somewhere along the line. This doesn't mean we're faking it; there's an art to living contentedly within our area of competence. But, inevitably, circumstances change.

None of us knows how secure we really are until the things we rely on for our sense of certainty are taken away. No one is above being temporarily rocked when big changes occur. But whether these setbacks or losses prove catastrophic to our confidence or merely require a recentering comes down to the work we have done at the deepest layer of confidence, which I call *core confidence*.

The folks at Oxford define two further aspects that get at the roots of confidence:

> *The state of feeling certain about the truth of something.*

> *The feeling or belief that one can rely on someone or something: firm trust.*

Some feelings are most sharply felt by their absence. If you've ever struggled to establish trust in a relationship with someone who repeatedly proved to be untrustworthy, you know exactly what it feels like when this level of confidence is missing. If someone has been lying to, cheating on, or disrespecting you on a regular basis, it can be hard not to internalize the emotions it brings out in you. You beat yourself up for feeling anxious and insecure, wishing you could summon more confidence in yourself. But if confidence is a feeling of certainty, your issues with confidence are justified. You're trying to locate a feeling of safety in a situation that's essentially unsafe. As long as you're relying on someone that untrustworthy, any real feelings of confidence are impossible.

That's why shifting the source of our certainty can have an immediate effect on our confidence. We stop attempting to find certainty trusting someone we know cannot be trusted, and realize instead that if anyone that close ever does betray us, we've proven ourselves to be strong enough to walk away and be OK. That simple shift moves our sense of confidence from the identity layer to the core. The identity layer says: "I'm confident (in part) because I have a relationship." The core says: "I'm confident I'll be OK even without a relationship, including the one I'm in."

The most unshakable relationship in life is the one we have with ourselves. Core confidence is about how we approach that relationship. The tweaks we make on the surface level of confidence alter how we appear to the rest of the world; changes at the core affect how we perceive ourselves. But core confidence isn't something that begins or ends with a slogan. If anyone ever asks us what our relationship with our self is like, most of us would have to admit it's complicated.

Your Relationship With Yourself

Wherever you look, there always seems to be someone ready to tell you that the secret to life is to love yourself. On social media, the advice feels less like a secret and more like an echo chamber. But if it's so obvious and ubiquitous that this is the one thing to do, what's keeping the rest of us from actually doing it? It's because, as advice goes, loving yourself turns out to be so damn hard to follow.

Falling in love, the way we do with other people, seems to take no effort. The hard part (if this book has proven anything) is learning to pump the brakes, so we don't scare someone away or rush straight into something we shouldn't. In Greek myth, Narcissus took one look at himself in a pool of water and immediately fell in love. Meanwhile, here we are, struggling just trying to like ourselves. For a lot of us, it feels intensely uncomfortable to be left in a room alone, let alone to somehow love the person you're stuck with having to be around for the rest of this life.

Advice that feels impossible makes us angry. We may smile and say, "You know, you're right," but inside we're thinking, "You imbecile, you think I haven't tried? It's bloody impossible." The instruction manual for *how* to actually achieve such a love feels like it's written on a secret scroll in a cave somewhere by an ocean we've never visited. That's what it always felt like to me. The problem with the "love yourself" shtick—much like the self-development mantra to "believe in yourself"—is that it makes us feel even more inadequate when we prove unable to do it, despite all our attempts. So when we hear others going on about loving themselves, we suspect they're lying or that something's wrong with us, or both.

Trying in Vain to Love Ourselves

When I ask live audiences "Why should we love ourselves?" I'm usually met with a few seconds of silence. People may recognize that it's something they should do, but coming up with real reasons to shout out in public is a much harder ask.

Eventually someone will say, "Because I'm a good person," or "Because I'm awesome," or "Because we deserve it." Notice that the third of these responses merely substitutes one platitude for another, begging the question, "And why do we deserve it?" Now we're back to square one, with people chiming in "Because I'm kind." Or loyal. Or generous . . . Hardworking . . . Selfless.

The problem with each of these justifications is that they suggest their inverse: If we deserve love based on our good qualities, does that mean we don't on our bad days? When we're unkind, disloyal, selfish, or lazy, are we undeserving of love? This logic—the one that makes us feel worthy of love when we're feeling virtuous—only winds up feeding our sense of alienation whenever we're out of sorts, exactly when we need the love that everyone says we're supposed to be feeling.

It's as if we only love a child when they come home from school with straight A's—a brand of conditional, goal-targeted love that leads to obsessive overachievement in later life out of a desire to *stay* worthy of love. Then there's the problem that no matter how many good qualities we have, there's always someone out there with more.

At this point, people in the audience are beginning to sense that this question is full of trapdoors, which they try to step over with vagueness. "We deserve it because we're special," they'll say, and I ask: "So are you saying we're all special?" And they say: "Absolutely!"

"But if we're *all* special then it kind of feels like no one is, doesn't it?" No matter how many people promote this idea, we know not everyone gets a gold medal—and others have ten. We've watched genetic marvels attracting all the attention. We've been eyewitnesses as people smarter than us made overachieving look easy. We've seen the parade of people inheriting millions, while others leap to the big time thanks to advantages afforded to one race or gender. We've seen people achieving more peace and joy than we can manage for ourselves. No one can convince us that opportunity, money, status, looks, or mental health are distributed evenly. No matter how special we tell ourselves we are, it seems clear that the best results come only to a few, and they're results that make a substantial difference in the quality of life.

When I joust with people in this way, I'm not trying to be intentionally difficult. I'm only mirroring the internal dialogue that prevents these aphorisms from making us feel better about ourselves.

When a child comes home from school dejected because she got picked last to play a sport she's not good at, the parent may console her by telling her she's special in other ways. "You're so intelligent!" they remind her. But the child says, "That doesn't make me good at basketball, and being bad at basketball is why I got picked last." And even that smart girl will inevitably find herself in a room full of people where her superior intelligence doesn't seem all that special, something my brother Stephen experienced when he arrived at Oxford University for his doctorate. And so we're back to square one.

In our adult lives, people we love may tell us we're special to them—that we deserve the best—but there's still a sharp child inside to whom this line still isn't making a lot of sense. On top of that, as adults we've suffered real disappointment and accumulated regrets that we are still beating ourselves up for. So when somebody says, "You're special and you deserve to find love," inside we're saying, "Yeah, right. Now give me some tips that'll help me on this dating app where I feel completely invisible."

I say all of this because I check out the moment I feel patronized by a piece of advice. These conversations are ones I had with myself for years before I had them out loud with audiences. What do we do when our looks fade, when we lose our job, when we get a C, a D, or an F in school or in life? How can we learn to love ourselves when who we are seems lacking? On what basis are we supposed to love ourselves?

What would "loving myself" even look like? A bubble bath and candles? Eating more salads? Not working so much? Or so little? And what happens when our best efforts make no difference? No matter how hard we work on our identity matrix, trying to become the most actualized, rounded version of ourselves, we still find ourselves looking in the mirror, cringing at the person who's looking back at us. Even when these efforts yield real results, and we begin to appear confident to the outside world, we still feel a growing sense of impostor syndrome—the suspicion that any minute, we're going to be found out for not being the person we have built ourselves up to be. It's a feeling that only grows the more we acquire, the more success we achieve. Now we're trapped—the deeper problem of our inadequacy is not being solved by our best efforts, but we can't let up, afraid that we'll lose the primary source of our worthiness.

Don't worry if you haven't figured out what it means to love yourself. Few have. And many claiming to are misleading you about the way to pull it off. This topic has been an obsession for me, because it's one of the biggest things I've struggled with. It may look like for fifteen years I've been helping people with their dating lives, but building this road map for myself and other people has always been my primary objective, not least because we can't have a sustainably happy love life without it.

In that time, I have learned two important things: The first is that core confidence is the answer to how to survive the profound reversals of our life. It is the answer to the deepest levels of insecurity and inadequacy that plague us our entire lives—that stop us from taking risks, that lead us to bad decisions, that rob us of our peace and happiness. The second is that people have fundamentally misunderstood the meaning of the term *self-love*. Self-love needs a rebrand.

Starting Over With Self-Love

We have tried in these pages to rebrand love, to move love from the world of feeling and plant it firmly in the territory of doing. It's the difference between *love*, the noun, and *to love*, the verb, a shift that's so important it's even right there in the title of this book. This change helps us set aside how we *feel* about someone and look instead at what they are actually doing—how much are they investing in us, and what are they doing to progress, nurture, and safeguard the relationship?

This shift is just as necessary when it comes to loving ourselves. Too often romantic love is the model for loving ourselves, and that's precisely why it's not working.

We have it backward. Loving yourself isn't the goal; it's the action. Self-love is the starting line. Core confidence is not just a one-time epiphany; it's a practice, with immediate daily application. It's actually something you can get better at.

Why doesn't the romantic-love model work for self-love? Esther Perel speaks of desire as the catalyst for love in intimate relationships. Desire comes first, which brings us close to someone, where feelings of love pull us in deeper. But as intimacy grows, desire fades. Mystery evaporates with proximity, the urge to chase subsides, and the veil (or the illusion) of perfection is lifted. That's the point where people start asking themselves if they're in the right relationship. The currents of desire are no longer taking them out to those oceanic feelings of love. Suddenly, love requires agency. The tides turn, and now the currents are pulling them toward—well, other people, who don't have the key to your apartment, and still have that air of mystery and excitement. Other people, observed at just enough distance, now seem flawless. Surely, you think, these glamorous strangers would never—well, here's where you insert a random drawback of your most recent beloved.

Looking through this lens, it's easy to see why self-love has felt impossible so far. What relationship is more ordinary than the one we have with ourselves? We've shared a bed every night of our lives. We know our every flaw. If familiarity breeds contempt, then what other emotion is there even room for? We come home to ourselves at the end of every day and take ourselves for granted. We heap abuse on ourselves, because who else will never leave?

In the world of romantic love, we start by liking someone, and then we fall in love with them. We know that process has started when two words in a text from them give us a shot of dopamine, and rolling around in bed with them floods us with oxytocin. But when we stop thinking of love in terms of hormonal waves of feeling, and start thinking of love as a verb, we can stop worrying about liking ourselves as a precondition for self-love. Loving ourselves comes first.

"Loving ourselves" is proactive here. In this rebrand, we have to start seeing the word *loving* in this phrase as interchangeable with "taking care of," "investing in," "encouraging," "nurturing," and "standing up for." *Self-love* is a verb.

The key question now is how, after a lifetime of regrets, failures, and self-contempt, can we get motivated to "love/take care of/encourage/nurture/stand up for" ourselves?

Reconceptualizing Self-Love

If we are tossing out the romantic model, we need a new one to replace it. To make it easy, let's start with one we already understand, the parent-child relationship. Remember the question that tripped up so many audiences: "Why should you love yourself?" Let's try that in the context of the parent-child relationship. Imagine asking a parent: "Why do you love your child?"

I've actually asked parents this question, and I can't remember ever getting in reply a list of qualities that make that child a great person. They rarely say, "Because she's smart, loving, funny, beautiful, and gets A's in school," as if the kid were in the running for Child of the Month. Some might. Most don't. Because that's not what their love is based on. They might say those things when I ask them why they're *proud* of their child, but not in answer to why they love them. And their love isn't really based on liking the kid either. There may well be days where their child is hard to like, but they still love them.

So what answer do they give when asked why they love their child? Usually: "Because they're my child." The tone of the response makes it clear that it's a silly question. That was a giant clue when I started looking for the roots of core confidence.

Siblings often have a similar connection. My mum is an identical twin. When I asked her why she loves her sister, she simply said, "Because she's my twin." Another clue.

These relationships, with a parent or brother or sister, don't rely on the person doing anything at all. They don't require them to be good, or to have done their best. These things may be hoped for, and they will certainly help the relationship, but ask a loving parent if on their child's worst day they still love them, and they'll scoff at the question.

This was an exhilarating realization. It felt like the essence of self-love, and I started looking for it everywhere. Listen to the way a child talks about his stuffed rabbit: "*MY* rabbit." I dare you to tell little Eddie that you have a better-looking, newer, more expensive version of Luigi, the stuffed rabbit he's been dragging around with him everywhere he goes. Luigi may be missing an eye, have dirt stains all over, and be oozing fluff from every seam, but Eddie and Luigi cannot be parted. Why? Because this isn't just a rabbit, this is *Eddie's* rabbit. It has nothing to do with what the rabbit can offer and everything to do with what Eddie has decided Luigi is to him. Luigi is Eddie's rabbit. You don't even need a child for this test. On your next outdoor walk, look out for the scraggly, crazy-looking dog with three hairs sticking out of its head and its tongue permanently hanging out to the left, and try offering the fully-grown adult holding the leash the opportunity to exchange their furry gremlin for a fluffier, more stately dog. We all instinctively know how that would go.

That's because the fundamental reason behind the love in all of these relationships is the same: "I love them because they're mine." And this realization turned loving myself, with all my flaws and shame, my regrets and self-resentment, all the fluff that's coming out of every seam, from an impossible ideal into something I knew exactly how to do.

Reclaiming Yourself

This may seem like a strange thing to say, but do we really think of ourselves as a person? Logically, we know we exist, that we are a person in the world, with a shoe size, a Social Security number, and places to be. But that's typically not the way we experience ourselves. Instead, we experience ourselves as a mind traveling around in a body we've dressed, peering out onto the rest of life and *other* people. It's *other* people we're looking at, talking with, having relationships with, taking care of, ordering coffee from, walking past in the street. But *me*? *What do you mean?*

Look at how much time we spend worrying about other people and how we treat them. Was I polite enough? Did I talk too much? Did I tip enough? I hope what I said yesterday didn't upset my sister. I need to call that friend to check in with how he is. Meanwhile, we barely consider how we treat ourselves. We may value being kind to others, but how often do we think of kindness as something we should extend to the person on our driver's license? We carefully monitor how much we ask of colleagues, then dump a completely unmanageable to-do list on ourselves. We encourage friends knowing it helps them thrive, then berate ourselves for underperforming. We shower people with gratitude for the things they've done for us, then barely acknowledge the bravery and sacrifice it's taken us to get to this point in life. Instead, whenever we have a quiet moment, we pinpoint the exact instances in our personal history where we have failed ourselves and others.

Most of us have arrived at this dehumanization unconsciously. It might be forgivable if we were horrible to everybody—at least that would be consistent. But to purport to care about people, then to systematically exclude ourselves from that same consideration? That is cruel. But like most cruelty, it takes place away from the public eye where no one's around to offer us any mercy or speak up on our behalf.

To everyone else, we quite clearly are a person. Not a single one of our friends thinks of us as some special entity deserving subhuman treatment. If we claim to love people, then we are a suitable candidate. There is no reason to apply a separate, harsher set of laws to ourselves. We are a person, a world citizen, a local fixture, a recognizable face, so how can we truly claim to care about people while we consistently pick out one single person and ignore their needs and mistreat them in specific ways we would never dream of using on anybody else?

If your compassion does not include yourself, it is incomplete.

—*Jack Kornfield*

Knowing this should nudge us toward basic decency. We can still acknowledge that we've screwed up. We've done bad things. We've hurt people.
We've let ourselves and others down in ways that are painful to admit. But
so has everybody else, and most of us don't think that should exclude them
from being treated with kindness and dignity. So end the special exemption.
Be kind—or at least decent—to yourself. It may not feel like self-love yet,
but it's a start.

Quick recap: We've established a few important things so far . . .

- If we love ourselves because of our strongest features and traits, it leaves
  us vulnerable to the argument that we shouldn't love ourselves on bad
  days when those traits aren't on show (or when someone with more
  of them shows up). That means we have to find deeper reasons to love
  ourselves.
- The romantic model of love is no help when it comes to loving ourselves.
  It's hard to "fall" in love with the person you know better than anyone—
  yourself. You have to see love as an action, not a feeling.
- Clues to how to love ourselves can be found in other models of love, like
  the parent-child relationship.
- Once we grasp the idea that we, too, are a person in this world, we
  realize that all the values of decency, kindness, respect, and compassion
  that we apply to other people must be extended to ourselves too.

We could stop there. If people simply followed this logic, they'd start
treating themselves at least as well as they do everyone else. And not just
people: I once invited my boxing trainer, Martin Snow, to speak at my retreat
in Florida—a risky move since there's no telling what the man is going to
say—and he said, "Do you feed your dog junk food, alcohol, and drugs? No?
Then why do you do it to yourself?" But we need to take one more step to
fully understand what self-love really means.

Here's the core truth: There are 8 billion people on this earth. You're one
of them. That doesn't just make it as important that you take care of yourself
as well as you take care of anybody else. It makes it more important. Because
of all those 8 billion, there is only one you've always been responsible for.

Imagine someone asking you why you love yourself, and you shaking your head just like the parent who says, "Because that's my kid." It has nothing to do with how great you are. No traits, attributes, or achievements are necessary. "Because I'm my person," you say, as if it were completely obvious. Because, when you think about it, it is.

How would you treat yourself if you realized "I'm the person who belongs to me"? At birth, you were given—by nature, or God, or whatever you believe—one person to take care of for the rest of your life. At first you weren't able to fulfill that role, which is why someone else had to start the task of raising you. They may or may not have done it well, but back then, keeping you alive was someone else's job. They were there to be your guardian until you reached the stage where you figured out the person who ultimately has custody of you: *you.*

Most of us have never thought about it this way. We may have felt a sense of responsibility to somebody else—a child, a sick relative, a sibling—but never for ourselves. Once we became an adult, we looked elsewhere for the care we got, or hoped to get, to a parent figure, a mentor, a romantic partner, a close group of friends. Many of us are still searching for somebody to take over the role of protecting and taking care of us. We want these people to verify that we are good enough, smart enough, desirable enough, and worthy of love. While it's true that building a community in adult life is essential for our well-being, this is more like an abdication of responsibility. It's like going through life trying to hand off the job we're supposed to do to somebody else. And the job description is simple: to actively love and nurture ourselves.

In shunning this fundamental duty, we have left our post. We're like Simba in *The Lion King*, the rightful heir who ran from the pride thinking that someone more capable would take care of them—protect them, nurture them, and make better decisions for them. But that's our job. This is why loving ourselves has to be taken much more seriously than waiting around for a feeling about ourselves. We have to make the decision to love ourselves like it's our job . . . because it is. It's not that the cavalry *isn't* coming. It's that *we're* the cavalry.

Why waste life worrying that someone has something we don't? All of that is ego, and it is a distraction. Yes, there are 8 billion people in this world, and in many ways, we may not be the best at this or that. But none of that matters. What matters is our one job: parenting the one individual in 8 billion who is ours. Comparison with other people is utterly pointless when we look at life this way; we can't exchange ourselves for another human. We only get *this* one, and our job is to give this creature the best life we can.

I don't know you, what you've done wrong in your life, who you've hurt, what regrets haunt you, what private or public shame plagues you, what your weaknesses are. I also don't know what your strengths are or what makes you an exceptional human being. But I don't need to know what's great about you. That's the point. I only know that you'd better love yourself every day, with all your might, because no one else has time to.

For years, I have treated myself badly, never feeling like I'm doing enough, working myself to the bone, being nasty to myself when I fall short, and rarely giving myself grace. I used to think that was me, my nature. But these days, in the moments I'm facing burnout, when I'm exhausted from having beaten myself up for a mistake I've made, showing myself not an ounce of compassion, I now think to myself: "You had one job! Where have you been?"

Loving ourselves is more than a feeling; it's an approach. It's doing hard things for yourself and showing up for yourself out of a sense of duty and responsibility. We have to stop looking for self-love's short-term rewards. Core confidence is a long-term investment. When a parent invests in a child for eighteen years, many of the fruits of that investment—the majority of them, in fact—will come later. As the child becomes an adult, they find fresh appreciation for the many things the parent did for them, and the relationship grows richer and sweeter with each realization. It's never too late. Raising ourselves is a similar long-term project that can begin at any age. We may find ourselves raising an awkward teenager at sixty. But as with any teenager, don't expect that love to come back to you right away. The rewards take time, but they will be real.

Having a high opinion of ourselves isn't necessary for this kind of self-love. (And it might just get in the way.) But it is possible to develop an affection toward ourselves, one born of empathy and compassion. The starting point for this empathy and compassion is self-forgiveness for the past.

Self-Forgiveness

Regret, with its constant loop of our worst moments, blinds us to the moment we are in and the people we are with. If we can't forgive ourselves—for our weaknesses, mistakes, shortcomings, failures, and omissions—we'll never find any real joy in the present we have or be able to summon the energy for the future we want.

There is one thing we all share: a past that's filled with mistakes. Every single one of us has done things that have cost us. In some cases, the cost is so high that it's hard to imagine how we'd ever be able to forgive ourselves and move on from:

- Not leaving someone sooner
- Not taking care of our health
- Letting our own destructive patterns screw up a relationship
- Procrastinating on something important until it was too late
- Making bad decisions—especially one that changed our entire life
- Hurting someone, or many people, including the ones we love the most
- Failing to learn an important lesson and then repeating the same mistake
- The feeling that we've wasted our lives

When we actually make a list of things we regret, we can wind up hating ourselves. It's hard not to hate someone who betrays us, but when that person is ourselves, the bitterness can be hard to shake.

All these bad decisions and self-betrayals leave us feeling like we've failed at our one chance to give ourselves a better life. And the spin cycle of self-blame all too often leaves us feeling angry and disgusted with ourselves, making our most private moments our most poisonous. When these feelings persist, it can even feel as if ridding the world of this poison would be an overall net gain.

Please, stop right there. Here's a reality check to help avoid this free fall. Answer this two-part test of how you treat yourself: A) When you do something right, do you spend any time acknowledging your contributions and celebrating the accomplishment? B) When you do something wrong or stupid, how long do you spend beating yourself up about it? I've asked this pair of questions all over the world, and most people say they'll spend anywhere from thirty seconds to twenty-four hours celebrating an accomplishment, then they'll turn around and spend days, weeks, years, and sometimes a whole lifetime beating themselves up for a mistake.

I've been one of those people. For as long as I can remember, I've beaten myself up to a terrible degree. It's been exhausting and at times it's made me ill. It's why I've thought so hard about this subject—to solve my own personal crisis of obsessive rumination. Having beaten myself up so often, and so intensely, my whole life, I finally realized I'd have no quality of life until I developed a conscious and robust model for practicing self-forgiveness. This is how I did it.

Separate Accountability From Blame

As a kid, I loved the original *Jurassic Park* movie. I remember watching it for the first time as a seven-year-old, wide-eyed at the opening scene of the rattling crate with the raptor inside. I walked away with the age-appropriate impression: Dinosaurs are great. Watching it for maybe the twelfth time, as an adult struggling with self-blame, a line in the movie I'd never really noticed suddenly stood out. It opened my eyes to a different way of approaching my past.

Dr. John Hammond, the owner of the park, is speaking to one of his staff who has made a mistake. Dr. Hammond (played by the late Richard Attenborough) says to him: "I don't blame people for their mistakes, but I do ask that they pay for them." I believe this one line holds the key to forgiving ourselves for the past and empowering ourselves to feel more confident in the present. And it focuses on a necessary distinction: the crucial difference between blame and accountability.

Accountability, from every point of view, makes sense. It empowers us to fix something, to do what we can to make it right. It creates a sense of responsibility for mistakes we've made and makes us realize there is a price to pay for having made them. Through accountability, we learn that there are consequences we have to live with and adapt to. Becoming an adult is about ownership, and making ourselves accountable is a way of owning what we've done up until now and the responsibility of fixing it. It is a way of making things better.

Blame, however, shares no such utility. In fact, not only does spending our energy relentlessly beating ourselves up for the things we've done serve no purpose, but I've also come to believe it doesn't make any logical sense. Here's why . . .

If You Could Have Done Better, You Would Have

Think about a moment in your life you regret; something you have struggled to forgive yourself for. You've probably replayed this scenario thousands of times, seeing exactly what you should have done instead of what you did. It's a maddening exercise that has you wishing for a time machine so you could take back what you did, and do what you didn't do instead.

I've played this game thousands of times only to come to see lately that I could never have done anything different. The idea that I could have is pure science fiction. Let's say you blame yourself for staying in an abusive relationship for two decades longer than you should have, believing now that you've "wasted your life." You hate yourself for being too weak to leave, and you never miss the opportunity to remind yourself of this weakness. But this ignores one thing: At the time, you didn't have what you needed to leave. You didn't have the resources. You didn't have the insight you do now, or if you did, you didn't have the tools to act. The key to having empathy and compassion for yourself, the crucial first step in self-forgiveness, is the realization that what you did at any moment was precisely the best you could at that time. That seems like strange phrasing for many of us, maybe because we carry around an imaginary ideal of what our best really is, imagining our best to be equivalent to our maximum effort, or our best response, on our most effective day, an expectation that inevitably puts us on the losing side of a never-ending race against our personal best. That's not what *doing our best* really means. Our best in any given moment is the action we were capable of taking based on where we were that day (and being able to forgive ourselves for it later if it wasn't necessarily the right thing). Doing our best doesn't mean doing something good. Our best may not be admirable, but for better or worse, our best is just what we are doing at the time.

The Philosopher's Cure for Self-Forgiveness

As I mentioned in the chapter "How to Rewire Your Brain," ego is more than hubris, an inflated sense of self. Ego may declare, "I deserve my wealth and good looks and exceptional children and my cryptocurrency in the Cayman Islands!" But ego works in the other direction too. If you think you are uniquely bad (vile, reprehensible, untrustworthy, malicious, and so on), and that you don't deserve to be happy because you betrayed your best friend and ruined New Year's and made the worst marital choice available, that's ego too. Both versions have more I's in them than Mississippi.

I've found a useful philosophy to toss around for dealing with both situations: hard determinism. (Don't worry, soft determinism's coming up!) It's an interpretation of observable reality that holds that every event is determined completely by preexisting causes and could not have happened any other way. It's popular enough at the American Psychological Association that they have their own definition applied to psychology: the position that all human behaviors result from specific, efficient causal antecedents, such as biological structures or processes, environmental conditions, or past experience.

In other words, our childhood, our body shape, our habits of mind, the town we grew up in, the lessons we learned there, the abuse we suffered, the mentors who took us on (and the ones who didn't) all form a cocktail of variables that have led directly to the next decision we're about to make. This makes some people uncomfortable because it doesn't leave much room for free will. That is why there are "soft determinists," the good cops to the hard determinists' bad ones, who agree that while, yes, everything we do is the effect of a previous action, those actions can be determined by human choice to the same degree as external forces. Either way, soft or hard, determinism is helpful when it comes to self-forgiveness, because it can help us to let go of this grand egotistical idea that we somehow don't deserve forgiveness.

I had a client, Randall, who came to me after working for a narcissist for many years. His boss, Mark, lied to him on a pathological scale, broke promises, abused his time and goodwill, manipulated him into thinking that he was incapable of working anywhere else, convincing him that staying was in his best interests because Mark would "take care of him." What's worse, to Randall, it was more than a working relationship. Mark had become a father figure to him, and a controlling one. He looked up to Mark, was inspired by him, and felt his boss was there for him in ways his father never was. Randall's father had been distant and emotionally withholding, never hugging him once, never telling him he loved him, spending no time with him when he was young. Now that Randall had a family of his own, his father showed a similar lack of interest in his wife and children. Randall had spent his entire adult life so far trying to fill that father-shaped void.

When Mark appeared, Randall could only see that Mark was giving him more than his father ever had. So when Mark didn't pay him on time, practically making him beg for his paycheck every month, when Mark showed up several hours late to meetings (or not at all), when Mark said things had been done when they hadn't and vice versa, Randall would tell himself, "He means well, and he's been there for me." Randall endured two decades of mistreatment before he came to me and finally put an end to his toxic working relationship with his boss and found another employer.

Unfortunately, leaving his narcissist of a boss didn't end Randall's sense of self-loathing for letting the situation continue for so long. I offered him the determinist perspective, trying to get him to see that the dominoes had been set in motion from the day he was born, thanks to his unloving father and his own particular blend of circumstances and genetics. In fact, it had even started before he was born, beginning with the mix of influences that led his father to treat his own son with such indifference.

At every stage, between his distant father and his manipulative boss, Randall did what he could with the tools he had. And these were times when Randall didn't have many tools to work with. What he did have, like you and me, was a nervous system he didn't choose, one that was unconsciously wired at an early age to cope with and survive what he was going through back then. And this nervous system led him straight to Mark. But with new tools, Randall was able to adopt a new perspective that allowed him to leave his job. It can feel like a small miracle when someone I'm coaching gets the dominoes of their life to fall in a different direction. And appreciating how truly hard that is—to deviate from our programming—is key to self-forgiveness. Randall had always done his best, and now, because of the work he was putting in on himself, his best was now better than before. That's beautiful.

This is one way you can turn self-love into a verb: Tell yourself you have always been doing your best. You may not have liked it at times, and it may not have been enough to get the result you wanted, but your best was exactly what you've been doing. Ruminating over what you could have done differently turns introspection into science fiction. There may be, somewhere in some infinite multiverse, a version of you who made a different decision, but that didn't happen in this one. Here, your best, for better or worse, is what you did.

As Sam Harris, the author and neuroscientist, points out, through the lens of determinism, hatred of ourselves or others makes no sense. Through this lens, if someone commits a crime, everything in their experience and genetics had been leading to that moment. We could choose to hate them for that crime, but we could just as easily direct that hatred to every previous event and genetic influence that contributed to their action. The person may well have to go to jail to be removed from society (accountability), but hating them (blame), from this perspective, makes no sense.

Adopting this perspective can make us feel as if we have no control in our own lives. If what I'm about to do is predetermined, then how can I change anything? But it's important to remember that the person who got us to where we are today is the old model. The new model has new inputs— new thoughts, new insights, new reference points. This book you are reading right now is a new input, and every new input brings the possibility of new decisions—decisions that give birth to new realities.

Don't Blame the Old Model

Did you own an early iPhone? Or an iPod before that? Remember the bugs? The way they crashed and turned off? The malfunctions that seemed calculated to get you to upgrade? When you finally did get that new model, did you unwrap the brand-new iPhone from its spiffy box and yell at it for all the ways your old iPhone malfunctioned? Of course not. You were excited to have the latest phone. Your old iPhone suddenly became a thing of the past. Why can't we do the same thing with ourselves?

To try another analogy: I like to think of my whole life like a relay race. In an actual Olympic relay, there are four runners, each of whom runs a quarter of the race. The first runner sprints off, baton in hand, and runs the best race he or she possibly can. At the end of that leg, the first runner hands the baton off to the next one, and away they go. Each runner has the job of running their best individual race within a larger race.

Now, let's say that the second of the four runners stumbles in their leg of the race and costs the team a few seconds. It's frustrating. It bothers the other runners, especially the third and fourth runner, who now have to try to make up the time the second runner cost the team. There's no doubt they have a harder race to run now as a result. But—and here's the point—we'd find it strange to hear that these other runners, frustrated about the second runner's performance that day, went home that night and shouted at *themselves* in the mirror. We'd think that such anger was misdirected, because the mistake didn't belong to them; it belonged to the second runner.

Imagine your life like this, divided into a series of legs in a relay. Each year when the clock strikes midnight on December 31, one year's runner hands off the baton to a brand-new one, who will run the next stage in the race, twelve months' worth, from New Year's Day on. Or you could imagine it the way I do: Every day a new runner wakes up, with the baton handed over by the runner from the day before. Every day, the job of the new runner is to run the best race he or she can for twenty-four hours.

Sure, some of the previous runners took shortcuts, ended up out of bounds, and made some serious mistakes along the way. They hurt people and themselves, they wasted time, made bad decisions, said things they didn't mean, sabotaged themselves, missed the chance to be courageous, failed to take risks. It can be frustrating, even infuriating, the way they have made our present life harder in a number of ways. (Our finances, for instance, or our love life.) Like the second runner in the Olympic relay, those stumbles have cost us time, and given us a harder race to run today. Cursing them for it is understandable. But cursing today's runner makes no sense.

Every runner starts with a clean slate, free of blame or baggage. After all, we expect a lot of them. Our job is to free up their energy as much as we possibly can so that they can run their best race, worry-free, until it's time to hand off the baton to the new runner. Today's race is hard enough without having to carry the baggage of past mistakes. Travel lightly.

None of this is about shirking responsibility. Today's runner is accountable for fixing the mistakes of the past—as Dr. Hammond said, this is our way of paying for our mistakes. We can't avoid that responsibility, because in the end, we're all running the same race, on the same team. If we don't accept the job of getting the race back on track today, then as today's runner, we are making a mistake all on our own. But as long as we feel accountable for running our best race today, we should feel pride in this new day's race, instead of feeling weighed down by the blame in the past. This is the essence of the distinction between blame and accountability.

On our retreats, when I take people through this way of conceptualizing forgiveness, they come to see that the hardest part of the race isn't fixing yesterday's problems, it's ending the unhelpful and stifling identification with the runner who created them. Once that baggage disappears, it's amazing how fast we can find ourselves running. And how much more enjoyable even hard races become.

As we stand at the starting line, having forgiven ourselves and ready to travel lightly, there's one more step we have to take that helps free ourselves from self-hatred, and lets us see that the way our life has unfolded so far is actually a good thing. It's a courageous and creative process. And more important than that, it's self-fulfilling. It's not that the positive story is true and the negative one isn't. It's that you're the one who gets to decide what things mean. That's what makes humans special in their ability to shape their emotions and direct their future.

Reframing, Resourcefulness, and Celebrating Your Ingredients

I don't really think anyone can grow unless he's loved exactly as he is.

—*Mr. Rogers*

As soon as I heard about the premise for the reality TV show *Chopped*—a brigade of chefs competing to make the best three-course meal out of identical baskets of mystery ingredients—I knew the show had identified two fundamentals of core confidence: acceptance and resourcefulness.

Sure enough, in the first episode I saw, the chefs had to make an appetizer that included Alaskan king crab, kelp jerky, salt water, and finger limes. All the contestants loved one of the ingredients—no points for guessing which—but their dish had to include them all. With twenty minutes to plate their creations, they had to accept the facts and work with what they had, and quickly.

Worrying about what you're stuck with is not what the show is about. Using ingredients creatively is. And there's no time to spare for the chefs to feel sorry for themselves. Almost as soon as the chefs recognize the ingredients, they have to begin shaping their dishes, knowing that they will be judged by their unique solutions to the riddle of their ingredients, and the speed and confidence they demonstrate in bringing it all to the table.

The hook of the show is the obscure, seemingly impossible ingredients they've all been stuck with. But the surprising things the chefs do with them are the reason we keep watching: to see someone turn impossibility into triumph in a race against the clock.

We could all use a little of that. It's too easy to think that success or happiness all comes down to our ingredients—our looks, our brains, our family, our advantages or lack of the same—forgetting that the show we're starring in is really about what small miracles we can pull off using only what we've got.

Too often we struggle with confidence because we're focusing on the wrong thing. We waste time fretting over our ingredients, which we consider subpar. But who can blame us? The message is hard to miss. Sometimes it's harsh and direct; sometimes it's subtle and roundabout. But the message is everywhere. Social media makes us measure ourselves against an impossible (and artificial) standard a hundred times a day. So when someone tells us we're *crazy* for feeling insecure about our looks ("Don't be silly, you're really pretty!"), it can feel like a form of gaslighting, because every time we open our phone, we confront an algorithm of beauty we clearly don't match up to. Online we can dive into the ocean of perfect butts, then look at our own and feel like a piece of kelp jerky.

"Your nose looks great!" we tell a friend considering plastic surgery for the distinctive asset she has grown to hate—because every perfect nose she's ever seen is clearly the opposite of hers. So is she really insecure, or is she just paying attention?

But when it comes to acceptance and resourcefulness, we don't need to like all of our ingredients equally. We don't have to like them at all. In fact, getting yourself to like an ingredient is just a blind alley, and risks fetishizing the importance of that one ingredient over the others. We got a random basket of ingredients. There's some Alaskan king crab in there and some kelp jerky. We may well learn to love kelp jerky, but here's what I know for sure: Any chef who can do something amazing and unexpected with kelp jerky is easy to love.

You Are Not Your Ingredients; You Are the Artist Using Them

When someone's a great chef, they don't just see a finger lime, or kelp jerky, or a carrot. They see the *potential* of a finger lime—every little way it could stand out or blend in. The more adept we become as a chef, the more we develop an affection and even an excitement for our ingredients. We discover a pride in showcasing ingredients that other people would have written off as useless or detrimental. Instead, we make our ingredients work *for* us—and our resourcefulness, which is at the center of core confidence, grows. On the identity level, confidence grows whenever things are working and going our way. But when we are in touch with our core confidence, we trust our level of resourcefulness to make anything work. Resourcefulness requires creativity. Where others see a roadblock, we must see a new ingredient, a new opportunity to display our shrewdness and ability.

BJ Miller is a palliative-care physician who comes across as wise and confident onstage. Nobody watching his TED Talk can deny his charisma as he recounts how a tragic event in his youth turned into the springboard for his career and his compassion. In 1990, as a sophomore at Princeton, he was out with his friends after a party and climbed onto a stationary shuttle train, where he reached up and 11,000 volts from an overhead wire unexpectedly shot through his body. The damage caused by that momentary impulse was severe: He suffered extensive burns, and he lost both his legs below the knee, as well as his left forearm. He woke up a week later to find that what he'd taken to be a long-lasting nightmare was in fact his unchangeable reality. All of it owing to one irrevocable moment in his life—one decision, one mistake.

And yet, Miller says he doesn't regret the event. Not even the injuries. He said, "Too much good stuff has come out of it. I was not headed toward a career in medicine before the accident, and I don't think I'd be as good a palliative-care physician if I hadn't had that experience. The gift was that it got me out of the habit of thinking about the future and comparing myself to others. It rammed me into the present moment. I'm actually grateful for that. I found a new confidence."

After suffering such extreme trauma, Miller could have easily given in to the idea that his life, as he knew it, was over. But instead he saw a different story, one that focused on what the event had given him. This is reframing— taking the non-negotiable circumstances of your life and making them your own—at an exquisite level. What I love is not just that Miller has clearly forgiven himself and run an incredible race in spite of this catastrophic life event, it's that he actually pinpoints the event as the catalyst for the positive direction of his life ever since.

This is an important part of reframing: recognizing the parts of ourselves that we could never have experienced without the very thing that we wish had never happened. We cannot delete our mistakes in life without deleting crucial and cherished elements of the person we have become. You may spend years in therapy trying to undo the damage your parents did, and that's admirable, but it's well worth considering the valuable parts of yourself that you only developed because your parents were the way they were. Maybe there was something incredibly useful you learned from them in spite of everything, or maybe you developed your own useful counterpunch in response to the things you hated them for or to the events they made you suffer through. Even the absence of a parent can produce qualities we would be scared to mess with. That doesn't mean we'd ever consider the worst parts of our lives to be a helpful medicine that other people need. But I know in my case, I wouldn't change them for fear of losing some of the things I'm now most grateful for.

Because if you could go back and remove your mistakes, tragedies, and pain, you would almost certainly erase yourself. The richness, complexity, and depth of your character today is as much forged in these incidents as it is powered by your achievements. You can't have one without the other. If you take away the trauma, you take away the treasure—the things that make you *you*. This is just as true right now: Your problems right now are shaping you into the person you will be proud to be tomorrow. Anytime a problem arises in your day, ask yourself: "Who would I have to become in order to deal with this?" The answer to that question gives meaning to the problem right away.

It's a unique superpower we have as human beings, that ability to create meaning and then use that meaning to reshape our lives. There are those who say that everything *has* a meaning, but I find that far less interesting. Trying to locate the meaning of something difficult or terrible in our lives is reactive. *Creating* meaning is proactive. It's storytelling. That's the essence of reframing. It's the essence of using your ingredients. Mel Abraham, a friend of mine who was diagnosed with cancer a few years ago, said to me: "I realized after the first year of looking for the meaning that the meaning wasn't in the past, it was in the future." In other words, Mel was going to create the meaning with what he did next. He was going to become someone and do something that made it have meaning.

Decide something right now: that from now till the end of your days, you will focus all of your energy on your resourcefulness, instead of judging yourself on the ingredients you find yourself working with. Remember, every day, a new version of you wakes up, and today's you has the task of doing the best they can, in the circumstances they have to work with. Do you have some tough and strange ingredients to work with? Great! What an opportunity to show the kind of artist you really are.

Now, you may point out that life isn't a TV show; in real life, people do get rewarded for waking up with a bowl of caviar. Good-looking people get the job. After work, their social life is booked solid. The kid from the good neighborhood, the Ivy League legacy, swims in a pool of powerful connections. That's all true.

This is why the only true judge is you. Only you know what you've had to overcome—your difficult parents, the formative moments when you were abused or cheated on, your struggles with your looks or body, your battles with addiction or bankruptcy or mental health, the loss of someone you love, or the opportunities you missed to have the relationships you've imagined for yourself. Only you know what you've done with everything you had to work with.

You can gain a great degree of confidence from your eagerness to take on the challenges of the future, but you should never lose sight of the resourcefulness you've already applied in the difficult circumstances of your past. Haven't you already done something beautiful with what you've had to work with? Think of all the things you've cooked up—starting with next to nothing. Think of how much you never gave yourself credit for because you were measuring yourself by the opinions of people who had no clue about your actual life.

Given that our standard-issue, ancient brain comes preprogrammed to scan the horizon for threats, there's a powerful instinct to move on quickly from the best meals we've ever concocted, no matter how perfect they were. But it's good to remember, whenever you do think back on your most inspired improvisations, that back when you put them together you were far less accomplished than you are today. You're a better chef now—wiser, more astute, even, dare I say, more seasoned. And it's likely because of the skills you've learned since, the tools and resources you've picked up, that today you have an even better assortment of techniques than you had back then.

This is why you should be conscious of how far you've come and remind yourself of that great distance as part of your everyday core-confidence routine. We're all in the habit of clinging to the side of the mountain, looking up at how far there is to go—or how much further up the mountain other people are. Few of us practice looking down on a regular basis to see how much we have had to traverse just to be here.

No one knows your life the way you do. Connect with the magnificence of your ascent so far, regardless of whether anyone else sees it as impressive from their perspective. To a person recovering from a paralyzing accident, supporting their own weight on two parallel bars and sweating out an inch of forward movement in physical therapy is extraordinary. And the fact that the majority of humanity is walking around with thoughtless ease has no bearing on the scale of that achievement. We have to cultivate an awareness of the tremendous power of what we have done working within our circumstances. The achievements that only we can measure form the basis for our confidence, no matter what those achievements represent to anyone else. In some ways, the fact that no one else can measure that achievement gives us an advantage. The only way to use that advantage is to learn to appreciate the view from where we have landed.

16

HAPPY ENOUGH

I asked my Instagram followers a very direct question not long ago: "What is your biggest fear for the future—the one that worries you the most?" At last count, 3,145 people had commented, most with an extraordinary level of vulnerability. But one comment from a woman named Danni stood out, and not just to me. It was the top comment, with 2,202 likes and 184 replies of its own:

> [My biggest fear is] That I'll stay single for the rest of my life—I know that might sound superficial or some people might think there are worse things . . . I know they'll say I need to love myself first. And I do, I do love myself. But I also have a lot of love to give and I love love! I have a fulfilling life, with a great job, wonderful friends and every day I live life for me. I am planning on traveling solo, etc., so my life isn't on pause waiting for "the one." But my biggest fear is that I'll never find "my person." People can say what they want, but romantic love fills spaces in our hearts that other love just doesn't.

Most comments voiced some variation of Danni's. ("Being old and dying alone"; "That I never find my person and spend my life single.") But something about hers got to the heart of it, which was that, no matter how well the rest of their life was going, it could not make up for the pain of being unpartnered. Her honest response seemed to checkmate the standard advice for someone struggling with being alone: find purpose, develop friendships, learn to enjoy your own company.

In *Letters to a Young Poet*, Rainer Maria Rilke wrote to a young man whose worries reminded him of his own of a few years before. Rilke recommended the virtues of cultivating solitude in life:

> There is only one solitude, and it is large and not easy to bear. . . . People are drawn to the easy and to the easiest side of the easy. But it is clear that we must hold ourselves to the difficult.

But I bet that even Rilke would have been stumped by Danni's comment. I can hear her saying: "Sure, I get that, Rainer, but I've done that already. You'll find a holiday with myself in my calendar, and plenty of solo reading time and bath time on weekends. I'm still ready to meet someone now."

Solitude is profoundly important, but it is not a fast-acting prescription for happiness, nor does it solve the need for the specific spark found in romantic connection. And how many of us have wondered, just like Danni, if we could ever be truly happy without it?

In the TV series *The Crown*, there's an emotional scene where Princess Margaret is spelling out to her sister, Queen Elizabeth II, whom she called Lilibet, the things she'd missed out on when she was prohibited from marrying the great love of her life, Group Captain Peter Townsend; all things that the queen had benefited from in her many years with Prince Philip. The conversation had an edge because it was Lilibet herself, in her role as queen, who'd forbidden her sister to marry Peter since he was not only a divorcé, but also a commoner who would be seen to be marrying well "above his station."

> Margaret: Without sun and water, crops fail, Lilibet. Let me ask, how many times has Philip done something? Intervene when you couldn't? Be strong when you couldn't be? Be angry when you couldn't be? Be decisive when you couldn't be? How many times have you said a silent prayer of gratitude for him and thought to yourself, "If I didn't have him, I'd never be able to do it"? How often? Peter was my sun. My water. And you denied me him.

How many of us feel like Princess Margaret and Danni, that we are missing the sun and the water in our lives either because of the love we lost—or the one we never found?

Many years ago, I felt this loss when I woke up from a dream where, for a brief moment, I experienced the kind of love I one day hoped to find. I'm the last person to wake up and say, "You must hear about this dream I had." But this brief and seemingly uneventful dream stayed with me.

I was standing in an elevator beside a woman. The two of us had just escaped from something—something dangerous—together. As the elevator slowed, there was a sense that whatever we were about to see, we would face it together. When the doors opened, she grabbed my hand, not afraid, but reassuringly, as if to let me know that we were going to be OK, no matter what, because we had each other. I felt both protective and protected.

Although I never saw her face, I knew this was my person. It was as if the dream had created a space for this person to become anybody—not a face to be found, a feeling to be relocated. I had never felt more at home. Whatever *it* was, I had found it, not so much love as everything that love provided: all I needed to face the world, a feeling that I would never let go of and that would not let go of me. Then the elevator doors opened, the light poured in, and I woke up.

My heart was breaking over someone I'd felt so close to and then immediately lost. I longed to be back in the dream, with that feeling of certainty and the person who shared it with me. I tried going back to sleep, hoping to find my way back, even just for a few more minutes. Still, even though I never had that dream again, the feeling had landed. The dream had revealed a void in my life and magnified it.

The desperation to return to the dream reflects the lack of control we feel so often in our love life. In other areas, we can at least identify things we can do to get us closer to a desired result. When we want to lose weight, we change our diet and exercise more. If we want more money, we save or invest. But it's maddening that our efforts in love fail to produce predictable results or ongoing returns. You could go on four dates a week for a year and not find someone you want who wants you back. Even if you do, and you give that person love, respect, and loyalty, there's no guarantee they won't cheat, lie, or leave.

For many of us, that uncertainty and lack of control is intolerable. So we exert control where we can—workaholism, gym addiction, food addiction, alcoholism, friendships, and family relationships. Sometimes we reject the entire world of love, so it can no longer reject us. But the desire to feel seen, accepted, and loved doesn't go away so easily. At the time of writing, we're beginning to hear about AI relationships, as people turn to software to create ideal companions—a reminder that the need for connection is universal and people will do whatever it takes to satisfy it.

What does AI offer that a normal love life can't? Control. An AI companion won't leave or cheat. It is guaranteed to be there when we need it, ready to listen and empathize (especially if its empathetic capacities can be programmed by clinical psychologists). It, if that's the right gender, provides a place to feel seen for those of us who have been rendered invisible by age, disability, illness, divorce, or changing life circumstances.

Can we be blamed for opting out of dating the hard way—in person, with actual people—and resorting to what Rilke calls "the easiest side of the easy"? Whether it's abstaining from relationships altogether, exploring AI ones, pursuing dating exclusively through a screen via dating apps, or just entertaining the person who is a dead-end "bit of fun"—these comforts, no matter how flawed, often feel preferable to nothing, which is too often the only alternative. How long does one keep standards high and wait for something better when something better never seems to arrive?

When I'm up onstage or online advising someone to ditch the casual partner who isn't giving them what they want, it often feels like I'm robbing them of the one comfort that helps them get by. Then I remember how many of these scenarios I've seen play out, leaving someone worse off than they were when it started, like a drug addict who first used in order to get high, then had to use just to not feel awful, only to wind up with the agony of addiction and withdrawal.

But when something as important to our happiness as romantic love is missing, how do we get by? By learning to be "happy enough."

I like happy enough. I've liked it for years now. Some will see that emotional state as "settling" by another name—a way of copping out on what we really wanted. For me, happy enough has not only served as an essential way of surviving life's inevitable disappointments and losses; it has also formed the basis for a deep sense of peace—the kind of peace that has served as the foundation for taking more risks, getting more involved, with greater results.

Happy enough begins with us first radically accepting where we are now, and then concluding that if nothing changed, we'd actually be OK. That doesn't mean there aren't things we want to strive for; it just means we aren't starting from a place of scarcity, but a place of peace. This, right now, is enough.

A younger version of me, with my Type A personality, might have written off this line of advice as a loser's mindset. But the more success I experienced, the more I found myself around people whose overriding philosophy seemed to be "never enough." I watched these people put themselves, and often their families too, through constant suffering to get more. I think of this as "the disease." Anytime I watch someone who can't stop, I think, "Uh-oh, they have the disease." Anytime I catch myself running to the next thing just for the sake of it, I tell myself, "Uh-oh, Matthew's got the disease right now."

Happy enough isn't accepting less; it's a philosophy rooted in gratitude and acceptance. This moment, this life, this body, this mind, this is enough for me to be happy. I may choose to try for more, because more might be fun, it might add comfort to my life, it might add new experiences, it might add new connections, but I am not putting myself through it from a place of lack, but from a place of calm. It's amazing how much this allows you to attempt more, because all of a sudden, you have nothing to lose. If the thing we are trying to get doesn't happen, we haven't risked or lost our happiness by not getting it. When we think of someone with nothing to lose, we often think of it in a negative sense, as in, someone who has nothing. But when we are happy enough, we have nothing to lose because we can look at our life today and recognize that it is already enough.

With this perspective, we can feel it would be lovely to have a relationship. We can be excited about the possibility. We can even acknowledge that having the right relationship might make us happier than we are now. But the absence of one doesn't prevent us from being happy enough to enjoy the life we have. That is power. Not power derived from a defensive or cynical place; power that comes from having agency in our own happiness, agency that coexists with an openness and the sense of endless possibility of a life lived with curiosity.

Happy enough is the bedrock of standards. When we are happy enough, we can cheerfully say no to bad treatment, disrespect, or behavior that simply doesn't fit with the culture of our life. We can say no to someone who has different intentions, regardless of whether we have someone to replace them. If you put a boat in a lake, the water will temporarily shift to make space, but remove it and the water resumes its natural level. There is no void that needs filling.

Happy enough doesn't need a replacement option in order to say no, because saying no doesn't leave a void. Life, as it is, is enough, so anyone or anything that is invited in must make life better or be left behind. Unhappy people say yes to people who make them unhappy because they think they or their life is worthless without them. People who are happy enough can objectively assess whether something is worth their time instead of feeling like a prisoner with no other options. Happy enough is the freedom to say no.

But how can we achieve being happy enough if we are overcome with pain and suffering? It could be the pain of a terrible heartbreak, tragic life circumstances, or the deep, ongoing ache of loneliness. Feeling trapped in our pain makes it seem impossible to connect with the idea of being happy enough.

Managing Pain

I wrote earlier in these pages about my own battle with chronic pain. Rarely have I spoken in public about how bad things got. I felt as if I could break down at any moment, so I dealt with the pain in private. As I said previously, this is why I started therapy, not out of any desire to grow, but from a desperate need to avoid drowning. I felt outside my own life, unable to connect to anything or anyone. At a distance, it may have looked as though things were going fine, but I was in trouble. I understood how people living in unrelenting pain and hopelessness can view death with a sense of relief.

One morning in therapy, the first words out of my mouth were: "I've decided I'm just going to live for other people, because I don't get any enjoyment from anything in my life anymore. All I think about is my pain." It was one of the darkest statements of my life. "Matthew," my therapist said, "that is hallmark depression." Maybe my depression was circumstantial, with its origin in chronic physical pain, but it was a distinction without a difference: The mental and emotional result was the same.

"Pain," he explained, "is very centralizing. That's especially true when it's pain in your head, because it feels so close." That was the perfect word: *centralizing*. The pain had taken over the landscape of my life, like a black hole. (Though I'm the last person who'd think that a pain in the head is more centralizing than a pain in your heart.) But even though it took years for me to see it, the pain did teach me an important lesson. Through the struggle with pain, I learned the tools for being happy enough, even in the hardest times. Happy enough made the hard times easier.

The Tools

Each of the tools that follow is based on a single, fundamental insight I learned from pain: The most painful thing about pain isn't the pain itself, but our relationship with it. So, first a word about that relationship.

My relationship with pain was toxic. When I felt throbbing in my head and ringing in my ear, I didn't just feel a physical sensation. It kicked off an entire chain reaction of catastrophic thoughts, with the final destination always some version of "I'm fucked." Here are some steps in my typical descent:

- You're never going to enjoy life again because of this pain. Nothing you love about life will ever be the same again.
- No woman is going to want you once they find out you have this weakness, which makes you pathetic, unhealthy, and unattractive. Women want a strong, capable guy, not some delicate and fragile creature who's always one wince away from collapse. This has robbed you of the confidence that once made you desirable.
- What do you expect? You did this to yourself. You didn't take care of yourself; you latch on to stress and anxiety, and now you're broken and beyond repair. For which you only have yourself to blame.
- You're never going to achieve the big things you once wanted to achieve, because this pain is going to dominate your life. And if you don't achieve those things, you'll be worthless.

It could get even darker, but you get the picture.

Notice the utter absence of self-compassion. When I needed a friend more than anything, I made myself the enemy, which quickly turned my everyday experience into a major artery of shame. My relationship *with* my pain, this spiral of self-recrimination, was a multiplier, making it ten times worse. In the pages that follow, you'll find the tools I've learned along the way that transformed my relationship with my pain, and in doing so, allowed me to be happy enough. In fact, I'm now happy enough that I can share all of this with you, something I could never have done when I was lost in it. Happy enough gives us the ability to make a difference again.

I'm confident these tools will work for you too. I didn't invent them, but I have molded what I learned from many different sources to create a fairly complete pain toolbox that I use daily.

Lose the Ceremony

I remember speaking to a mentor at the height of my physical symptoms. I told her that eating certain foods or drinking alcohol seemed to make them worse. I'd have a sip of wine and immediately start feeling pain, dizziness, and the ringing in my ear got louder. I've never been a big drinker, but I love food, a glass of wine, a good cocktail. I associate these things with some of my best experiences in life, like travel and adventure. I explained in a completely defeated voice—my emotional baseline in that period—that I could never have those things again because of my symptoms. I'll never forget what she said to me: "Look, we don't know where your symptoms are going to be in one year, let alone five, so let's lose the ceremony of 'I can never do this again,' which we don't even know is true, and just focus on what's best for right now. Some of these things seem to cause pain, so let's not do that for now, at least until we get things to a better place."

When she told me to "lose the ceremony," she was really telling me to stop the catastrophic thinking, which was making me far more unhappy than the reality that I couldn't have a jalapeño margarita that evening. The same is true in our love lives. When we are lonely, our mind will often characterize the situation in the extreme. ("I'm going to die alone!") And that's the thought that sends us into panic and depression. Lose the ceremony!

Everything Changes

The corollary to my mentor's advice to lose the ceremony is the simple fact that you really have no idea how you will feel in a year, or how your life is going to change. Pain, like everything else in life, changes. Sometimes it lessens or goes away altogether. Sometimes it's still there but doesn't affect us the same way because we learn to change our relationship with it and manage it differently. At a certain point, aren't they the same thing? Don't judge your future based on how you feel right now. Everything changes, and it's changing all the time.

The next time you're writing the script for your entire future based on what's going on today, remember, your only job is to manage the situation today the best you can, while remaining open to the surprises the future will inevitably hold.

Surrender

As Eckhart Tolle said, "Acceptance of the unacceptable is the greatest source of grace in this world." While the future may hold surprises, sitting around hoping and waiting for them is a bad idea. The only way to live is to lean into our current circumstances. I learned how counterproductive it was for me to wake up every day hoping that my symptoms were going to change. This didn't mean I had to give up looking for ways to alleviate them over time. But I had tried so many things and wound up so devastated each time they didn't work that hope itself had started to become corrosive. To counteract my cynicism and despair, I learned to tell myself, "Maybe in a few years I won't have these symptoms, but for now I do, and life is too short to not enjoy it in the meantime, so let me accept them and learn how to make the best of my life while they are here."

Something about this acceptance immediately lessened the grip that pain had on me. I was no longer fighting it. There's a story in Greek mythology about Prince Ilus, who founded the city of Troy. He made the mistake of looking upon a sacred object sent down by the gods, and was blinded by it instantly. In Stephen Fry's retelling of the story, he writes: "He [Ilus] was wise enough in the ways of the Olympians not to panic. Falling to his knees he cast up prayers of thanks to the heavens. After a week of steadfast devotion he was rewarded with the restoration of his sight."

Others may see little to learn from a story that depicts an unrealistic miracle, but I see one of the most important lessons I've ever learned. For me, Prince Ilus represents the person who has learned that he can be happy enough even if he doesn't get his sight back. Perhaps he even knows instinctively that he will be sure to learn from this new experience that life has given him, so he gives thanks. He found gratitude inside the calamity. The reward for that approach to his plight is grace. His sight is restored. That miracle, though, is not what I find interesting about the story. He was already seeing clearly by approaching his situation from a place of gratitude and surrender.

Surrender won't always reverse our circumstances, but it does transform our relationship to them. The condition of Prince Ilus' mind was far more important than the circumstances of his life. Through surrender we transform our lens for seeing life itself. We accept what is, even if it means taking the path that others resist. By doing so, we have created a new relationship with the situation itself, one that no longer causes the pain it used to. Acceptance on this scale is not passive. It's a conscious action that requires decisiveness. It says: Let me make peace with What Is, then do everything I can to make What Is better. Once we say, "This is how it is; it couldn't have been anything else," we are free to ask, "How can I make the best of this?" When we are done fighting the situation, we finally free up energy that can be used to explore its hidden benefits.

Choose Your Pain

I remember psychologist Guy Winch telling me of an experiment done on rats, and it went something like this: Rat A was voluntarily allowed to run on a wheel, and another, Rat B, was confined to a wheel that was connected to Rat A's wheel. Anytime Rat A chose to run, Rat B was forced to run involuntarily. Afterward, Rat A showed all the positive effects of exercise—decreased stress, higher serotonin—while Rat B showed a marked increase in the stress hormone cortisol. Both were doing the same amount of exercise. So why did one have a neurologically positive experience and one of them negative? Rat A chose, Rat B didn't.

The pain we *choose* benefits us. The pain we stay a victim of hurts us. This leaves a clue as to how we can renegotiate our relationship with pain. We can actually go beyond surrender and choose our pain for ourselves.

We may not have chosen to be single, or heartbroken, or lonely, but we can act as if we chose them by figuring out what unique benefits they are giving us. This is a form of retroactive choice that turns us from Rat B into Rat A. We become grateful for the exercise life has made us do. I came to realize that by learning to manage my relationship with my physical pain, I had created a template for managing my relationship with life that would serve me in every part of my life and future. I could never have achieved this if I'd been able to simply make my pain disappear. This lesson has become one of my most prized assets.

Imagine that you've been given a menu with all sorts of difficult life situations that create pain. Next to each one is the list of treasures and benefits that can be had by going through that difficult situation. Now imagine seeing your situation on that menu, the one that has caused you immense pain. You look over to the next column and see the list of all the benefits this pain gives you, the ways it has made you stronger, more interesting, more capable, more resilient, more compassionate, more equipped for other struggles. Now connect with the fact that these treasures are already yours, and there are still more of them to be discovered in this situation. You may not have chosen this situation at the outset, but now that you're here, imagine yourself retroactively choosing it from the menu because of its amazing unique benefits . . . benefits you couldn't get any other way.

People choose pain from the menu in life all the time: They climb literal mountains, they go to the gym, they try to build a business, they choose to write a book (!) Some of these may appear to have more obvious benefits than the pain we are going through in life. But that's not the case. The benefits of the pain we put ourselves through are not inherently more valuable than the benefits awarded to us through the struggle created by our circumstances in life. From my perspective, I have to argue that the value I've received from the pain I didn't originally choose is far greater than the value I chased after with the pain I chose.

By choosing to see our difficulty through the lens of its unique benefits, we rewrite the story and the meaning of our pain, and in doing so, we transform ourselves from Rat B into Rat A.

Pay Attention to the Modulations in Your Pain

Some days or hours, your loneliness will reach a 10. Others, it will be at a 3. That's a big difference. I know when I'm experiencing pain at a 10, I am in danger of losing objectivity. At the peaks of pain, we tend to have a poor recall of recent moments when we've actually felt fine. This temporary blindness can leave us incapable of seeing that our immediate maximum pain is temporary. We put too much importance on our bad moments, which leads right back to catastrophic thinking and then despair.

Here's a reasonable prediction: Sometimes you'll feel a little better. Sometimes a lot better. Keeping a log of these variations is important. It reminds you that how you feel at your worst is not any kind of final truth, and that feeling better is possible. But a log also helps because it gives you a record of what you did that helped you feel better than you do in your worst moments. Knowing how to reduce your pain from a 10 to a 7, or a 7 to a 4, is life-changing. And once you have a couple of these formulas at your disposal, you can replicate that result.

I used to think about my pain twenty-four hours a day. Then I began to notice instances when I hadn't thought about my pain for the last ten minutes. Not much to someone who's not in pain, but a significant feat when the pain is constant. That let me know that there really were times when I could live without thinking about pain. And if I could do it for ten, surely I could do it for twenty, perhaps even an hour! Once I reached an hour, my goal was simple: Make more of those. In the worst breakup, it's on your mind twenty-four hours a day. But one day you'll go an hour without thinking about that person. Recognizing that feels like hope, which helps you focus on making more of those. At the very least, the next time you're pitched into despair, you'll remember that there's an hour coming where you won't think about them at all, and that thought alone can be enough to let the light in, take a deep breath, and calm yourself down.

Practice Maximum Self-Compassion

Surely feeling bad is bad enough. Why then do we make it worse with all the stories we tell ourselves, like "It's all my fault," "I'm such an idiot for landing myself in this position in the first place," "I'm getting what I deserve," or "No one wants me because I'm worthless"? This is exactly when we have to practice the kind of self-compassion we talked about in the previous chapter on core confidence.

Self-compassion is saying to ourselves: "I feel bad/sad/hurt/lonely/in pain. That on its own is a horrible thing to feel. I should take care of myself today and help myself to feel better." On days when my physical pain was at its worst, I felt incapable of getting anything done. I would torture myself over the fact that I wasn't being productive that day, then I would shame myself for having pain in the first place, and try to find a way to blame myself for having created the conditions in my life for it to occur. It all added up to a suffocating message: "You're not going to get anything done today. And that's going to mean you get left behind in life. And it's all your fault."

I had to learn to talk to myself in a completely different way, which meant shedding all the doomsday stories I'd created around this pain, and instead seeing my pain as just a fact of that particular day, which sucked for Matthew.

My new monologue, which took a while to learn, looked like this: "Matthew is in pain today. That's really hard for Matthew, especially because he has a lot on his plate. How can I help Matthew today? Can I find more time for him to rest? Can I get some other people to help with his workload? Perhaps I can give him permission to delay or even fail at some things today while we get him the rest he needs to have a better chance at doing well next week. Or perhaps it's not true that we will get nothing done today. Maybe with a little encouragement and gentleness, we could still get some important things, or just some minor things, done."

This is what self-compassion looks like in action. The next time you feel lonely, tell yourself: "Feeling lonely is a hard thing to go through, so I feel bad for [insert your name], who feels so lonely today. That's really tough for her/him. How can I help [your name again] feel better? What does she/he need in order to have a better day tomorrow? How can I best support [again!] through this feeling right now?" See yourself as a friend you are helping make their way through pain. And, ideally, saying your own name several times helps you get enough perspective to treat yourself that way.

If a bee stung you unexpectedly right now, it might hurt, but you wouldn't attach any special meaning to the pain. It would just be a painful sensation. That's really all it ever is. Emotional pain like loneliness is just another variation of sensation. If we shed all of the stories we use to shame and blame ourselves, we are left to simply treat a difficult sensation in the body. That slight adjustment makes it much easier to practice the self-compassion that leads us out of or away from that sensation.

Reset Your Expectations

A key component of self-compassion is being willing to reset the expectations we put on ourselves according to the current situation. This is especially true during hard times. As a compulsive goal-setter, one of the most difficult things I had to learn to do was to make peace with what I just couldn't accomplish on my hardest days. I had to start making allowances for bad days, and tempering my demands on myself accordingly. Sometimes I needed to slow down. Sometimes I needed to get less done. Some days I needed to do nothing.

It's hard to do this if we're always comparing our output to what we see (or think we see) other people doing who may or may not have the same struggles we face. It's just as hard if the person we're comparing ourselves to is us, back when we weren't suffering the things we are now, or back when we had fewer responsibilities.

Forget what everyone else is doing, or what you were able to do in another time. Progress means completely different things depending on your situation. To the deeply depressed, getting out of bed in the morning is a heroic act. We have to decide what represents a great day for us, and stop worrying about whether our day, or *life* for that matter, matches up with someone else's.

Keep Perspective

Sam Harris once said, "If you think things can't get worse, that's just a failure of imagination." Your circumstances today might be a dream compared with what could go wrong in your life but hasn't. If you didn't have your biggest problem in your life right now, there's no guarantee you wouldn't have an equally difficult or even worse problem in another area. Everyone struggles. How many couples who seemed to be part of a dream marriage are now going through a divorce? How many people have life-changing accidents that force them to learn a completely new way of relating to their bodies? How many young people have a disease and don't have anywhere near the years you still have to go out and find a relationship?

There will always be uncertainty, and some new pain you have to learn how to coexist with. Don't take it too seriously. Even in the moments when your pain is at its worst, it doesn't mean there's anything wrong with you. Our pain isn't unique; it's just our particular Rubik's Cube to solve. Own it, master it, see what you can learn from it, and it will be the springboard for everything you become that you are proud of about yourself.

Ironically, as I write this section of the book, my physical symptoms happen to be particularly bad. It's a familiar feeling. Tension behind my right eye, throbbing in my ear accompanied by a ringing that is louder than normal, pressure all through the right side of my head. Difficulty concentrating. I'm not sure why it's worse this morning. As anyone with chronic pain will know, different things can trigger it. If I'm getting sick, it shows up in my head and ear first, like an early storm detector. It might be that I'm overstressed without realizing it, and my head and my ear are warning me. This time of year I can also get allergies, another trigger. I don't know what's setting it off at an 8 out of 10 today instead of a very manageable 2 or 3. And in a way, it doesn't matter. I've learned to be happy enough at an 8 too, with the exact tools I've talked about in this chapter.

In a moment like this, I used to get utterly demoralized, even panic. The stories would come rushing in: "I'll never be over this. It will haunt me for the rest of my life. I thought I was doing better with this, but it's back with full force. It's hopeless. I can't do this." That phrase, "I can't do this," was the most dangerous phrase of all. It signaled total overwhelm, which made me check out altogether. In the past, it made me give up on whatever I had to do that day, crawl back into bed, and spiral into an emotional abyss because I couldn't see a way out. Not that there's anything wrong with crawling back into bed (it might be just what we need!), but thanks to the tools I've mentioned, that's not a necessary part of my response to pain right now.

First, I notice the pain as an independent sensation, without attaching any immediate meaning to it—I don't shame myself or blame myself for it. (In any case, even if I did something to create it, the *me* who did that was an old runner, not the Matthew who has woken up today.) I don't start catastrophizing by thinking about all the things I will struggle to do today. These are just the facts: Matthew is feeling pain. That's it.

Second, I'm calm. Calm because I've experienced this before and come out the other side. I know that pain modulates, with good days and bad days, good hours and bad hours. So it will not stay at an 8 forever. There was a time before my head pain when the ringing in my ears alone sent me into full panic and then a black hole of numbing depression. Now I rarely even think about it. Sometimes I even enjoy it a little—isn't that weird? I lie with a fan on most nights, or some kind of white noise, but sometimes on the road, I don't have access to one, and I lie in bed at night and my ears ring and the quietness of the room makes the ringing feel really close inside my head, and it feels almost cozy to sit there and hear it. It's like an old friend who has taught me so much, and I say, "Ah, there you are, old friend. Pull up a chair; come sit with me."

I've become well acquainted with my symptoms. We've been through so much together. They've been my teacher. And they've made me a better coach and leader. They've been a continuous and unavoidable master class in empathy, and a crucial window into the lives of those who have it much worse. So much of what I value most in myself, I have learned from this old friend. So I feel grateful.

Then from this state I set about doing the things that may help. Have you exercised in the last few days? No, well that's part of it, silly. Have you been eating well? No, OK. So let's get some good food in you today. Have you been creating a lot of stress and anxiety about this book? Yes, OK, well, it's just a book, let's not take it all so seriously. Most of all, I evaluate whether I'm going through life right now with a clenched fist, and if I am, I unclench it. I tell myself that whatever gets done gets done, and whatever doesn't doesn't, and that that's the best I can do right now.

Then I say a message of thanks to myself:

> Thank you, Matthew, for coming as far as you have over the last seven years with how bad you've felt so much of the time. Thank you for every day you got out of bed when it was hard; for all the ways you still helped people and your family; for all the ways you chose to grow out of this experience; for all the times you never gave up; for the strength of character you showed in learning to live with this; for the versatility you showed in recognizing that this was a time to learn acceptance instead of fight. Thank you, Matthew, my friend, for taking care of us in this era, for doing everything you could not to let our life fall apart, and for actually using the experience to become a richer human being with more to give than ever before.

One of the reasons I didn't like to talk about my pain publicly is that other people feel an urge to rush in with solutions. They are desperate to give you a fix that can make your pain go away. But what they don't realize is that I've already successfully managed my relationship with this pain, which is why I don't need them to find me a solution.

What I hope you get from all this is that the chronic pain you feel from heartbreak, or longing for a partner, is not only manageable, but can be one of your most illuminating teachers, and a tremendous source of strength and gratitude. That is the truth of this pain. Your job is to connect to it. And if you need a helping hand, here are some truths about the pain of looking for love to get you started:

TRUTH: Being in a relationship is no guarantee of happiness either, and there are plenty of people who seem happy in public who are suffering immensely in private. Relationships do not automatically equal happiness.

TRUTH: Even being in a relationship that makes you happy doesn't guarantee you'll never be alone again. We may find the person we've always been looking for only to have life take them from us. The path to togetherness is not linear. The only relationship we are guaranteed till the day we die is with ourselves.

TRUTH: You have learned so much already through this pain. You have had to become stronger on your own. You have had to learn how to fully experience solitude. You have had to learn how to self-soothe. You have formed deeper friendships in the absence of a romantic relationship. You have had to take care of yourself. And if you've done none of these things yet, your pain brought you to a point where you can now begin, by reading this book to start with (and look, you're almost done!), a journey you never would have taken if you didn't feel that pain.

TRUTH: You have access to a whole different level of empathy toward others who experience this kind of pain. So now you can express the kind of sensitivity and compassion that others may not be able to. You can connect to people who are suffering (which is nearly all of us, something you are now that much better at picking up on) and really help them.

TRUTH: You are learning how to be happy enough with or without a relationship, and that is a form of invincibility. That's core confidence at its essence, knowing you'll be happy enough no matter what happens to change in your identity matrix. If the wrong person comes along, you'll be able to say no to them. When someone promising comes along, you'll be present enough to actually enjoy it, instead of suffering the constant anxiety that they may one day leave and take your happiness with them. Happy enough is what allows you to actually enjoy the happiness of the relationship you're in.

TRUTH: Your life is awesome, just as it is. There are so many things to be grateful for—including the complaints you don't have because of terrible things that haven't happened to you. Everything is a bonus.

Happy Enough Makes Us Attractive

With the help of the tools and truths above, you can create an entirely different lens for your life than most people have. This doesn't just result in you loving your life more: It transforms how you are seen by other people. The problem with chronic pain, be it emotional or physical, is that it wires our brain for negativity, anxiety, panic, resentment, overwhelm, and hopelessness. These states have a double-negative effect: They give us a negative experience of life, but then that negative experience changes us in ways that make it so much harder to attract the people we want in our love lives. When we're constantly mourning what we're not getting in life, being anxious or panicked over the things we can't change, or completely preoccupied with trying to manage our pain, we put out an energy that pushes people away.

This makes it harder to find whatever we're looking for. It's not our fault that we've had to contend with all these things: We didn't choose our looks, our genetics, our influences, the relationship patterns our parents passed down, the abuse we suffered at the hands of a terrible partner. And then we find out that as a reward, we attract much less interest from other people whenever the pain we still suffer from gets to us. That's the kind of cycle that creates tremendous resentment and bitterness.

This is why it's common, and understandable, for people to spiral downward. Because life is hard. It takes bravery to choose to be creative and attempt to make something remarkable out of such ingredients. But there are special rewards for those who do, because as I said earlier, life has a way of rewarding great chefs. We don't control much. But we do control one thing: our energy. And that energy turns out to be the greatest asset we have in attracting other people. Making ourselves happy with, and making the best of, our situation is one of the most powerful and beautiful ways to attract another person.

The tools I've mentioned can help us achieve a manageable, even positive, relationship with our pain. Once we have landed there, we can do what all great people do: create magic.

Where Magic Lives

Most people go through life chasing after magic. These magic seekers chase dream careers, dream partners, dream houses, dream countries to live in. Whatever they imagine is going to bring them the magic they're looking for, that's what they chase after.

My parents first took me to America when I was thirteen. Like so many Brits when they save up enough to travel to the States, we headed to Orlando, Florida. Destination: Universal Studios and Walt Disney World.

If you're more sophisticated than I was (and still am, to be honest), you might find these giant theme parks cheesy and commercial. I had the time of my life! I felt utterly depressed boarding the plane back to England, and I promised myself I'd be back.

This wasn't a wish I grew out of. Being there, I felt something within me awaken. In all that synthetic, manufactured escapism, I'd found a kind of magic that resonated with me on a deep level, from the way the staff ("cast members," as Disney calls them) came up to greet me, to the intricate set designs that transported me into new worlds. I remember visiting Universal Studios' Halloween Horror Nights and being astonished at how much effort had gone into creating the immersive haunted houses, and streets overrun with actors dressed as everything from demons to demented clowns jumping out at every corner.

We really are the strangest species.

I was deeply affected. And clearly, so are many people who travel halfway across the globe to visit these places, even though there are theme parks closer to home that they could go to. But while the others may offer rides, these two places create their own world. They do this by telling great stories, and by obsessing over all the little details that conjure an entire immersive experience, something you could never get anywhere else. Maya Angelou (who sometime later recorded the narration for Disney's Hall of

Presidents) was right when she said, "People will forget what you said, people will forget what you did, but people will never forget how you made them feel."

I have such affection for the young boy who didn't want to leave. It wasn't just that I far preferred going on rides in a sunny theme park over going back to school in a wet and dreary England. Part of me had come alive. I'd felt something I didn't want to lose: an excitement and emotional connection. Why couldn't all of life feel like this?

Magic had taken root in those places. As Florida fell away beneath my window seat as the plane took off, I was devastated to return to my world. How many of us have felt that way—that by losing a relationship, the magic in our lives was disappearing? How many of us have spent months after a great date bending over backward for someone with no interest in getting that magic back?

We've all fallen into the magic-seeking trap. But at some point, we have to change from a seeker of magic into an author of magic. This requires a shift of focus, from looking for it outside of ourselves, to becoming a source of it. When we author the magic, we become the magic in someone else's life because of how they feel around us and in our worlds.

There are so many ways to create magic: When we take a bad situation and find beautiful meaning in it, the way a great chef does with tough ingredients; when we help someone else in a tough situation discover the potential to turn it into something great; when we stop trying to copy other people's specific brand of charisma, confidence, or appeal, and set about discovering and creating our own; when we express our passions to the world; when we create something out of love, whether it's a book, an artwork, a room in our house, a beautiful friendship, or a sofa fort for the kids; when we recognize what's special about others and we let them know; when we smile at someone, or make them laugh: These are all ways of authoring magic.

One of the greatest ways to be the author of magic is through a generosity of spirit. When we reach out to someone with a text or a call, recognize their efforts, notice what's special about them, or encourage their potential, we show them that in a world moving at breakneck speed, there's someone who truly sees them, who is bearing witness to their journey. If you leave people better than you found them, you are a source of magic in this world. This is different from people pleasing, which is rooted in fear. It is giving love from abundance. And in giving love, we feel filled with it. We're no longer seeking it; we are it.

I know people who will never be satisfied with a hotel if there's a better one they could have stayed in; never happy with the partner they have as long as someone better-looking can walk into the room; never happy with the money they have so long as there's more they can get. Those are the "never enough" types I wrote about earlier. But one of the greatest ways to be happy enough is to be happy *with* enough.

My cousin Billy is one of the best people I know at this. Let me tell you about his hat, which is what he would do if he met you. He once bought a "Kwik-E-Mart" hat, named after the famous store in *The Simpsons*. Billy wore this hat all the time. When it came to that hat, he was not shy about his feelings. ("Everywhere I go, Matt, I just know there is no better hat. It's such a great hat.") Any friend of Billy's knows: The man is an author of magic. I went to his bachelor weekend recently in Madrid. All twenty of the friends he had invited stayed in a three-star hotel in the middle of the city. It had a tiny roof deck, with an ice-cold pool that most of the lads weren't brave enough to get in, and some deck chairs that we arranged in a circle on the concrete tiles so we could hang out and talk. There are people who stay in the Four Seasons in Madrid and complain that it's not as nice as the Mandarin Oriental six minutes away. Those are the magic seekers. Billy is a magic author. He walked around that roof deck, while all of us sat around talking, and he kept saying: "How lucky are we? This little roof deck is perfect! Chairs out in the sun, views over the city, a pool for when we get too hot. It worked out so well." I love him. This has always been and probably will always be the quality in him that I admire the most. Like everyone else who meets him, it makes me want to be around him. Billy didn't just learn to be happy with enough; being around him makes enough feel like more. It's common to hear people say Billy is the luckiest guy they know because great things always seem to land in his lap. Now, I have no doubt that the energy he brings to his life has a way of making more great things come his way. But I still think they missed it . . . because Billy's real magic trick, the one he performs on both the exciting days and the everyday ones, is that everything feels great when we see it through his eyes. That's Billy's magic hat.

Being an author of magic is essential to a love of life, because nothing on the outside in life is a guarantee. People will come and go. Careers will change. We will lose people we love. We will encounter sickness. We will have to move out of a house that was our pride and joy. We will lose things we never thought we'd lose. But our magic is something we control—it is a guarantee as long as we commit to authoring it.

At any point we can make a decision to stop waiting for magic to arrive in our lives and start creating it. We can all become the magic in our own lives. And becoming the magic often ends up being the indirect way we get the results we sought in the first place. My personal passion for taking the life tools that were helping me and turning them into videos I didn't know anyone would watch landed me in America. My wife, who always dreamed of finding love, spent years working on her inner peace, a beautiful mindset, and strong standards, which happened to be the things that made me fall in love with her. This backs up what Oxford professor John Kay argues in his book *Obliquity*, that our goals in life are best achieved indirectly.

It's also important to connect to the magic you already have. It's not all about what you are going to create in the future—sometimes in order to feel confident, we need only connect to what we already are, which in the harder seasons of our life we have a way of forgetting. Whenever I see someone going through a terrible heartbreak, I know they think they've lost the thing that's most valuable in their lives. I have to remind them that 50 percent of what they miss about that relationship is themselves. Think of your last breakup. How much of what made that relationship special was you? Your sacrifices; your compromises; all the ways you showed up and gave attention to the details of that relationship to make it special; your gifts; your surprises; the ways you anticipated their needs; the questions you asked that created true vulnerability and forged a deeper bond between the two of you; the moments you looked out for them and made them feel safe and loved; how you loved them so purely that they felt accepted even for the parts of them that weren't easy to love (perhaps reading this is making you realize you were far more than 50 percent of the relationship). In heartbreak we tend to overvalue what someone else brought to the relationship while failing to see how much our efforts contributed to why the relationship was special, or simply lasted as long as it did in the first place. This is just another way we place our power outside of ourselves. How much of the magic you miss about your past relationships (or wish you'd had) is actually *your* magic that is still with you? You may have lost a person, but you didn't lose the magic. The magic is you. And you need no excuse to unleash it again.

"To Die Will Be an Awfully Big Adventure"

Happy enough is not just a philosophy for those of us who haven't found something we were looking for. It's an essential working model for those who have. Even if we are in a season of our lives where we have the things we wanted, there's no guarantee they won't be taken from us. In fact, it's practically a certainty that at some point some of them will. And when that happens, we will have to learn to love our life all over again.

A certainty of life is that we will die. While we are alive. And not once, but many times. Heartbreak is the death of the future we'd counted on having with someone. Divorce is the death of a mutual promise. Disappointment is the death of a cherished idea. Infertility is the death of the precise way we had planned to create a family. Failure and rejection are the death of ego. You and I have experienced some of these deaths already. There are more to come.

If you've read J. M. Barrie's *Peter Pan*, the book that inspired the movies and plays, you know it makes for heart-wrenching adult reading. Several times while I was reading, I found myself welling up, but there's one line in particular that's always stuck with me. A battle with Captain Hook has left a wounded Peter strewn over a rock in a lagoon with a rising tide. Barrie writes about Peter contemplating his imminent death:

> Peter was not quite like other boys; but he was afraid at last. A tremor ran through him, like a shudder passing over the sea; but on the sea one shudder follows another till there are hundreds of them, and Peter felt just the one. Next moment he was standing erect on the rock again, with that smile on his face and a drum beating within him. It was saying: "To die will be an awfully big adventure."

What death have you recently experienced, or are experiencing right now? The death of a relationship? The death of a cherished ideal of how your life would be by this point? The death of an old identity you'd held on to until now? The death of your ego? How might these deaths hold the key to your next great adventure?

Sometimes loss opens us up to something even better, something we never could have seen in our previous life. We lose a relationship we couldn't bear to be without, and the loss makes way for someone even better. Other times pain rewards us with the person we become. Pain is the great transmuter. The old version of us dies, a bigger one comes back. In *The Lord of the Rings*, Gandalf is pulled into the depths of Moria and we're sure he's dead. We were right, but not in the way we thought. Gandalf the Grey is gone, but Gandalf the White came back. At the heart of confidence is this realization that we do in fact survive such fractures. We are broken vessels that still work.

None of this means we cannot mourn the deaths we experience in life. Sadness is part of our lives and shouldn't be discounted as an experience, even a desirable one. Who hasn't watched a movie or listened to a song knowing it would bring on tears or melancholy? And how many times have you caught yourself thinking, in the midst of your tears, "Finally—what a relief!" Living doesn't just happen in the good times. Experience is living, and hard times are just another experience. It all counts.

Yet we should be wary of the urge to fetishize our sadness, as if the last loss we experienced is the one irreducible truth of our life. In fact, as soon as one story ends, countless others line up, ready for the telling. Can we make enough space between ourselves and our sadness to see them? Letting go of our sadness doesn't create a void; it makes room. Happy enough isn't passive. You aren't settling for the life you've been given; you're settling *on* the life you have, and resolving to live these new stories whose starting points can be located precisely where you stand right now.

There's no way to know the ways your life could change before the next year passes. Whether or not you've found love yet, you could be telling a very different story. This is why curiosity is a driving force for being happy enough. Yes, happy enough makes us content with what we have in the present moment. But curiosity prevents us from thinking that all we have this minute is all we'll ever get. Curiosity says, *Hold on, I just don't know! I have no idea what's coming!* I don't know who I'll be next year, or five years from now. I don't know how I'll feel about this heartbreak in as little as six months, maybe even next week. I don't know about the opportunities coming to me that I can't imagine right now. Isn't it kind of exhilarating *not* to know?

Wherever we are right now, let's not waste time wishing for the kind of wholesale change that doesn't exist, like a do-over or a clean slate. Did we *ever* have a clean slate? We started out with the mess our parents handed down to us, some of which we'll surely pass on, nearly unchanged, to the next generation. A clean slate turns out to be just another mirage of ego— like the spotless record or the perfect score. Life without mistakes or regrets is impossible. But you can rely on progress, which is messy, and must be fought for, inch by inch. Very little in life is easy. When we try to love life, it doesn't always love us back. In spite of it all, stay committed to that relationship, and to the one you have with yourself. Both are relationships you will be in till the end. Experiment with life, and with those decades-old assumptions about yourself. Attempt new ways of being. Have fun with it. Sculpt your beautiful mess into something you feel a little prouder of each day. The changes today may be modest, but the results over time will be miraculous. As they already are: Look at what you've been through, all you've had to overcome. All that and you're still here; you're the kind of person you turned out to be. What else could a person like that do?

ACKNOWLEDGMENTS

First, to my incredible wife, Audrey. I was lucky enough to marry Audrey not in the hope that she would be with me in the hard times, but with the deep security of knowing she already had. Thank you for ever returning my focus to what is truly important in life since the day we met. And for being patient with me as I have managed the stress of this process, and the life that was happening in between. This book, and the organization behind it, couldn't be what it is without your extraordinary ability to read human behavior, empathize, and generate ideas that help people. Thank you for being an honest champion of everything I do. You make everything better, whether it's my work, or my life.

Thank you to my publisher and dear friend Karen Rinaldi, and her passionate team at Harper Wave, including the wonderful Amanda Pritzker, Kirby Sandmeyer, and Tina Andreadis. Karen published my first book over ten years ago, which also gave me the honor of being the first book she published at what was then her new imprint. Every year since, Karen would ask when the next book would happen, and every year she would wait patiently as I told her I wasn't ready. Thank you for waiting, Karen. Thank you for believing in me all those years ago. And thank you for loving me enough to have hard conversations with me when you knew I could do better. It's been a ten-year journey, friend. I look forward to many more years of sharing both our joys and our war wounds, and laughing about it all together.

Thank you to my editor and writing coach Kevin Conley, who has worked tirelessly with me for the past two years to create a book we are both incredibly proud of. Without your guidance, I could never have written to the standard I have. Thank you for not only being a true partner in the process, but for generously educating me on how to be a better writer. In doing so, you have given me a gift I take with me beyond this book.

Thanks to Michele Reverte, who helped me from day one in compiling material, editing, proofing (often with little notice!), and passionately supporting me in this process. One could not ask for a more supportive friend to work with.

To my team at my company, 320 Media LLC, I'm so grateful to you all for the hard work you put in that enables us every day to lift people up all over the world, and help them find the perspectives and the strategies to love their lives a little more each day. Special thanks to my executive team, Audrey Le Strat Hussey, Chet Gass, Lauren McNeill, Daniel Hyde, and Suzanne Willis, for all of your effort in these past couple of years; to Jameson Jordan for your loyalty and love, and the hard work and creativity it took to create the huge body of videos we have produced together over the past ten years; and to Stephen, Harry, Billy, Celia, Courtney, Charlotte, and Vic for all the ways you've led your teams to create magic in this company. Thank you to my beloved assistant and dear friend, Annik, for always being there for both my family and me, and for thinking of everything I don't. I couldn't do it without you.

Thank you to my advisor, friend, and CEO Dan Hyde. Every now and again, someone comes along at a time in your life where, in hindsight, you have no clue what you would have done had they not been there. Dan was that person for me. There are those who give you the wisdom you need, and those who help you execute that wisdom. Dan has been both. I'm grateful for your support every single day, and I'm proud to call you a friend—you've gone over and above for me in ways I'll never forget. Special thanks also to my friend James Abrahart, who has been a light for me in dark times, and constantly checked in on me when I needed it the most.

Shout-outs to a few other friends: Lewis Howes, who has brought more friendships into my life by inviting me into rooms I was not previously a part of, who has been generous with his own hard-won resources, and who has had many a life-affirming conversation with me in various saunas across America. Jesse Itzler, for the perspective, the wisdom, and the hill. Dr. Ramani, for your belief in me, your expert insights on people, and your presence as a teacher on my programs.

Thanks to my family, who are a constant reminder that if you have love at the center of your life, the rest is a bonus, or just ego. Love allows you to take big swings in life because at home you already feel safe. Thank you for making me feel like George Bailey, the "richest man in town."

To my mum: You may not know this, but your growth at this stage in your life has been the single biggest inspiration to me in the past two years, and the greatest validation I could ever hope to get for the path I chose. You are proof that it's never too late to grow and learn new ways of being. And such growth is not just an act of bravery, it is an act of love for others around us. I'm so proud of you, Mum. I will never stop being grateful for the unending love you have shown me my whole life, but it's such a privilege to now get to be grateful for the love you are showing yourself.

Lastly, I want to say "thank you" to all of you who in my audience have supported me over the past fifteen years, both old and new. Those who come to my events, watch the videos, support my programs, and cheer me on. Thank you for being kind enough to give me love, even while you have been seeking it for yourselves. Many of us have been friends for a long, long time now. We've grown together. The stories and the questions you've vulnerably shared have helped me shape this book into what it is. You've been patient with me as I grew and changed and made discoveries about myself. It's hard growing at the same time as having your thoughts out there over so many years. But you've always encouraged me and been generous with me anytime I was willing to go back to the drawing board in my own life. I'm so grateful for our relationship, and I look forward to growing together for many years to come.

RESOURCES FOR YOUR
LOVE LIFE JOURNEY

What Should You Read Next?

It means so very much to me that you've taken the time to read my book. I'm not a fast reader myself; finishing any book is a real time commitment, so I'm truly grateful you chose to spend your time with me. I'm committed to making these insights, tools, and support free and accessible to all. So if you've enjoyed *Love Life*, and you'd like to read more things I write, I'd like to extend you an invitation.

My free weekly newsletter contains my latest writings and content, and by being part of it, you'll also be first to hear about my new projects.

As a fun way to start, when you sign up, I'll send you a special unpublished *Love Life* chapter. This didn't make it into the book due to space constraints, but it's a chapter very close to my heart.

You can sign up at:
matthewhussey.com/newsletter

Join the Love Life Club

You've read about some of our Love Life Club members' stories inside this book. If you want to know more, the Love Life Club is my online community and membership program where I coach people every month. This book is a wonderful starting point, but if you'd like comprehensive support and guidance for putting it all into practice, the Love Life Club was created for that purpose. It is a community built on healthy mindsets, growth, and loving support.

You can join now at: matthewhussey.com/club

Come See Me Live

One of my greatest passions has always been, and probably always will be, live events. They are a chance for all of us (myself included) to step away from routine, try something new that changes us, and do more than just learn—creating a memory. There's nothing like being at a live event, and we've spent years crafting an atmosphere and a culture at our events that is truly unique to us. I design my events to be the same way I hope this book was—entertaining, insightful, and a place everyone can feel at home.

We've been running both in-person and virtual live events for nearly two decades now. I invite you to join one for yourself, and I look forward to the possibility of meeting you.

Register for an upcoming event here: matthewhussey.com/live

ABOUT THE AUTHOR

Matthew Hussey is a *New York Times* bestselling author, speaker, and coach specializing in confidence and relational intelligence. His YouTube channel is number one in the world for love life advice, with over half a billion views. He writes a weekly newsletter and is the host of the podcast *Love Life with Matthew Hussey*. Hussey provides monthly coaching to the members of his private community at LoveLifeClub.com. Over the past fifteen years, his proven approach has inspired millions through authentic, insightful, and practical advice that not only enables them to find love but also feel confident and in control of their own happiness. He lives in Los Angeles.